Panchayati Raj System

Panchayati Raj System

Towards Sustainable Rural Livelihood and Development

Edited by
DR. M.R. BIJU

KANISHKA PUBLISHERS, DISTRIBUTORS
NEW DELHI-110 002

KANISHKA PUBLISHERS, DISTRIBUTORS
4697/5-21 A, Ansari Road, Daryaganj
New Delhi-110 002
Phones : 2327 0497, 2328 8285
Fax : 011-2328 8285
E-mail: kanishka_publishing@yahoo.co.in

First Published 2008

ISBN 978-81-8457-055-7

PRINTED IN INDIA

Published by Madan Sachdeva for Kanishka Publishers, Distributors, 4697/5-21A, Ansari Road, Daryaganj, New Delhi-110 002, Typeset by Sunshine Graphics, Delhi, and Printed at Nice Printing Press, Delhi.

Contents

List of Contributors

Dr. Suresh Misra is currently working with Haryana Institute of Public Administration as Professor of Public Administration and Head, Faculty of Public Administration. He is currently associated with the Capacity Building of Afghanistan Civil Services in associated with USAID.

Dr. Sanjay Arora is an active Researcher in the field of Natural Resource Management mainly focusing on sensitive environment of foothills of Himalayas for more than 7 years. Dr. Arora is a recipient of Young Scientist Award and SCSI Leadership Award. He has presented his diverse research in national and international conferences and visited Thailand, Israel and Italy on scientific assignments.

Dr. M.R. Biju is the Director of Asian Institute of Development Research and Editor of South Asian Journal of Socio-Political Studies (SAJOSPS) and Reader in the Post-Graduate and Reaserch Department of Political Science, Sree Narayana College, Kollam, Kerala. Currently he is heading a major research project of the Ministry of Panchayati Raj, Government of India. He is also working as Member, Associate Board of the Renowned Management Journal – Economics and Management (E+M) Published by the Technical University of Liberce, Czech Republic.

Dr. Reepunjay Singh is currently working as Sr. Lecturer in Geography, Government College, Ajmer, Rajasthan.

Sonia Deoval is a UGC Doctoral Fellow in Geography, Government College, Ajmer, Rajasthan.

Dr. G. Palanithurai, Co-ordinator in Rajiv Gandhi Chair, Gandhigram Rural Institute is an academic activist working with the people in rural areas for building the capacity of the leaders and people to reinvent sustainable grassroots democracy. He is heading the Department of Political Science and Development Administration, in Gandhigram Rural University, Tamil Nadu. He is a member of the expert committee constituted by the Government of Tamil Nadu, to monitor the training programme for local body leaders.

Dr. Aditya Kumar Patra is a Master of Arts and a holder of Ph.D Degree from Berhampur University. He is in the Department of Economics, Kalinga Mahavidyalaya, G.Udayagiri, Orissa.

Dr. V. P. Raghavan is currently working as Director, DCSMAT Business School, Pullikkanam, Idukki, Kerala. He has awarded with UGC-IUC Associateship in Humanities and Social Sciences at Indian Institute of Advanced Study, Shimla.

Dr. Lingaraj Patro started his career as Lecturer in Zoology in 1987 at Aska Science College, Aska, Ganjam, Orissa, under Berhampur University. Now, Dr. Patro is working as Head of the Department, Zoology, K.B.D.A.V. College, Nirakarpur, Dist-Khurda, Orissa under Utkal University, Bhubaneswar.

Jhum Jhum Das started her career as Lecturer in English at Women's College, Orissa since 1989. She published some papers in different National Journals. She participated and presented papers in different national seminars, Symposia and Workshops.

Professor R. K. Khitoliya is graduated in Civil Engineering from Banaras Hindu University. At present Dr. Khitoliya is working as Professor of Civil Engineering and Head, Post-Graduate Environmental Engineering Department in Punjab Engineering College, Chandigarh and teaching upto post-graduate level. He has been Convenor, Board of Studies in Environmental Studies – Panjab University, Chandigarh. He has provided consultancy to more than hundred river valley projects in India and abroad. His areas of interest are Geotechnical investigations and Materials Characterization, Environmental Legislation, Environmental Management, Sustainable Development and Environmental Impact Assessment.

Dr. P. N. Sankaran, holds a Masters in Economics, a Bachelors in Law and a Ph.D in Co-operative Credit (University of Kerala). He is currently Professor of Economics (and Research Coordinator, SCMS Centre for Socio-Economic Research-

SCENSER), School of Communication and Management Studies-Cochin (SCMS-Cochin), Kerala. He was Chair Professor Rural Management, St. Joseph's College of Business Administration, Bangalore, Reader in Economics, University College, Thiruvananthapuram, Kerala and Chief, Decentralized Planning, Kerala State Planning Board.

Dr. A. Subbiah is working as a Reader in the Post-Graduate and Research Department of Commerce, Sri SRNM College, Sattur. Tamilnadu, affiliated to Madurai Kamaraj University, Madurai, Tamilnadu.

A. Muthumani is working as a Lecturer in the Post-Graduate and Research Department of Commerce, Sri S R N M College, Sattur. Tamilnadu, affiliated to Madurai Kamaraj University, Madurai, Tamilnadu.

Dr. K. Prabakkar Rajkumar, Lecturer, Department of Commerce, Periyar University, Salem, Tamil Nadu. Currently he is heading a major research project of the U.G.C.

Dr. C. Karthikeyan is currently working as Deputy Director at Sree Narayana Guru Institute of Science and Technology, Mannam P.O., North Paravur, Ernakulum Dist., Kochi, Kerala.

C. Siva Murugan is currently working as Lecturer at Research Centre in Economics, Aditanar College of Arts and Science, Tiruchendur, Tamilnadu.

Dr. V. Anbumani is currently working as Reader of Economics, Bharathiar University, Coimbatore.

Dr. Rajesh Kumar is currently working as Reader, Department of Public Administration, Kurukshetra University, Kurukshetra.

Dr. M. Rajivlochan, Teacher at the Department of History, Panjat University. He Specialises in Contemporary Indian History.

1
Introductory Note

Dr. M.R. Biju

Since an overwhelming majority of India's population lives in villages, a holistic development of its rural life is a requisite for the acceleration of the pace of overall economic development of the country. Rural development programmes are designed to facilitate a multi-faceted growth of the rural poor by extending the benefits of development to them. It also aims at the improvement of their living standards by providing them opportunities for the fullest utilization of their capabilities through their active participation in the process of goal-oriented change. Rural development also tends to reduce migrational pressure on cities and towns. It also enables the use of human and national resources in the rural areas and to reduce area-wise differences. Evidence indicates that in India, public and governmental interest in rural development has been growing rapidly and a strong and various commitment towards it on the part of our polity-makers is clearly visible. The government has initiated a number of programmes to resolve the chronic problems facing village in India. In fact efforts to improve the rural economy were initiated soon after independence, particularly after the constitution came into force. Notably, in the early phases, despite some efforts at involving the people though democratic decentralization community development and panchayati raj rural development programmes were virtually synonymies with agricultural development. This followed the prevailing worldwide thinking and India's excessive concern especially till the green revolution in the late 1960s with food sufficiency. In the seventies, however, it came to be realized that rural development is much broader in scope than merely agricultural development. Besides, it was recognized that development in agriculture was not a panacea for all ills and that development should not be confined to a single area of change, however significant it may be. Therefore, if the strategy for rural development had to be made effective, a multi-pronged approach to rural problems was imperative. A package programme of rural development had to be devised, a multi-dimensional approach taken up and multi-institutional efforts had to be initiated.

Social Structure and Sustainable Rural Development

Rural India now contains 72 per cent of the population, and some 70 per cent of the labour force is engaged in agriculture. Despite the land reforms of late 1940s and early 1980s, the distribution of land ownership in rural India has been grossly unequal. In the early 1970s, over 96 per cent of India's household owned less than 20 acres of land; 43 per cent owned less than 5 acres; and 24 per cent owned no land at all with the percentage of landless labour increasing. The disparities in land ownership are revealed in the fact that 10 per cent of the rural families hold 70 per cent of the cultivable land.

As has been indicated earlier, the social structure in India consists of powerful status groups based on religions, castes and language. Although a class system has also begun to emerge in India, it still remains tenuous. The slow process of industrialization and urbanization had led to a highly uneven pattern of class-growth. Status group continues to cut across class lines. As a result, the development of class identities and political mobilization based upon class appeals has been securely inhibited. India's urban based class structure is small compared to the rural society. The 15 million industrial workers in the organized sector of the economy make up only 10 per cent of the total work force of 150 million. Of these, only 3 per cent, or 5 million, work in large modern factories. The industrial work force moreover is not only small, but its portion of the total labour force has also remained remarkably stable over the past several decades.

In comparison to this the size of the urban population represents a consumer market larger than the entire European Union. These changes in the rural/urban population and the merging class structure have meant the evolution of new administrative policies, strategies and institutions. In the past forty years, there has been a proliferation of a number of administrative institutions, authorities and agencies both at the center as well as states to cater to the strategies of integrated rural development, and the needs of growing urban metropolises, incredibly crowded, lacking in adequate housing, transportation, water and electricity sewage and sanitation facilities. The administrative strategies evolved have ranged from technological and scientific innovations in the field of agriculture production to the establishment of institutions of democratic decentralization and a host of specified agencies for regulating industrial development, large, medium and small scale and a host of institutions for providing a number of services for good urban life have come into operation. Because of a growing concern for environmental degradation a number of regulatory agencies have come into being to protect the environment from further degradation, although with little success. All these developments have further meant a keen political competitions among various segmented social groups and cultural communities based on language, religion, region and caste, creating additional pressures on the administrative systems. The existence of a number of multifarious agencies with conflicting and overlapping jurisdiction have not only highlighted the problems of unified direction, control and coordination, but have also raised afresh the basic issue of centralization and the relative autonomy of various units of administration.

In the Era of Liberalization

The Government of India has adopted policies of globalization, liberalization and market economy in the wake of the serious economic crisis owing to a steady decline in exports, negative growth rates in industry and agriculture, and 0.3 per cent decline in the domestic production of crude oil. Among the long-term domestic factors contributing to high cost and low productivity were: *(a)* the inadequate returns and continuing losses from the massive investments in the public sector undertaking, and *(b)* economic populism resulting in increasing state subsidies, especially in fertilizers and writing off loans to farmers and hidden payments incurred through lower tariff rates of state undertakings in power and transport sectors.

India's adoption of a programme of globalization, market economy and competitiveness came after more than six months of negotiations with the World Bank starting in January 1991. The package of reform measures announced by the newly installed

Narasimha Rao Government in July 1991 consisted of two separate economic policies: *(a)* a macro-economic stabilization programme (IMF inspired) essentially focus on reducing the twin deficits on the balance of payment and on the state budget, and *(b)* a comprehensive programme for structural change of the economy (World Bank Inspired) in the fields of trade, industry, foreign investments, public sector and the financial sector among others.

'Globalization', 'competitiveness' and 'liberalization' come to India as a booster, and through the backdoor of "economic reforms". The sanctity of economic reforms had been derived from it. It was argued that progress is taking place through globalization, and economic reforms are the only means to join in this process. Hence economic reforms are the only alternative for human security and India's future. Globalization as a phenomenon involves two different entities *(a)* finance capital through multinational corporations and *(b)* new technologies such as computers and telecommunications. It was argued that the growth and internationalization of finance capital is good and desirable for projects because it promotes growth of technology. Globalization provides a useful means to develop technology necessary for the production of goods and services that improve our well-being.

The post-1991 economic reforms were initially launched under compelling balance of payments crisis. At the same time it was felt that by adopted market-oriented and globally competitive restructuring policies somewhat similar to those of Southeast Asian countries, the Indian economy could grow much faster and become more self-reliant in managing its balance of payments and could at the same time speedily accelerate growth and reduce the level of poverty, thus contributing to human security including freedom from hunger, disease, ignorance, unemployment and homelessness.

The Pre-Reform (1991) Scenario

The structural adjustment policy and economic reforms were introduced in the Indian polity at a time when the domestic inflation raged at an annual rate of 17 per cent. The growth rate of gross domestic product (GDP) in 1991-92 stood at 0.6 per cent. The industrial sector also showed the same growth rate, while the index number of agricultural production had declined from 148.4 in 1990-91 to 145.5 in 1991-92 with foodgrains production declining from 176.4 million tonnes in the previous year to 168.4 million tonnes. In the view of the fast deteriorating economic situation the fight of capital had started from the country. This resulted in a severe balance of payment (BOP) crisis, the foreign exchange reserve touching the bottom line of $ 1 billion - from 4.4 months of inputs to 1.1 months in 1990-91 – to attain that growth and to reduce poverty on a sustainable basis, a series of measures have since been undertaken to bring back the macro-economic balance of the economy and to initiate the necessary structure adjustment programme for improving efficiency in resource use. In this perspective, the emphasis in policy objectives has shifted to higher 'growth', with the expectation that higher growth will automatically percolate as benefits to the poor.

Reform Package

The New Industrial Policy of 24 July 1991 spelled out the process of liberalization. It stated that foreign investment and technology collaboration was welcomed to obtain higher technology to increase export and to expand the production base. The number of industries reserved for the public sector was reduced to only eight, and compulsory industrial licensing was restricted for only eighteen industries. The policy indicated the need for more dynamic relationship between domestic and foreign industry than before in terms of technology and investment. The direct approval of investment upto 51 per cent of foreign equity in high priority industries was made without any bottleneck. Liberalized Exchange Rate Management System was evolved to help in the free working in the foreign exchange market and secure convertibility of the rupee. Coupled with changes in industrial licensing, the financial and banking sectors were also revamped. The directional paper of the Planning Commission (1991) had clearly indicated that the public sector should make investments of an infrastructural nature in areas where private participation is not likely to come quickly, but it should withdraw from areas where no public purpose is served by its presence. The paper stated that in large part of public sector operations, where commodities or services are produced and distributed, unless it is necessarily for protecting the poorest in society, the main operating principle should be that of the market economy.

The Role of the State

In the context of the new economic policy in operation since mid-1991, a controversial question that has often been raised is about the role of the state. State is not only required to achieve a balance between the functions of security, equity, ecology, development and safety, but also to provide an equilibrium between stability and growth. It is wrong to assume that under liberalization, the state folds up. The rolling back of the state on the economic issues necessitates a re-defining of its new role and a re-examination of its structures and process it may no longer remains to be the owner of strategic industries, but it is still a regulator – a pro-consumer regulator that oversees and prevents the abuse of the market and to provide the legal, physical and human infrastructure. It has to concentrate on 'Development dynamics' that would benefit primarily the poor and the disadvantaged.

To Protect the Living Standard of Poor

In order to protect the living standard of the poor during the transition period and provide for human society, the complimentary social measure reflecting india's commitment to good governance were also conceived to ensure equitable distribution of both the gains and costs of economic reforms. Since over half of India's population continued to live below the poverty line. A number of direct attacks on poverty were launched during 1980's. Prominent among these were special programme for backward areas, such as subsidized food supplies though a Public Distribution System (PDS), concessional loan schemes for marginal farmers and agricultural labourers, employment-oriented programmes sponsoring different employment schemes like Jawahar Rozgar Yojana (JRY), Nehru Rozgar Yojana (NRY), that are geared mainly towards urban housing improvement. After the introduction of the policy of globalization, market economy and liberalization, and despite the fiscal austerity, the government committed itself to increased outlay for clearly targeted social sector expenditure and rural development during the overall plan period 1992-97. In particular, employment creation and human capital development in rural India through (both Poverty Alleviation Programme [PAP] and Social Services, such as primary health care, elementary education and rural water supply-cum sanitation) were to be expanded and broadened. However constraints on budgetary resources forced the government to postpone the provision of extra-funds for those programmes, and on the contrary to curtail them along with all other public expenditures. However, in February 1992, a National Renewal Fund (NRF), meant to provide assistance to workers who would become redundant as a result of the adjustment programme was created. Together with the rural development and social sector programmes, NRF was intended to constitute a comprehensive and permanent Social Safety net, providing adequate shelter for those who would be temporarily affected by India's SAP.

Employment Generation for Poverty Alleviation

During the last one and a half decade, poverty alleviation and employment generation programmes which have been in operation of several years have been redesigned for generation of self-employment and wage employment of rural areas and restructured to improve their efficacy and impact on the poor. An outlay of Rs. 9650 crore has been provided in 1999-00 (BE) as against 9345 crore in 1998-99 (BE). The former Integrated Rural Development Programme (IRDP) and allied programmes such as training of rural youth for self-employment, Development of Women and Children in Rural Areas (DWCRA) and Million Wells Scheme (MWS) have been restructured into a single self-employment programme called the Swarnajayanthi Gram Swarozgar Yojana (SSGY) from April 1999. Simultaneously, Jawahar Rozgar Yojana (JRY) has been restructured and streamlined with effect from April 1999 and has been renamed as Jawahar Gram Samridhi Yojana (JGSY). The other ongoing programmes include, National Social Assistance Programme (NSAP), Urban Employment and Anti-Poverty Programme (UEPP). The Swarna Jayanti Shahari Rozgar Yojana (SJSRY) has subsumed the earlier three urban poverty programmes viz. Nehru Rozgar Yojana (NRY), Urban Basic Service for the Poor (UBSP) and Prime Minister's Integrated Urban Poverty Alleviation Programme (PMIUPEP) and has become operative from December 1997.

Decentralised Governance and Sustainable Rural Development

The concept of decentralisation has now-a-days emerged as a dominant and vibrant trend in global politics. In 1998, the World Bank estimated that all but 12 out of 75 developing and transitional countries with populations greater than 5 million had embarked on a process of political devolution. At the heart of this transformation are a number of complex yet inter-related themes. One is an ideological shift, in which the legitimacy of central state-led development has been challenged on the grounds that it produces systems of governance that undermine national economic performance and effective public policy (Gore, 2000; Johnson and

Start, 2001). A second is a (remarkably widespread) political agenda, which asserts that the decentralisation of public administration and the introduction of locally elected bodies will produce systems of governance that are better able to meet the needs of poor and politically marginal groups in society. A third and related theme suggests that democratic decentralisation is a political strategy that national elites have used to maintain legitimacy and control in the face of political disintegration. Here it can be argued that economic liberalisation, political regionalism and the rise of powerful inter- and sub-national actors have weakened the traditional nation state and created the conditions under which more local identities could emerge (Giddens, 1998).

Assertions in favour of decentralisation are often founded upon a wider critique of central state planning, which holds that large and centrally-administered bureaucracies represent an inefficient and potentially destructive means of allocating resources (and generating wealth) within society. Two assertions are generally used to substantiate this claim. One argues that central state agencies lack the 'time and place knowledge' to implement policies and programmes that reflect people's 'real' needs and preferences. A second and related assertion is that time and place gaps give local officials unlimited ability to distribute resources and extract 'rent' as they see fit. Such outcomes are believed to be particularly prone in poor countries, where government represents a vital source of wealth, and mechanisms to ensure accountable governance are often poorly enforced. In theory, decentralisation would undermine these opportunities by creating institutional arrangements that formalise the relationship between citizens and the state, giving the former the authority to impose sanctions (such as voting, recourse to higher-level authorities) on the latter. Decentralisation is also thought to create the conditions for a more pluralist political arrangement, in which competing groups can voice and institutionalise their interests in local democratic forums. Finally, it is argued that decentralisation creates institutions that are more amenable to local needs and preferences. However, a problem that is well-recognised in the literature on decentralisation is that the devolution of power will not necessarily improve tbe performance and accountability of local government. Indeed, in many cases, decentralisation has simply empowered local elites to capture a larger share of public resources, often at the expense of the poor.

In 1993, the Government of India passed a series of constitutional reforms, which were intended to empower and democratise India's rural representative bodies—the *Panchayats*. The 73rd Amendment to the Constitution formally recognised a third tier of government at the sub-State level, thereby creating the legal conditions for local self-rule—or *Panchayati Raj*. Since this time, the process of decentralisation has been highly variable, ranging from ambitious attempts at *Gram Swaraj* (or village self-rule) in Madhya Pradesh, political *de-centralisation* in Karnataka and *peoples plan* in Kerala. Early experiences have also revealed considerable uncertainty and confusion about the precise political, administrative and fiscal powers *Panchayats* have in relation to the States, line ministries, and local user groups. This, in part, reflects the fact that the 73rd Amendment gave the State governments considerable autonomy to interpret and implement the constitutional reforms.

Decentralisation—Basic Concepts

Decentralisation can be usefully understood as a political process whereby administrative authority, public resources and responsibilities are transferred from central government agencies to lower-level organs of government or to non-governmental bodies, such as community-based organisations (CBOs), third party non-governmental organisations (NGOs) or private sector actors (Craig Johnson, 2003: Crook and Manor, 1998: 6-7; Rondinelli *et al.*, 1989; Meenakshisundaram, 1999; World Bank, 2000a: 3). Conceptually, important distinctions can be made among:

Deconcentration, in which political, administrative and fiscal responsibilities are transferred to lower units *within* central line ministries or agencies (Crook and Manor, 1998: 6-7; Rondinelli *et al.*, 1989; Meenakshisundaram, 1999: 55; emphasis added); **Devolution,** in which sub-national units of government are either created or strengthened in terms of political, administrative and fiscal power (Blair, 2000; Crook and Manor, 1998: 6-7; Rondinelli *et al.*, 1989); **Delegation,** in which responsibilities are transferred to organisations that are '*outside the regular bureaucratic structure* and are only indirectly controlled by the central government,' (Meenakshisundaram, 1999: 55; emphasis added); **Privatisation,** in which all responsibility for government functions is transferred to nongovernmental organisations (NGOs) or private enterprises independent of government (Meenakshisundaram, 1999, 56). Such transfers can involve the power to decide the allocation and distribution of public resources, the power to implement programmes and policies and the power to raise and spend public revenues for these and other purposes. These three powers we can classify broadly as political, administrative and fiscal decentralisation.

Political decentralisation transfers policy and legislative powers from central government to autonomous, lower-level assemblies and local councils that have been democratically elected by their constituencies. **Administrative decentralisation** places planning and implementation responsibility in the hands of locally situated civil servants and these local civil servants are under the jurisdiction of elected local governments. **Fiscal decentralisation** accords substantial revenue and expenditure authority to intermediate and local governments.

However, democratic decentralisation implies more than the downward delegation of authority. Crucially, it entails a system of governance in which citizens possess the right to hold local public officials to account through the use of elections, grievance meetings and other democratic means. Blair (2000: 21) captures the essence of this important idea: Democratic decentralisation can be defined as meaningful authority devolved to local units of governance that are accessible and accountable to the local citizenry, who enjoy full political rights and liberty. It thus differs from the vast majority of earlier efforts at decentralization in developing areas, which go back to the 1950s, and which were largely initiatives in public administration without any serious democratic component. A defining feature of any democratic system is that decision-makers are under the 'effective popular control' (Mayo, 1960:60) of the people they are meant to govern. How this is accomplished, of course, constitutes a major dilemma for theorists and proponents of democratic development. Nevertheless, a number of defining features can be observed. Mayo (1960: 61-69) identifies four:

- popular control of policy makers, both by regular elections and by the pressure of social interest groups;
- the institutionalisation of all adult citizens in voting (i.e. one person, one vote);
- political freedom in the eyes of the state;
- policy decisions made on the basis of majority rule.

Beyond these very basic principles, democracy also implies a wide range of rules, norms and customs through which citizens can exercise 'effective popular control' over public officials. Included here would be an independent judiciary, a free press, systems of transparency, and freedom of association and speech (Luckham *et al.*, 2000; Putzel, 1997b).

Retrospect and Prospect

The forgoing analysis given in the beginning of this chapter provides a summary of the various measures taken by the government the field of rural development. Despite the serious commitment on the part of the government, the benefits of the programmes do not seem to reach the indented targets and they fail to serve fully the purpose for which they were launched. It has been observed that, more often than not, the rural development programmes are implemented without testing their local suitability. Theoretical perfection of a scheme is regarded as the criterion for the soundness of a programme, which should not be the case. Factors such as psychological receptivity, local conditions and constraints and lifestyle are often ignored while designing the rural development programmes.

Most of the rural development programmes, though indented for the poorest of the poor, have not fully helped in alleviating their problems. There is a lacuna in the identification of the really poor, with the result that the rich farmers have benefited much more from these programmes. The programmes have, no doubt, generated a ray of hope for the underprivileged sections of society, but they have, as yet, not brought about a perceptible rise in the income of these sections. Further, some other programmes have succeeded only partially because of the low motivation level among the villages. The basic problem of being unable to arouse popular participation has plagued most of these programmes. Little wonder, most of the programmes did not affect the rural poor substantially. It was found that the village level workers, who ought to have worked as the rural animators, did not truly accomplish their role satisfactory. An impression exists that a VLW is of greater help to the rural elite than to the rural poor. A look at the rural development programmes will also show that some of them have been launched by various political leaders with only an inadequate understanding of the complexity of the problems faced by the rural poor. It appears that, sometimes, they were simply forcing the programmes down the villagers' throats. Programmes with catchy slogans have also been launched in an haphazard manner just before elections and, hence, have been implemented in a half-hearted way.

A number of programmes, such as the TRYSEM, JRY, DWCRA, etc., are employment-oriented. Yet, they hold little or no interest for the rural youth who perhaps feel that there is little future for traditional cottage industry. These programmes offer only manual jobs, whereas the youth today want opportunities that are gainful and yet decent. Some programmes also suffer because of lack of adequate trainers. The involvement of the rural poor in the process of rural development is low, particularly in the planning and implementation of such programmes. On the other hand, top-level planners and administrators, generally, have not held a 'correct' perspective of the values of traditional Indian society and, very often, they offer solution which do not have much bearing on the holistic development process in rural areas. For instance, a beneficiary may be supplied with a buffalo, but due to the poor water resources in the village or absence of a veterinary doctor, the animal may die. Or else, the villager may be forced to sell it. Involvement of beneficiaries can help in making programmes more realistic.

There are several cases of default on the part of the beneficiaries also. There have been cases when the beneficiaries, financed by a bank for buying an oil engine, sold the engine off without the permission of the bank. The concerned banks do not have adequate staff to monitor and provide after-case service to the beneficiaries. Hence, the process of recovery by banks, including taking legal action against the defaulter, must be made effective.

A number of voluntary agencies are also involved in rural development. They are mostly dependent for their funds on the government those procedures are often slow and time-consuming, or on foreign donor agencies, whose grants may not be available on a regular basis. There is also lack of communication between the government and these agencies. As a result, the government funds may lapse because the agencies sometimes have no knowledge of these funds and when to avail themselves of them.

Financial institutions, chiefly the banks and cooperatives have a very crucial role to play in the success of the rural development programmes. It has been found in many cases that the loan sanctioned by the bank was inadequate and not timely, resulting in the diversion of funds for some other non-productive purposes. It was also found that some cooperative societies were charging the farmer more than the authorized interest rate. The banks also do not actively participate in the identification of the beneficiaries. They do not carry out pre-sanction inspection of the village before financing an activity. For instance, it has been found that, sometimes, an electric motor pumpset was financed without consideration of availability of electric power.

Regarding the involvement of the rural poor, all experiments in rural development including most of the present-day rural development schemes, emanate at the top. It is necessary that emphasis is laid on planning from the bottom and the exclusive reliance placed on the pyramidal structure approach has to be given up. Because of this approach to planning, the programmes also tend to have very high administrative costs. New technology, such as high yielding seeds, tractors, oil engines, etc., has no doubt been introduced in the agricultural and irrigation sectors, but it has helped the already rich farmers rather than the small and marginal farmers and agricultural labourers who have very little land to begin with. Had the measures of agricultural growth been preceded by land reforms, this problem could have been tackled more rationally.

Moreover, the organizational dimension needs a reappraisal. With a number of models of rural development administration experimented with and applied over the last for decades and more, it is time that the respective efficacy of each was intensely examined. Since the last one and a half decade, our general understanding of government and governance has been changing at a very fast pace. The forces of globalization, liberalization and the revolution in information technology have shattered many a myth hitherto held sacrosanct about the government and more specifically concerning its primary institution of governance the public administration. No longer can governments afford to support, rigid, bureaucratic, reactive, rules driven administrative organizations. Rather, today's administrative system must be flexible, consultative, result-oriented and proactive-encouraging and supporting creativity and innovation from the bottom to the top in order to govern and provide services to the citizens at large. There has been a considerable rethinking the way the governments now conduct their business, and they are looking more and more towards innovative solution to respond to an increasing number of complex new environmental and global problems and pressure, which are further accentuated in a developing, multi-linguistic, and a multi-cultural country like ours having diversity of social and religious systems.

Dr. M. Rajivlochan in his concluding paper has made an empirical escavation on the formal processes of Local Waster Supply System.

Against this backdrop this collection of seventeen articles contains indepth and illuminating discussion on various aspects of the Sustainable Rural Development under Panchayati Raj viz., Sustainable Rural Development and Millennium Development Goals, Participatory Watershed Management Approach, Role of Panchayats Towards Sustainable Rural Development, Role of Panchayats Towards Sustainable Social Development, Rural Development and NREG Act, Social Action, Gender Equity, Kudumbashree Projects, Interweaving of Economic Growth, Environmental Protection, Rainwater Harvesting, Rural Labour Banks, Income and Assets Generation, NABARD Refinance Assistance, Trusting Attitude in Rural Talent, Community Participation in Rural Development, Role of Artisans in Rural Development etc.

These introductory remarks remain incomplete without expressing gratitude to these who have been kind enough to help me in the preparation of this volume. I am extremely thankful to Shri Madan Sachdeva who brought out this volume in an elegant form and am also grateful to my wife Jaya, daughter Aishwarya and son Anantha Padmanabha for kindly sparing me the time for completing the volume.

2

Sustainable Rural Development and Millennium Development Goals: Challenges and Opportunities

Dr. Suresh Misra

Gandhiji said that India lives in villages. In spite of globalization, liberalization and rapid urbanization three quarters of India still lives in villages (72.20 per cent in 2001). Given the rapidity with which urban population is growing, this share will come down drastically in the decades to come... But if we count out the section of the urban population, which resides in towns and cities, but is rooted in villages, the rural population would continue to stay high... While a quarter (27.80 per cent) of population of India is classified as urban (in 2001), only 20.83 per cent of the labour force lives in cities. Rural areas thus sustain four-fifth of the total labour force (main workers) of the country. Over 64 per cent of India's population is engaged in agriculture compared that with 2 per cent in the United States. Most of India's farming families live in absolute poverty. They practice subsistence agriculture, only producing enough to feed themselves.

A decade after economic reforms, in 2003, according to NSS Household Consumer Consumption and Expenditure and Employment—Unemployment situation in India, the all India average monthly per capita consumer expenditure (MPCE) was Rs.554 for rural India. Those below Rs. 470 constituted fifty per cent of the rural population in India. For urban India it was Rs. 1022, that is about 84 per cent higher than rural areas. The proportion of rural households living in kutcha structures was 21 per cent.

A mere 5 per cent of the population controls 25 per cent of the agricultural land. The remaining land is broken up into very small family plots, some smaller than a single acre. The current fragmentation worsens under the land inheritance methods, dividing a man's land among all of his sons. The land reform measures following independence might have rectified some of the problems and inequities in the system. However, not surprisingly the large landowners also wield political power and have effectively blocked all attempts to reapportion agricultural land. The situation is not likely to change for decades to come.

The share of rural activities in the Gross National Product of the country is, however, secularly declining. Agriculture's share in the GDP in 1951 was 65 per cent; it declined to 45 per cent in 1971 and to 31 per cent in 1993. The agricultural growth rate has remained around 1.4 per cent in the last two decades. Naturally then, the per capita income of rural population is far lower than that of its counterpart living in urban areas. There are more poor in rural than in urban areas whether one looks at poverty in terms of absolute number or in terms of per cent of population below the poverty line. A substantial number of urban poor have deep roots in rural areas.

When we look at the question of poverty in terms of access to work opportunities and basic needs, the rural parts of India are in far worse situation. Self-reliance which made rural people meet their basic needs in the most adverse circumstances stands totally destroyed. Government, which professed and promised to uplift them from the miserable living conditions, have failed to do much if the records of the last five decades is any indicator. The less said about the implementation of the rural development schemes the better it is. Corruption has become the major cause of worry. The panchayats in large number of states continue to remain dormant and the local level bureaucracy still controls the rural development process. Why rural India remains under developed in spite of sixty years of Independence needs to be understood? Perhaps we have misunderstood the very notion of rural development. Poverty, unemployment, hunger, subsistence agriculture and poor public services are the hallmark of our rural development process.

Causes of Rural Underdevelopment

Distorted Notion of Development

The most fundamental factor is the ruling paradigm of development in general and rural development in particular. Enough has been written on this theme, and several attempts have been made to redefine development far more broadly and comprehensively than done hitherto. Development for a long time (until 1970s) was co-terminus with economic development as evident from per capita national income, industrial growth, urbanization, etc... How the income was distributed, what impacts economic growth had on the quality of life of the poor, and on ecology and environment were not pertinent concerns.

On becoming independent, India adopted a hybrid development style of mixing the styles pursued in the USA, Western Europe and the then Soviet Union. In this model of development, rural functions and villages were treated as historical relics of a dying civilization. Ultimate answer was industrialization and urbanization. As such rural development policies remained populist, designed to push agricultural production upto feed the growing number of people and industries.

Given the above world view, rural development was equated with agricultural development. The logic ran something like this. Increased agricultural production will generate surplus for export to urban markets, within and outside the country. The rural incomes and wages will go up. This in turn will promote consumption of goods and services in rural areas. Surplus agricultural labour will move to the urban industries making urban centers the engines of economic growth. In due course of time India will get urbanised and only a small percentage of labour force will be left in rural areas to take care of a highly mechanised agriculture.

Rural-Urban Divide

Rural and urban areas were treated as two different worlds inhabited by two different sets of people. A typical villager was considered to be an ignorant, conservative, traditional peasant unwilling to change and adapt urban ways of life. As against this, an urbanite was supposed to be dynamic, risk taking, rational and willing to learn and change. The outcome of these notions is the present hiatus between rural and urban development policies in India.

Rural and urban centers in reality constitute a continuum of human settlements. They are sub-systems of a single system with considerable amount of overlapping of functions, problems, and perquisites of development. They are interring dependent and complimentary too. To divide them into watertight compartments is to ignore their potentials and to subvert the future of both. Today the rural and urban worlds in India are too far away from each other in terms of income, assets, occupational structure and quality of life. True there are rich as well as poor people in rural as well as urban centers, and the depth of poverty in both the places is highly degrading. But the rural areas are much worse off; they are struggling hard to save their souls.

How has this rural-urban divide come into being? It is a phenomenon of the last two hundred years or so. In ancient and medieval times there was nothing of this sort. There were large cities earlier too yet they were few in number. The villages were self-reliant and were well-served by small townships. It is pertinent to note that most of the productive functions were rural based. Even the industrial goods were produced in rural areas. Large and intermediate size cities were clearing houses for these goods. The picture was not rosy, but it was not so depressing either. With the advent of the British and the capitalist enterprises, the situation changed drastically and a new rural urban relationship mediated by international capital developed.

Consequences of Rural Underdevelopment

Lack of adequate and appropriate development in rural parts of India has had several consequences. Some of these have further deepened poverty in villages and some others have wider ramifications. A few of them are discussed below:

Decreasing Access to Land

Land in its broadest sense is the most vital resource of rural India. Its importance further increases in the context of rapid growth of population particularly in rural areas. The first task of any meaningful rural development policy, its quality and to ensure the access to land for all those who were denied the same. Another major task would be to diversify the rural economy to such an extent that dependence of the people on agriculture declined.

Agricultural census returns have consistently shown iniquitous distribution of arable land in India. In 1971, the country had 71 million operational holdings which increased to 105 million in 1990-91. The average size of holdings however declined from 2.28 ha in 1970-71 to 1.57 ha in 1990-91 indicating increasing pressure of population on land resources. When we look at the size of distribution of holdings, we find that 69.9 per cent of holdings were small i.e. less than 2 ha in 1970-71. The proportion increased to 78.9 per cent in 1990-91. The share of marginal holdings (less than one ha) also increased from 51 per cent to 59 per cent. In 1970-71, almost 70 per cent (69.90 per cent) of the total operational holdings accounted for only 20.9 per cent of the area operated. The situation changed only marginally in 1990-91 when 78.7 per cent of the holdings accounted for only 32.2 per cent of the area operated.

Poor Quality of Rural Life

Rural underdevelopment has produced a vicious circle of poverty and unemployment; it does not allow people to get out of it. Today the small and marginal farmers are committing suicide as they are in severe debt. They have very little options left, a few migrate to over-crowded cities but the cities offer nothing better and they return only to repay the debt they had taken to go to the cities. Only those who are educated and skilled make migration a success story. The rest are condemned to live in slums and jhuggi jhopadies and to eke out a living from what is known as informal sector of the urban economy. No less than 30 per cent of the rural people of India live below the poverty line. But the quality of life of the other 70 per cent is no better. But even 30 per cent means 300 million people which are too huge to be ignored. These are the people without food security; who cannot afford to send their children to school; who have no money for health care; who have just a roof over their head; and who are partially or completely dependent on government support direct or indirect.

Apart from these the public service delivery mechanism is very poor in the rural areas. Sectors like education, health, environment, sanitation, and infrastructure continue to be largely neglected, even though crores of rupees are being spent in the name of the rural poor. In a recent report of the Human Resource Ministry, Government of India it has been found that nearly 33,000 primary schools in India do not have students. Many of these schools must be in the rural areas. In a study on Corruption in Education by UNESCO's International Institute of Educational Planning states that teacher's absenteeism in India is among the highest in the world. While the global average of teacher absenteeism is about 20 per cent, in India it is 25 per cent. While in Bihar two of every five teachers were reported absent, the figure in UP was reported to be one in every three. These are the two states where the bulk of the population still lives in rural areas. The condition is no better in other states.

Environmental Degradation

Rural underdevelopment has left no option for the people but to consume natural resources in far larger amounts than ever before. Having no other sources of livelihood, they have encroached upon the forests, pastures and water bodies destroying the ecological balance which once was the hallmark of rural space. Many plant and animal species are lost forever and many more are on the verge of extinction. The situation is highly disturbing in region of fragile ecology such as the Himalayas, Western ghats, coastal zones, deserts and reverie tracts and degradation, depletion of underground water resources, deforestation and loss of biodiversity have emerged as major concerns of the people. Rural areas are no longer the preserves of nature. Man's reach has extended to highest mountains and deepest oceans. So long as he remains cut off from nature and treats it as material resource to be used as and when needed to satisfy his ever increasing wants, ecological balance would remain disturbed.

We need to reorient our rural development programmes and policies. The need is to eradicate poverty, target hunger, promote gender equality and empower women and improve the quality of services being delivered in the rural areas. The Millennium Declaration Goals must be the guiding force if we are serious about improving the quality of rural life. The MDG's should help us achieve a sustainable rural development.

Millennium Declaration Goals

In 2000, the member states of the United Nations adopted the Millennium Declaration as a renewed commitment to human development. The Declaration includes eight Millennium Development Goals (MDGs), each with quantified targets, to motivate the international community and provide an accountability mechanism for actions taken to enable millions of poor people to improve their livelihoods.

About 70 per cent of the MDGs' target group lives in rural areas, particularly in Asia and Africa, and for most of the rural poor agriculture are a critical component in the successful attainment of the MDGs. Thus, a necessary component in meeting the MDGs by 2015 in many parts of the world is a more productive and profitable agricultural sector.

The Millennium Declaration adopted by the General Assembly of the United Nations in September 2000 reaffirmed its commitment to the right to development, peace, security and gender equality, to the eradication of many dimensions of poverty and to overall sustainable development. These are intended for the member countries to take efforts in the fight against poverty, illiteracy, hunger, lack of education, gender inequality, infant and maternal mortality, disease and environmental degradation. The Millennium Declaration adopted 8 development goals, 18 time-bound targets and 48 indicators.

The Millennium Development Goals are:

1. Eradicate extreme poverty and hunger.
2. Achieve universal primary education.
3. Promote gender equality and empower women.
4. Reduce child mortality.
5. Improve maternal health.
6. Combat HIV/AIDS, malaria and other diseases.
7. Ensure environmental sustainability, and
8. Develop a global partnership for development.

The first Millennium Development Goals—India Country Report for the year 2005 captures India's achievements, challenges and policies with reference to the goals and targets and reveals that there have been substantial improvements in the lives of people of the country over the years. This has been possible due to the planned implementation of programmes despite the enormous and complex problems and diversities of our nation. The Central and State Governments have set up goals more ambitious than the MDGs. With the well-thought out planning, comprehensive development strategies devised in the national policy, and matching implementation process, it is hoped that India will be able to meet the challenges and achieve all the MDG targets much earlier than the targeted dates.

India's position with reference to the various goals is given below:

1. To achieve the goal of eradicating extreme poverty and hunger, India must reduce by 2015 the proportion of people below poverty line from nearly 37.5 per cent in 1990 to about 18.75 per cent. As on 1999-2000, the poverty headcount ratio is 26.1 per cent with poverty gap ratio of 5.2 per cent, share of poorest quintile in national consumption is 10.1 per cent for rural sector and 7.9 per cent for urban sector and

prevalence of underweight children is of the order of 47 per cent. National Rural Employment Act is a positive step to reduce the poverty ratio further.

2. To achieve universal primary education under Goal-2, India should increase the primary school enrolment rate to 100 per cent and wipe out the drop-outs by 2015 against 41.96 per cent in 1991-92. The drop-out rate for primary education during 2002-03 is 34.89 per cent. The gross enrolment ratio in primary education has tended to remain near 100 per cent for boys and recorded an increase of nearly 20 percentage points in the ten years period from 1992-93 to 2002-03 for girls (93 per cent). The literacy rate (7 years and above) has also increased from 52.2 per cent in 1992-93 to 65.4 per cent in 2000-01.

   To ensure gender parity in education levels in Goal-3, India will have to promote female participation at all levels to reach a female male proportion of equal level by 2015. The female male proportion in respect of primary education was 71:100 in 1990-91 which has increased to 78:100 in 2000-01. During the same period, the proportion has increased from 49:100 to 63:100 in case of secondary education.

3. Goal 4 aims at reducing under five mortality rate (U5MR) from 125 deaths per thousand live births in 1988-92 to 42 in 2015. The U5MR has decreased during the period 1998-2002 to 98 per thousand live births. The infant mortality rate (IMR) has also come down from 80 per thousand live births in 1990 to 60 per thousand in 2003 and the proportion of 1 year old children immunised against measles has increased from 42.2 per cent in 1992-93 to 58.5 per cent in 2002-03.

4. To achieve Goal-5, India should reduce maternal mortality (MMR) from 437 deaths per 100,000 live births in 1991 to 109 by 2015. The value of MMR for 1998 is 407. The proportion of births attended by skilled health personnel has been continuously increasing, (from 25.5 per cent in 1992-93 to 39.8 per cent in 2002-03) thereby reducing the chances of occurrence of maternal deaths.

5. Insofar as Goal-6 is concerned, though India has a low prevalence of HIV among pregnant women as compared to other developing countries, yet the prevalence rate has increased from 0.74 per thousand pregnant women in 2002

to 0.86 in 2003. This increasing trend needs to be reversed to achieve MDG 6. The prevalence and death rates associated with malaria are consistently coming down. The death rate associated with TB has come down from 67 deaths per 100,000 populations in 1990 to 33 per 100,000 populations in 2003. The proportion of TB patients successfully treated has also risen from 81 per cent in 1996 to 86 per cent in 2003.

6. Goal-7 aims at ensuring environmental sustainability. As per assessment made in 2003, total land area covered under different forests has been 20.64 per cent due to Government's persistent efforts to preserve the natural resources. The reserved and protected forests together account for 19 per cent of the total land area to maintain biological diversity. The energy use has declined consistently from about 36 kilogram oil equivalent in 1991-92 to about 32 kilogram oil equivalent in 2003-04 to produce GDP worth Rs. 1000. The proportion of population without sustainable access to safe drinking water and sanitation is to be halved by 2015 and India is on track to achieve this target.
7. Goal-8 is regarding the developing global partnership for development. It is basically meant for the developed countries to provide development assistance to developing countries... The Government of India holds the following views regarding the role of the developed countries in achieving this goal:
   - The financial support needed to achieve the targets under this Goal had been estimated for the least developed land locked and small countries by a high-level panel on 'Financing for Development at an additional amount of US $ 50 billion which would be required for this purpose every year till 2015.
   - However, a huge gap still exists for those countries between the development assistance required to meet the MDGs and what has been pledged by the developed countries so far.
   - Recent months have seen new commitments toward reaching the internationally accepted 0.7 per cent of Gross National Income (GNI) target. We have reminded that these potential increases still leave development assistance donor countries as a group well short of 0.7 per cent.

- It is also a matter of satisfaction that actual disbursements of ODA, in recent years, have shown a welcome reversal of the declining trend that lasted for almost a decade since the early 1990s. In this regard, it is important to realize that unless aid commitments translate into actual delivery, securing MDGs will remain elusive goals. We do hope that all the developed countries would scale up the ODA to realize the goals reaffirmed at the Monterrey Consensus.
- It has also been our consistent position that additional resources for implementing the development agenda should be channelized through the existing multilateral agencies. Moreover, allocations must be based on pre-defined and transparent criteria. Our own development experience clearly indicates that, ultimately, it is the availability of untied additional resources for use in accordance with national development strategies, which is most beneficial for recipient countries.
- To deal with the problems of debt, the Heavily Indebted Poor Countries (HIPC) Initiative was launched by the World Bank and IMF and endorsed by 180 governments. In regard to the HIPC Initiative, India is of the view that the Initiative should be met by additional funding from the developed countries and the flow of concessional assistance to other countries should not be reduced. India also opposes the concept of "equitable burden sharing" since some of the non-Paris Club creditor countries are themselves poor countries.
- We have supported the G8 initiative on irrevocable debt cancellation for the HIPC countries, which has now been adopted by IMF and the World Bank as the Multilateral Debt Relief Initiative (MDRI). We have always been supportive of all efforts being extended to the low-income countries (LICs), including those in Africa, where debt burdens are serious threats to attainment of the MDGs.

8. With regard to one of the targets of the Goal 8, i.e. in cooperation with the private sector, make available the benefits of new technologies, especially information and communications, India has made substantial progress in recent years. The overall tele-density has remarkably

increased from 0.67 per cent in 1991 to 9.4 per cent in June 2005. Use of Personal Computers has also increased from 5.4 million PCs in 2001 to 14.5 million in 2005 and there are 5.3 million internet subscribers as on March 2005 (2.3 internet users per 100 populations and 0.5 per 100 internet subscribers).

9. The National Employment Guarantee Act, Sarva Siksha Abhiyan, Total Literacy Campaign of the National Literacy Mission, 73rd and 74th constitutional amendments providing reservation for women, commitment for women empowerment in the NCMP, National Health Mission, Total Sanitation Campaign and Bharat Nirman are some of the important steps taken by the Government which will help in achieving the Millennium Development Goals.

Making Sustainable Rural Development Work

No doubt the target should be to reduce poverty, improve the health and education facilities, combat diseases but given the nature of rural areas it is not possible to have a single pattern of development all over the country. The MDG's should be integrated with the very nature of rural structure. Some of the areas which could help in bringing about a sustainable rural development through the MDG's could be as follows:

Land Use Planning

Land is the most vital resource of rural areas. Rural land should be classified on the basis of its suitability for various uses—agriculture, forestry, pasture, public uses, habitation, etc... Each micropolitan region should have a land use plan and the same should be made a legal document. Each village should also have a land use plan which should detail out the suitability of each piece of land (plot) for various crops, tillage practice, irrigation, and mix of chemical and organic manuring.

Each village should have a forest land, something like the Deoban of older days or biodiversity reserves of modern times. The forest land should cover at least 5-10 acres of land depending upon the size of the village. It should be a common property, only dead wood should remain on it, so that in due course of time minor wild animals can get shelter. And each micropolitan region should have a biodiversity reserve of 10-15 ha. Each village and micropolitan region should have water management plan, along with the land use plan.

Misuse of water has become a major problem in the world. In India water scarcity has assumed serious proportions. The first step in this direction would be revive/restore the dead ponds and other water bodies. The second step that is urgently needed is to ration canal water to discourage flow irrigation that is leading to rise in water table. Drinking water should get priority in water resource planning.

Each micropolitan region should evolve a production plan which should meet the following requirements: (1) Food requirements of the region; (2) Agro-industrial requirements of region; (3) Export crops; (4) Input requirements (water, chemical fertilizers, manuring etc.); and (5) Training of the people. Efforts should be made to persuade the farmers to follow the plan indicators. The production plan should also include potentials of energy manure and seed production. Potential markets for village products should get due attention.

Self-Reliance

Each village must produce its own foodgrains, vegetables, fruits, milk and milk products as well as red and white meat (wherever relevant). But in case it is not done because of the physical and ecological constraints, it should be achieved at the micropolitan level. Any residuals should be met at the supra-micropolitan level so that practically each district would be self-reliant in food and raw materials it needs to run its processing and service industries. Each micropolitan region should ultimately generate its own electricity, manage its waste, produce manure, and have its own marketing outlet; run its own school, gramin bank and health service. It should have its own water supply system as well as excreta disposal.

Each household in the village must be engaged in one or the other non-farm functions—services or processing of agricultural produce. Each village should aim at selling nothing without processing. This may never be achieved, because lot of agricultural commodities has to be consumed fresh (fruits and vegetables). But to keep such a perspective will be helpful in diversification.

Ecological Regeneration

It is yet to be realised that environmental reconstruction can become a highly paying proposition. Community forests with selective cuttings can generate lot of resources. Pasture land with regulated entry of animals can promote dairying, and leaving water bodies intact provides avenues for aquaculture of plants and fish. Rural areas should become green again and its sanitation should reach the standards of at least Harappa and Mohenjodaro which flourished in India over 4000 years ago, within the next two decades or so.

Micropolitan Planning

Indian planners should not be neglectful of villages and rural areas as they have been in the past. They should adopt the concept of modular cities and modular micropolitan regions and prepare plans for each city and village with sustainability as the basic requirement. Each district should have a sustainable micropolitan regional development plan of action, so that the message can spread out to other parts. And each state should have an experimental action plan for a city with modular units.

Summing up

The basic objective of sustainable rural development is to develop a balanced and ecologically sound microregional economy and polity. In an ideal setting and within a span of 20 years (i.e. by 2025) the rural economy should derive 30 per cent of its income from crop farming, 25 per cent from processing activities, 30 per cent from services and 15 per cent from remittances from outside and government.

In country like India, where the majority of the population still lives in rural areas, improving the quality of rural life should be on top the priority. The productivity and the service delivery mechanism need to be improved and targeted programmes to achieve the MDGs should be charted in full sincerity. The need is also to restructure the service delivery mechanism in the rural areas. We also need to address the issues and problems being faced by institutions of local governance. Integrating MDGs with the activities of the panchayats may help to some extent. For India to make impact on the world map the rural areas need to be taken care of.

REFERENCES

National Sample Survey Organisation; Household Consumer Consumption and Expenditure and Employment—Unemployment Situation in India, Jan–Dec., 2003, New Delhi.

United Nations: The Millennium Development Goals Report, 2007, New York.

Government of India, Ministry of Rural Development: Performance Budget of Department of Rural Development, 2002-03, New Delhi.

P.N. Sankaran: Rural and Urban Development: A Partnership Perspective, Kurukshetra, Vol.53, No. 2, Dec. 2004, New Delhi.

S.N.Mishra: A Case of Rural-Urban Integration, Kurukshetra, Vol. XL.VI, No. 1 & 2, Oct., 1977, New Delhi.

3

Participatory Watershed Management: Approach for Sustainable Rural Livelihood

Dr. Sanjay Arora

India is primarily agricultural country. Out of the total geographical area of 329 million hectares, 165 million hectares comes under cultivated area and of this cultivated area only one-third receive irrigation and the remaining area depends on rainfall. Except for the high rainfall region in the east, north-east and some costal districts, the rainfall in most parts of the country is characterized by medium to low and even very low leading to droughts. Not only the total rainfall, but also its distribution during growth period is important for a crop, but both are dependent on chance. Substantial areas of India periodically experienced droughts leading to considerable loss of agricultural production, livestock, besides causing misery to people inhabiting these areas. Fifty-four districts in the country together with parts of another 18 districts contiguous to them are identified as drought prone.

This rainfed agriculture contributes about 45 per cent of food production and about 40 per cent of population are dependent on this rainfed agriculture. It was estimated that about 235 million tons of food production would be required to meet the demand of sowing population by 2025 AD, even with all possible efforts to bring more area under irrigation. Not only is that, around 60 per cent of the nation's cattle wealth concentrated in these rainfed areas. Course cereals, pulses, oilseed crops and cotton are the principal rainfed crops. Unlike the irrigated crops, the rainfed crops, were not affected by the green revolution. Impact of the green revolution came into focus largely because of tremendous boost to irrigated agriculture and use of improved variety of seeds. But the gains in agricultural production did not reach the vast rainfed areas of the country and development of dry land farming did not get the attention it deserved. The result was though the objective of overall food production was increased, it created unintended serious agricultural, socio-economic and ecological imbalance. Low and unstable production continued to haunt large areas of rainfed agriculture. The main reasons include inadequate rainwater conservation, intensified scarcity of soil moisture availability, generally degraded infertile soils, and poor entrepreneurial base of rainfed farmer. All these results in poor socio-economic conditions of the farmers in the area.

Rainfed Area Development

The Government has made numerous efforts like All India Coordinated Research Project for Dryland Agriculture (AICRPDA), Integrated Dryland Agricultural Development Project (IDADP), etc did not receive adequate financial support and priority. The resource base of farmers in drylands is very poor and their credit worthiness is almost zero. Hence, the transfer of technology to farmers field was very slow and low due to operational, institutional, geopolitical and socio-economic constraints. The idea of 'watershed approach' or 'area approach' was conceived, designed and developed to test strengths and weaknesses of dryland technology based on the experience gained in demonstrations at farmers fields, Operational Research Programme (ORP), Lab-to-Land Programme, Krishi Vigyan Kendra (KVK) etc. The watershed programme was initiated during 1983-84 by Government of India, financing through different state governments. Model watershed projects were formulated and implemented with the involvement of Indian Council of Agricultural Research (ICAR) as pilot projects. ICAR through Central Research Institute for Dryland Agriculture (CRIDA) was made responsible for testing technologies developed at Dryland Research Stations. These projects generated valuable information, which culminated in the launching of the National Watershed Development Programme for Rainfed Agriculture (NWDPRA) in the Seventh Five Year Plan covering 99 districts in 16 states. These watersheds are distributed in different agro-climatic zones with varying topography and soil types, which provide appropriate conditions for evaluating the performance of dryland technologies. The main thrust of the watershed programme is to conserve the rainwater or soil resources to an eco-zone through appropriate technology development.

Meaning of Watershed

A watershed is a basin-like landform defined by peaks, which are connected with ridgelines that descend into lower elevations and small valleys. It is a ridge of elevated land dividing two areas that are drained by different river systems. A watershed carries rainwater falling on it drop by drop and channels it into the soil, rivulets and streams flowing into larger rivers and in due course to the sea. The important fact about watersheds is that the activities carried out in a watershed affect the people living downstream.

A watershed is the entire region drained by a waterway that drains into a lake or reservoir or the total area above a given point on a stream that contributes water flow at that point. A single watershed may include different areas under forests, glaciers, deserts and/or grasslands. A watershed may be nearly flat or may include landform features like hillocks, hills or mountains. Watersheds come in all shapes and sizes. They cut across village, district, state, and national boundaries.

Definition of a Watershed

A watershed is a geo-hydrological unit that has been described and used as a physical-biological unit and also, on many occasions, as a socio-economic-political unit for planning and management natural resources (Sheng, 1990).

Land elevation, not political borders, defines watershed boundaries. Generally a watershed can be sub-divided into sub-watersheds. It is bounded by the ridge line, which starts from and closes at the same common draining point duly encircling the watershed.

Various definitions have been proposed over the recent years for the term 'watershed'. While the definitions use a wide variety of words, they all mean practically the same thing. Since big watersheds consist of many smaller watersheds, it is necessary to define the watershed in terms of a point. This point is usually referred to as the watershed 'outlet'. With respect to the outlet, the watershed consists of all land area that sheds water to the outlet during a rainstorm (McCuen, 1969). A watershed is a topographically delineated area that is drained by a stream system, i.e. the total land area that is drained to some point on a stream or river. Generally a watershed can be defined as an area from which runoff resulting from precipitation flows past a single point into a stream, river, lake or an ocean. The terms watershed, catchment area or drainage basin are used synonymously. The watershed boundary is called drainage divide. Rains received on opposite sides of drainage divide do not contribute runoff and reach to the adjoining areas.

Watershed Management

Watershed development consists of conservation, regeneration and the judicious use of all the resources—natural (like land, water, plants, animals) and human within the watershed area. Watershed management seeks to bring about the best possible balance in the environment between natural resources on the one side and man and animals on the other. Since it is the man who is primarily responsible for the degradation of environment regeneration and conservation can only be possible by promoting, awakening and ensuring the participation of the people who inhabit the watersheds. Watershed management is defined as the integrated use, regulation and development of water and land resources of a watershed in order to accomplish sustainable use of land, water and vegetation. The emphasis is on soil and water conservation.

Principles of Watershed Management

The main principles of watershed management are as under (Mahnot and Singh, 1993):

(i) Utilizing the land according to its capability.

(ii) Maintaining adequate vegetative cover on the soil for controlling soil erosion, mainly during rainy season.

(iii) Conserving maximum possible rainwater at the place where it falls, on arable land by contour farming.

(iv) Draining out excess water with a safe velocity to avoid soil erosion and storing it in ponds for future use.

(v) Preventing erosion in gullies and increasing ground water recharge by putting nullah bunds and gully plugs at suitable intervals.

Watershed Management and Multiple Use Concept

A multiple use perspective is required to achieve sustained and integrated watershed management, particularly in those areas, where large rural population depend upon a variety of resources produced in upland watersheds. It may be noted that much of the intensive farming, grazing, and timber harvesting that take place in most of the areas is leading to watershed degradation, loss of bio-diversity and adverse downstream impacts.

Watershed inhabitants in many areas practice multiple use, which involves the production of goods that they require such as food, fibre, fuel and fodder. Most of the development activities are closely associated to the development and use of water resources. Thus, multiple use is being practised on various watersheds, but whether multiple use is being properly managed for upland and downstream inhabitants is a matter of concern.

The main aim of multiple use management is to manage natural resource mixture for the most beneficial combination at present and future uses. It is not necessary that every watershed is managed for all possible natural resource products simultaneously. Instead, most of the watersheds are utilized for various natural resource products depending on levels of supplies and demand. Multiple uses can be accomplished by one or more of the following options (Brooks *et al.*, 1997):

(i) Concurrent and continuous use of several natural resource products obtainable on a particular watershed requiring the production of several goods and services from the same area.

(ii) Alternating or rotating the use of various natural resource products on a watershed.

(iii) Geographic separation of uses or use combinations, so that multiple use is accomplished across a mosaic of land management units on a watershed, with any use to which it is most suited. It is important that effective multiple use management should accommodate to the extent possible the full spectrum of today's requirements while providing for tomorrow needs.

Types of Multiple Use Management

There are two types of multiple use management viz. resource oriented and area oriented. Resource oriented multiple use management represents the alternative uses of one or more natural resources. For instance, timber can be managed for lumber, fuel wood and pulp. Such management depends upon the knowledge of interrelationships—showing how the management of one natural resources affects other uses of the same resources or how one use of a natural resource affects other uses of the same resource. Resource oriented multiple use management needs thorough understanding of the production capacities of natural resources.

Area oriented multiple use management represents the production of a mix of products and amenities from a particular area. It is important that area-oriented multiple use should consider the physical, biological, economic and social factors related to resource product development in a given area. Area oriented multiple use gets the information required to describe resources potentials from resource oriented multiple use and then relates this to the dynamics of local, regional and national demands. Brooks *et al.* (1997) show multiple resources from land area that result in several products (Table–1). It may be noted that area oriented multiple use management is not necessarily intended to replace other forms of land management but to complement them.

Table–1
Multiple Resources from Land Area Resulting Several Products

Resource	*Products*
Water	Irrigation, Municipal are Industrial, Recreation
Timber	Lumber, Pulp, Wood, Fuel wood, Recreation
Forage	Livestock, Wildlife, Recreation
Wildlife	Consumption, Recreation
Minerals	Depends on the Type of Mineral

Watershed Size

Watershed is an area from which the runoff flows through a common point on the drainage system. Naturally, the size of the watershed may vary from a few square meters to thousands of square kilometers and is categorized accordingly (Table–2). However, a particular size of a watershed depends upon the objectives of development. For a major and medium irrigation projects watersheds of thousands of square kilometers may be considered. On the other hand for a small storage structure on the farm, the size of watershed may be only a few hectares. For agricultural purposes, the criteria for deciding the size may be time and money available for integrated development of a watershed. Size of the watershed would be affected by the possible major components of development such as afforestation, pasture development and cultivation. The physiographic conditions such as valleys, undulating foothills, and rugged hilly areas would also influence the selection of appropriate size of the watersheds. Larger watersheds can be selected in the plain valley areas or where pasture or forest development may be the major objectives. In the hilly areas or where intensive agriculture development is planned, the size of the watershed may be small. For land management point of view, a convenient size of watershed may vary from 500 ha to 1000 ha. However, these limits should not be taken rigidly. On an average, a size of 2000 ha is considered reasonable for agricultural development with regard to ease of surveys, investigations and effective planning keeping in view the local conditions and completion of the project within a reasonably short time (Tideman, 1996).

Table–2
Types and Sizes of Watersheds

Hydrologic unit	*Area (size) hectares*
Macro-watershed	50,000–2,00,000
Sub-watershed	10,000–50,000
Micro-watershed	100–1,000

Objectives of Watershed Management

Watershed management is concerned with the wise use of soil, water and vegetation of a watershed area to obtain optimum production with minimum hazard to the natural resources. The basic objective of watershed management is to solve the problems of soil and water on the basis that all the resources are interdependent and must therefore, be considered together. Watershed management aims to improve the standard of living of common man by increasing his earning capacity through offering all facilities required for optimum production.

The main objectives of watershed management programmes may be outlined as under :

- *(i)* Recognition of watershed as a proper unit for judicious utilization and development of all lands. The land should be treated according to the requirement and by adopting suitable methods that will control soil erosion, conserve water, improve farm income, encourage wildlife and prevent flood damage to the lands.
- *(ii)* Prevention and retardation of floods through construction of reservoirs and other impounding structures.
- *(iii)* Provision of adequate water supply for agricultural, industrial and domestic purposes.
- *(iv)* Abatement of soil, water and air pollution.

(*v*) Creation of recreational facilities with more lakes and streams suitable for picnic, camping, swimming, boating and fishing.

(*vi*) Utilization of natural resources for improving agriculture and allied occupation or industries in order to improve socio-economic conditions of local people.

The objectives of managing a watershed should be clearly and precisely defined. Different objectives call for different techniques, manpower, inputs and approaches for proper planning and execution.

Components of Watershed Management

Development activities in a watershed have to be taken up in a holistic and integrated manner on an area saturation basis. It not only seeks to stop the ongoing degradation of natural resources but also to conserve, enhance and utilize the natural resources for production on a sustained basis. In the process, all natural resources such as land, water, vegetation, livestock and also people within the watershed are to be developed. The following indicative lists of components of watershed management are interactive and interdependent and they could be included when a plan is prepared for watershed management. According to revised Guidelines for Watershed Development issued by Department of Land Resources (DoLR), Ministry of Rural Development, Government of India in 2001 the components of watershed are:

- Land development including *in-situ* soil and moisture conservation measures like contour and graded bunds fortified by plantation, bench terracing in hilly terrain; and nurseries for fodder, timber, fuel wood, horticulture and non-timber forest produce.
- Afforestation including block plantations, agro-forestry and horticultural development. Shelter-belt plantations, sand dune stabilization, etc.
- Drainage line treatment with a combination of vegetative and engineering structures.
- Development of small water harvesting structures such as low-cost farm ponds, nala bunds, check dams and percolation tanks and ground water recharge measures.
- Renovation and augmentation of water resources, desiltation of tanks for drinking water and irrigation.

- Pasture development either by itself or in conjunction with plantations.
- Repair, restoration and upgrading of existing common property assets and structures in the watershed to obtain optimum and sustained benefits from previous public investments.
- Crop demonstrations for popularizing new crops and crop varieties or innovative crop management practices.
- Promotion and propagation of non-conventional energy saving devices and energy conservation measures.

Selection of Watershed Site

The Hanumantha Rao Committee recommended the need to adopt the watershed approach in the implementation of area development programmes so that the development efforts of different agencies working in the watershed are sharply focused on a single eco-system and technical expertise can flow to a definite area and local people can be involved in its management.

The watershed projects would be implemented in the districts and the blocks that have been notified by Government of India under the respective area development programmes. The villages are selected keeping the following points in view:

- Those villages from where people's participation is assured through voluntary donations/contributions in terms of labour, raw materials, cash, etc. for the developmental activities as well as for the operation and maintenance of the assets created.
- For investments on community works/development of common property resources such as pasture lands, social forestry, community nurseries etc. on public or private lands, at least five per cent of the cost of investment shall be contribution from the community.

The contribution may come from the village community/ panchayat or users who are likely to derive benefit from these investments.

For investments on individual works on private property, at least ten per cent of the value of work/ investment must come from the beneficiary/users. A resolution from the Gram Panchayat to the effect that the village community/Panchayat is willing to take over, operate and maintain the physical assets that will be created as a part of the watershed development project.

A resolution from the Gram Panchayat to the effect that the Gram Panchayat in the case of common property resources like fisheries, tanks, common pasture lands, community forests/wood lots etc., other community assets created under the project, shall be willing to share the benefits from these assets with the Scheduled Castes, Scheduled Tribes, women and other persons below the poverty line in an equitable manner.

Where some Voluntary Agency/Krishi Vigyan Kendra (KVK)/ other government or private institutions like Agricultural University Research Stations, Public Undertakings, Cooperatives, Private Sector Companies/Organizations, Banks etc. are working and willing to take on the responsibility of project implementation. Where the village community has already been successfully organized into homogeneous groups for thrill, and credit activity under Development of Women and Children in Rural Areas (DWACRA), social forestry, joint forest management committees, community-based welfare, prohibition, etc. have been successfully organized in the recent past.

- Where water is allocated on priority basis and other facilities are provided to 'serve' the lands of marginal farmers and women.

Criteria for Selection of Watershed Village

In each selected village, a watershed of approximately 500 ha shall be identified and selected by the Watershed Development Team (WDT) in consultation with the Panchayat/Village community. The following criteria may be used in the selection of the watershed:

- assured people's participation through contribution of labour, cash, material etc for its development as well as for the operation and maintenance of the assets created
- acute shortage of drinking water
- a large population of scheduled castes/schedule tribes dependent on it
- preponderance of wastelands
- preponderance of common lands
- actual wages are significantly lower than the minimum wages

- the chosen watershed is contiguous to another watershed which has already been developed/is selected for development
- five hundred ha., preferably covering an entire village, is a general norm and, if on actual survey, a watershed is found to have slightly less or more area the total area may be taken up for development
- in case the watershed area falls in two or more villages the watershed should be divided into village-wise sub-watersheds and activities should be/undertaken simultaneously.

Watershed Management for Rural Development

The environment is an area wherein the human community lives and makes its livelihood. When the economic and natural conditions of the community deteriorate, the community tends to overexploit and degrade the natural resources which, in turn, further aggravate poverty. Degradation of any of the natural resources reflects in the degradation of other resources and the degradation of natural resources directly leads to fall in productivity. The inhabitants of problem areas progressively become poor, with progressive degradation of natural resources resulting in a vicious cycle. It is, therefore, necessary to understand the relationship between the poverty and the degraded environment the villagers live in. Human beings and their activities are the cause of environmental destruction and they alone can undo the damage. Sustainable natural resource management is possible through improvement of environmental conditions with the active participation of all the inhabitants of the concerned environment/area. Indian villages are the suppliers of food for more than one billion people. Nevertheless they are the victim of the unpredictable monsoons and market prices for their produce and ever increasing food requirements. All these lead to more intensive use of available land, which results in creation of vast stretches of wastelands, barren land, degraded land, water logging etc. In India, about 57 per cent of area is suffering from different soil degradation as a result of over-population, harsh climate conditions, overexploitation, improper use of soil resources, deforestation, etc. A populous country like India cannot afford to let these lands remain waste. Ministry of Agriculture (Government of India) has prepared a Wasteland Atlas of India on a 1:50000 scale in which 584 districts in 29 States and Union Territories were covered.

Of the total geographical area covered under this atlas, 19.42 per cent is wasteland.

More than half of the area of Himachal Pradesh, Manipur, Nagaland and Sikkim States is wasteland. Twenty-five to 50 per cent of total the geographical area of Assam, Jammu and Kashmir, Meghalaya and Rajasthan States is wasteland. In the remaining states, wasteland constitutes less than 25 per cent.

The governments at the Centre and at the State level formulate and implement a number of area development programmes with a view to restoring the environment and also to convert these problem areas into productive lands adopting various approaches. All these area development programmes have been brought under the Watershed Development Project (WDP). Since 1995-96 the Ministry of Rural Areas and Employment, Government of India, has been implementing the WDP in about 10,000 watersheds of the country. Further, a number of State governments and non-governmental organisations are also executing a number of watershed development programmes utilising funds given by national and international funding agencies.

Approach for Watershed Development and Management

It is a well-known fact that land and water resources interact at the instance of people to produce food, fodder, fibre, timber and inputs for the agro-based industries. The physiography of the land, slope, nature and depth of soil cover, present land use, hydrogeology, climate, socio-economic and legal aspects, etc. and the hydrological features of the land area determine the productive interaction between these two resources. Because of these factors that there has been an increasing effort in India in planning and implementation of soil and water conservation programmes in problem areas on watershed basis since 1996. The technological advancements will no doubt, constantly improve the output from a unit of land and a unit of water. The natural resources of soil and water are vulnerable to deterioration and degradation under improper use of watershed. In order to maximise the benefits of application technological innovations, it is necessary to protect and use of natural resources like soil and water judiciously. Appropriate soil and moisture conservation practices are, thus, basic foundations upon which maximum efficiency of technological developments can be obtained from soil and water resources. The soil, vegetation and water resources are the basic resources, which interact and establish in a watershed. Hence, all these three resources have to be managed, collectively and in an integrated way. Watersheds being natural hydrological units, hence they respond more effectively to the various engineering, biological and cultural treatments. As it is a known fact, that no two watersheds are identical. However, they have common characteristic parameters, which can be judiciously modified with an intention of obtaining the required results. In the watershed approach all these parameters can be made use of according to their nature, problems and potential.

Water is the best index of watershed management and thus, provides an excellent monitoring mechanism. As there is a specific natural ridge line for each watershed to drain into the drainage system it is easy to study and evaluate the impact of the programme by making observations at the outlet of the drainage system. Such measurements are relatively easy to make and they also integrate the effects of erosion over large or small area. Maintenance of works carried out in the watershed is also easy as it is possible to have a close watch over them by making observations at one point only. Central and State governments are turning to the watershed approach as a means of achieving greater results from their area development programmes because managing area development programmes on a watershed basis makes good sense—environmentally, financially and socially. The watershed approach can be adapted to convert and make productive use of problem areas like drought prone areas, wastelands, waterlogged, degraded and sailne areas. The advantages of adopting the watershed approach are explained hereunder:

(i) *Environment Friendly:* Watersheds are defined by natural hydrology. They represent the most logical unit of planning for managing natural resources. Keeping the water in the central point, the develop professionals are able to gain a comprehensive understanding of the overall conditions in the watershed and the factors which affect those conditions. The watershed approach is comprehensive enough to cover all the factors that affect a watershed. It facilitates determining the action required to be carried out to protect or restore the natural resources of the watershed.

(ii) *Saves Time and Money:* For the success of the watershed approach, those departments which work within the watershed including Central, State, local government, NGOs and village community have to work together to improve the conditions of the watershed. Improved communication and coordination of all their efforts will avoid duplication, supplement and complement each other's activities, which ultimately saves time and money and restores normalcy quickly.

(iii) *Greater Peoples Participation:* The watershed approach can also lead to greater awareness and participation from the watershed community. Once individuals become aware of and interested in their watershed, they often become more involved in decision-making as well as in the protection and restoration efforts. Through such involvement, watershed approach builds a sense of belonging, community ownership, helps to reduce conflicts, and increases commitment to the action necessary to achieve the objectives of the programme. It strengthens teamwork, which brings private and public partners together.

Implementation of Watershed Programme

A date of commencement of the project is the date of sanctioning of the project. It may be important over a period of 5 years.

ZP/DRDA

At the district level, the ZP/DRDA is the nodal agency for the implementation of all area development programmes under the supervision and guidance of the State Government and the Government of India. It shall approve the selection of watersheds, appoint the PIA, approve the action plan/treatment plan of the project etc. The CEO or the PO, ZP/DRDA shall maintain the accounts of the watershed project and shall sign all statutory papers such as Utilization Certificates (UCs), Audited Statements of Accounts, Progress Reports, Bonds etc. The ZP/DRDA will be entitled to recover funds from any institution/ organisation/individual and take appropriate action under law if the project is not properly implemented or funds are misutilised or not spent as per the guidelines.

Watershed Development Team (WDT)

The WDT is a multi-disciplinary team responsible for the technical and financial supervision of the project activities. The team consists of field level officials drawn from various disciplines like forestry, soil, horticulture, social sciences, etc. These officials are key functionaries in the sensitization of SHGs/UGs in particular and the watershed community in general.

Watershed Association (WA)

The WA consists of all the members of the village whose land is located within the watershed area and all those members who derive sustenance from the watershed area. The WA will meet atleast twice in a year to monitor and review the progress, approve the statement of accounts, formation of UGs/SHGs, resolve differences or disputes between different UGs, SHGs or amongst members of the UGs/SHGs, approve the arrangements for the collection of Public/voluntary donations and contributions from the watershed community and individual members, lay down procedures for the operation and maintenance of assets created, approve the activities that can be taken up with the money available in the WDF, nominate members of the WC from amongst the UGs/SHGs by a system of rotation, and take disciplinary action of removal of members from the WC or UGs and whatever other disciplinary action it deems fit. The WA will elect its own president who shall be different from the office-bearers and members of the WC. The Watershed Secretary shall assist the president of the WA in the discharge of the responsibilities entrusted to the WA.

Watershed Committee (WC)

The WC is directly involved in the implementation of the programme right from the preparation of the action plan the checking, the measurements of the work executed and payment of wages. The WC also determines the mechanism for the sharing of the usfructs and the post-project sustenance arrangement. It functions under the direct supervision and control of the WA. The WC may consist of 10-12 members who will be nominated by the WA from amongst the UGs (4-5), the SHGs (3- 4), the Village Panchayat (2-3) and a member of the WOT. While making nominations, it may be ensured that the WC has adequate representation of women, members from the Scheduled Castes/Scheduled Tribes/Shepherd Community, etc. The WC also appoints a Watershed Secretary. The WC and the WDT will choose the work/activities as per the requirements of their watershed treatment plan.

Project Implementation Agencies

In case the Panchayats are not adequately empowered then the ZP itself can either act as the PIA or may appoint a suitable line Department like Agriculture, Forestry/Social Forestry, Soil Conservation etc. or an agency of the State Government / University/ Institute/NGO in the District with adequate experience and expertise in the implementation of watershed projects or related area development work as the PIA. An NGO-PIA shall normally be assigned 10-12 watershed projects covering an area ranging from 5,000 to 6,000 ha. However, in exceptional and deserving cases, an NGO-PIA may be assigned a maximum of 12,000 ha at a time, including ongoing projects in all the programmes of similar nature in a District and a maximum of 25,000 ha in the State.

The PIA will provide necessary technical guidance to the Village Panchayat for the preparation of development plans for the watershed through a PRA exercise. It undertakes community organisation, trains the village communities, supervises the watershed development activities, inspects and authenticates project accounts, encourages adoption of low cost technologies and builds upon indigenous technical knowledge, monitors and reviews the overall project implementation and sets up institutional arrangements for post-project operation and maintenance and further development of the assets created during the project period.

The ZP/DRDA shall be the authority competent to decide on the suitability or otherwise of the PIA for taking up projects under the WDP. However, the State Government may consider changing the PIA in any of the projects on specific grounds with the prior concurrence of the DoLR, Government of India. In order to avoid the tendency to overemphasize certain activities related to the specialty of the PIA selected, particularly in the case of line Departments like Agriculture, Soil Conservation, Forestry etc., the ZP/DRDA should ensure that subject matter specialists from various line Departments at the District and Block levels are involved in the preparation of the plans.

Each PIA shall carry out its duties through a multi disciplinary team designated as the WDF. Each WDT should have at least four members, one each from the disciplines of forestry/plant sciences, animal sciences, civil/agricultural engineering and social sciences. At least one member of the WDT should be a woman. One of the WDT members shall be designated as the Project Leader.

Village Panchayat

At the field level the Village Panchayats shall implement the projects under the overall supervision and guidance of the PIAs and also as per the guidance and under the control of the Gram Sabha. The Village Panchayat shall carry out the day-to-day activities of the project and will be responsible for coordination and liaison with the WDT and the ZP/DRDA to ensure smooth implementation of the project. The Village Panchayat shall maintain a separate account for the watershed project and all receipts from the ZP/DRDA shall be credited to this account. This account shall be operated jointly by the Village Panchayat Secretary and the Village Panchayat Chairman. The Village Panchayat Secretary will be responsible for convening meetings of the Village Panchayat and Gram Sabha and for carrying out all their decisions. He will maintain all the records and accounts of the project activities. If required, the Village Panchayat may appoint two or three volunteers to provide assistance to the Village Panchayat Secretary in the implementation of activities as per the action plan/treatment plan of the watershed project.

The Gram Sabha will meet at least twice a year to approve/improve the watershed development plan, monitor and review its progress, approve the statement of accounts, form UGs/SHGs, resolve differences/disputes between different UGs, SHGs or amongst members of these groups, approve arrangements for the collection of public/voluntary donations and contributions from the community and individual members, lay down procedures for the operation and maintenance of assets created and approve the activities that can be taken up with money available in the WDF.

Self-Help Groups

The Village Panchayat shall constitute SHGs in the watershed area with the help of the WDT from amongst the landless/assetless poor, agricultural labourers, women, shepherds, scheduled caste/scheduled tribe persons etc. The Gram Panchayat will set up a revolving fund not exceeding Rupees one lakh to be given as seed money for vocational development by the SHGs at a rate not exceeding Rs. 10,000/- per SHG for undertaking income generating activities. The seed money must be recovered from the SHG members in a maximum of 6 installments on a monthly basis. This can be reinvested in the same or other SHGs.

User Groups (UG)

The Village Panchayat shall also constitute UGs in the watershed area with the help of the WDT. These groups shall consist of landholders who are likely to derive direct benefits from a particular watershed work/activities. The UGs shall be responsible for the operation and maintenance of all the assets created under the project through which they derive direct or indirect, individual benefits.

Watershed Secretary and Volunteers

The WDP shall have a Watershed Secretary. He will be a full-time paid employee of the WA. He should preferably be a graduate from the same village or from some nearby village and agree to live in the watershed area during the project period. He will work under the direct supervision of the Chairman of the WC and will be responsible for convening meetings of the WA and the WC and for carrying out all their decisions. He will maintain all the records and accounts of the WC and the WA. He will also help the UGs/SHGs to maintain their accounts. He will be assisted in his responsibilities by Watershed Volunteers from the Watershed area/village. The establishment cost for the Watershed Secretary and the Watershed Volunteers shall be charged to the administrative overheads component of the project and paid through the WDT.

Van Rakshaks

To take care of plantations on public/community/panchayat lands, the Village Panchayats may engage local unemployed youth from below poverty line families as "Van Rakshaks" on a honorarium. The Van Rakshaks (or volunteers) are not to be treated as employees of the Government. The honorarium of the Van Rakshaks may be increased or decreased by the Village Panchayat based on the survival rate of plantations. The Village Panchayat shall also ensure the collection of usufructs from these Van Rakshaks.

Mobilization and Training

Community mobilization and training are prerequisites for initiating development work in watershed projects. Prior sensitization and orientation training on watershed project management should be imparted to all concerned functionaries and elected representatives at the district, block and village levels before they assume their responsibilities. If the PIA happens to be the ZP/DRDA or a line department, NGOs may be involved for community organisation and training.

Activities for Watershed Development

A meeting of the Gram Sabha shall be convened for preparation of an action plan/watershed treatment plan, on the basis of the information generated from the benchmark survey of the watershed areas and detailed PRA exercises. The prepared action plan/treatment plan for the integrated development of the watershed area under the guidance of the WDT will be submitted to the PIA. The PIA, after careful scrutiny, shall submit the action plan for the approval of the ZP/DRDA. The approved plan shall be the basis for the release of funds, monitoring, review, evaluation etc. by the ZP/DRDA, State Government and Central Government. The items that can be included in the action plan/watershed treatment plan are:

(i) Development of small water harvesting structures and other ground-water recharge measures;
(ii) Renovation and augmentation of water sources and desiltation of village tanks;
(iii) Fisheries development in village ponds/tanks, farm ponds etc.;
(iv) Afforestation;
(v) Pasture development;
(vi) Land development;
(vii) Drainage line treatment;
(viii) Repair, restoration and upgradation of existing common property assets and structures;
(ix) Crop demonstrations;
(x) Promotion and propagation of non-conventional energy saving devices, energy conservation measures, biofuel plantations etc.

The WDT, while drawing up the action plan/watershed treatment plan, should ensure that project work involves only low-cost, locally available technologies and materials, are simple, easy to operate and maintain. The watershed treatment plan should give emphasis to rain water-harvesting activities and undertake massive plantation work on community as well as private lands. The focus should be on employment and income generation activities so as to benefit the poor in the project area, in addition, the action plan should specify the following:

(i) Physical targets to be achieved (year wise) under the project;
(ii) Definite time frame for each major activity;
(iii) Technological interventions for the proposed activities;
(iv) Success criteria for each activity;
(v) Exit protocol.

After the approval of the action plan by the ZP/DRDA, it would be the responsibility of the PIA to get the same implemented through the Village Panchayat with the active support and supervision of the WDT members.

Participatory Rural Appraisal

In seventies and eighties, PRA dominated the scenario but for the basic flaw of non-participation and non-involvement, basic mode of PRA, however, remained obstructive.

Outsiders used to go to the rural areas and obtained data from the local people. The data, the information and the knowledge were extracted from it. The outsiders or the investigators remained central. In late eighties, participatory rural appraisal (PRA) techniques evolved. It presumed investigators as learners, catalysts and facilitators. In PRA, the knowledge is generated and articulated in a participatory way in which interviewing, mapping, diagramming, transecting, presentations and analysis are carried out by the rural people themselves. They identify the priorities, they give shape to their information, knowledge, attitudes and aptitudes and they own informations. PRA evolved as a forum of PRA in which the onus of initiative shifted from the investigator to the villager. PRA effort is a creative approach to information sharing and a challenge to prevailing pro-conceptions about the rural people's knowledge.

What is Participation?

Participation has a long history in development projects in involving people in certain aspects of plannings and implementation in a programme. In the earlier programmes, initiatives in this regard distorted participation, created dependence and misleading impressions. Patronising participants in the name of participation resulted in failure of a programme after the project period was over. Jules Pretty developed typology for participation as under:

1. *Passive participation*: People participate by being told what is going to happen or has already happened.
2. *Participation in information giving*: People participate by

answering questions posed by extractive outsiders using questionnaire, surveys or other approaches.

3. *Participation by consultations*: People participate by consulted and the outsider agency listening to the views and define and modify the programme in the light of people's responses.
4. *Participation for material incentive:* People participate by providing resources (for example labour) in return for food, cash or other material incentives.
5. *Functional participation*: People participate by forming groups to meet pre-determined objectives related to the project, which can involve the development or promotion of externally initiated social organisation, but remain dependent on external initiative and facilitators.
6. *Interactive participation:* People participate in joint analysis which leads to action plans and formation of new local institutions or the strengthening of existing ones.
7. *Self mobilisation:* People participate by taking initiative independent of external institutions to change systems. Such self-initiated mobilisations and corrective actions may or may not change existing, inequitable distribution of wealth and power.

The project implementing agency should keep in mind various aspects of participation while promoting involvement and participation of the community in the watershed management programme.

Functions of PRA

1. Menu of methods.
2. The primacy of rapport through behaviour and attitudes.
3. Visual sharing.

Basic Principles of PRA

1. *Reversal of learning:* To learn directly and face to face from the local people gaining insight from their local physical, technical, social and psychological knowledge.
2. *Learning rapidly and progressively*: Conscious explorations with the use of flexible methods and improvising, iterating and cross-checking the methods with the process of time.
3. *Upsetting biases* by patient listening, probing and learning through concerns, values, beliefs and priorities.

It means flying to gather information with trade-offs between quantity, relevance, accuracy, credibility and timeliness.

Fundamentals of PRA

(i) *Triangulation:* Cross-checking and progressive approximation to the truth. Normally, findings from different methods, places, times, disciplines, investigators are assessed and compared.

(ii) *Seeking diversity:* Looking for learning from explanations, oddities, discreteness in any distribution. By maximizing the diversity, the information is enriched. It is important to notice and investigate the contradictions, anomalies and differences. The objective is to seek variability rather than averages.

(iii) *Villagers as performers*: The facilitators initiate a process of participatory analysis and the villagers take up the task of facilitating investigation, analysis, presentation and learning.

(iv) *Self critical awareness:* Facilitators continuously and critically examine through behaviour.

(v) *Personal responsibility:* Facilitators take personal responsibility for what is done rather than relying on the authority of the rigid set of rules.

(vi) *Sharing:* Sharing of information, ideas, knowledge, experiences between the facilitators and the villagers.

The use of PRA techniques in watershed areas in last one decade has shown that:

(i) Villagers have a great capacity and skill to map, observe, compare, estimate, quantify, link, score, model and diagram;

(ii) The facilitator's behaviour and attitudes are important and that early relaxed rapport is easily established;

(iii) Participatory diagramming is popular and powerful and visual sharing makes it more participative; and

(iv) PRA techniques and tools are very powerful and popular in conveying the field realities.

The basic PRA include:

1. Learning from the community.
2. Facilitation to enable the community to do more or all the investigations, analysis and planning, so that they own the outcome and are empowered.

3. Respect for behaviour, attitudes and knowledge of the community and confidence in their ability to do things.
4. Collecting and sharing the information and field experiences between the facilitator and the community.

Upsetting of the bias through self-awareness and in the community by actively asking the poorest, the least visible and the least articulate.

PRA, as a process emphasizes on the establishment of a more equitable relationship between the facilitator and the community. There is conscious effort made to empower the community. Empowerment is through the creation of a participatory research process in which local people are viewed as active agents rather than objects. The objective of the participatory process is to facilitate local people doing their own analysis through own situations. PRA is exploratory and helps in assessing needs anti prioritising problems. Planning formulation, feasibility studies, monitoring and evaluation can be undertaken by using PRA techniques.

Important Tips for PRA Practitioners

1. PRA is a continuous process. Hence, PRA techniques should be used in the first, second, third and fourth years of watershed development and this process of gathering information should also be done during monitoring and evaluation.
2. There are numerous PRA techniques and tools available to choose and opt from. A judicious selection of such techniques should be done for a particular activity.
3. PRA techniques should be used on different groups in watershed areas. This would facilitate cross-checking and triangulation and also facilitate rapport-building with different sections of the society.
4. The facilitator should always keep time for the use of PRA processes and techniques in the watersheds.
5. Make a checklist everyday before going to the field. This would help in encompassing different techniques.
6. Act as a team, i.e., be united and handle all areas together with other PIA members and the community.
7. Be accommodative and inventive in handling techniques and tools. These techniques should be adopted to the field situations prevailing and existing in the watersheds.

8. Promote team building in the community. Identification of self-help groups and user groups should be an automatic outcome.
9. Be flexible in the approach, so as to suit the needs and demands of the community/groups.
10. Explain the objective and methodology to the group in great details before starting the technique.
11. Make these techniques and tools as a game for the community, so that the community owns the technique and evolve, modify, rectify and include relevant aspects in the techniques on its own.
12. Constant consultations and facilitations should be promoted. The community should not feel left-out and ignored when it has started using the techniques. Cross-checking of information should also be taken into consideration when the processes are going on.
13. It is always helpful and useful to choose a permanent and unanimously accepted spacious place in the village.
14. It is preferable to start the techniques in early morning. Though, the community should decide the timings or the techniques.

Benefits of PRA

1. *Empowering poor and the weak:* PRA give confidence and authority to present need based proposals, to make demands and to take actior by the poor and the weak.
2. *Diversification:* PRA increases and interplays of diverse and numerous perspectives of the community.
3. *The community process:* PRA helps in identification, appraisal, planning, implementation, monitoring and evaluation—all in a participatory mode in watershed management.
4. *The research priorities:* PRA helps in identifying the research priorities and initiating participatory research.
5. *Organisational changes:* PRA helps in indicating changes and modifications in the organisation, so that it becomes closer to the community's aspirations.
6. *Policy review:* PRA helps in generating insights into the community and the facilitator so that policy reviews in the watershed programmes and management is possible.

Participatory Rural Appraisal Exercises

On return from training, the WDT members will conduct three-day PRA exercises in all selected villages. All the members of the team will move as one unit and use techniques like participatory mapping/modelling, transact, matrix ranking, timeline, seasonality diagram etc. to gather first hand information about the village community and the watershed and their problems and achievements. The PRA exercise should lead to diagnosis of the important problems and a common understanding of the village community's priorities. This should enable the WDT and the village community to arrive at a common outline of an action plan for the next three to six months.

The information generated over PRA exercises should be cross checked with other sources of data and further supplemented with more detailed scientific surveys such as contour survey, hydrological surveys, benchmark, remote sensing surveys, soil classification, land capability analysis, monitoring surveys with satellite image and GIS at regular intervals, specific design analysis or resolution of specific technical problems through research/action research/ operational research assignments and such other technical inputs as well help achieve better results for all or any of the development activities.

Community Organisation Programme

WDT members should organise small self-help groups with membership ranging from 15 to 30. Each group should be homogeneous having a common identity such as agricultural labourers, women, shepherds, Scheduled Castes/Tribes, farmers or a common purpose/activity such as thrift and credit, dairying, rope making/basket weaving, sewing and tailoring, vegetable vending, etc. The SHGs may be constituted within 3-6 months of the starting of the community organization programme after which they will continue to function and grow. The WDT may also use the revolving fund of Rs. 50000 at its disposal to advance funds to SHGs as matching contributions to help them grow quickly and undertake more income-generating activities. WDT members should organise small self-help groups with membership ranging from 15 to 30. Each group should be homogeneous having a common identity such as agricultural labourers, women, etc. or a common purpose/activity such as thrift and credit, dairying, rope making/basket weaving, sewing and tailoring, vegetable vending, etc. The SHGs may be constituted within 3-6 months of the starting of the community organisation programme after which they will continue to function and grow. The WDT may also use the revolving fund of Rs. 50000 at its disposal to advance funds to SHGs as matching contributions to help them grow quickly and undertake more income-generating activities.

Watershed Development Plan

After general discussion of the watershed development concept at the WA, each UG shall prepare an Action Plan in consultation with and guidance of the WDT members and WC members with time and cost estimates, design and execution procedures for each individual work/activity to be taken up in the watershed. This Action Plan will also clearly define the respective roles and responsibilities of the users and the manner in which the work/activity would be executed. These individual work plans will be submitted to the WC which will then prepare an integrated Watershed Development Plan in consultation with the WDT and submit the same to the WA. The Watershed Development Plan should also identify the mechanisms and the sources that would be used by the WC and the PIA to monitor and review the progress being achieved. The WA shall submit the Plan, with the recommendations of the WDT to the ZP/DRDA for sanction and release of funds. This approved Watershed Development Plan shall become the basis for the ZP/DNDA for release of project funding monitoring, review and evaluation of the Watershed Development Project.

Development of Forest Lands in the Watershed

Some watersheds may include, in addition to arable land under private ownership, forestlands owned by the State Forest Department. Forest lands forming part of such watersheds may also be treated simultaneously as given below:

(i) The Divisional Forest Officer concerned should give technical sanction for the treatment plans.

(ii) The treatment plans should, as far as possible be implemented by Village Forest Committees in close coordination with the Village Panchayat.

(iii) The micro-watershed development plan for the forest areas should be in conformity with the Forest Conservation Act and the approved work plan for the area.

(iv) Where the major part of the watershed is covered by forest

lands, the Forest Department at the district level should be encouraged to take up the development work as the PIA.

(v) A forest official should invariably be included as a member of the WDT wherever forest land falls within the watershed.

Indigenous Knowledge in Watershed Programme

It is an accepted fact that the traditional approach towards rural realities has been lacking in several aspects. Misinterpretation, misjudgement and misrepresentation of situation have resulted in wrong precipitation and knowledge about field conditions. Various participatory learning and action techniques were adopted to bypass such problems. Rapid rural appraisal and participatory rural appraisal are growing families of methods and approaches to enable local people to express, emphasize, share and examine their knowledge of life and conditions to plan and to act. Rapid rural appraisals (RRAs) were evolved to be cost-effective and quick techniques. Indigenous technical knowledge (ITK) was observed in the villages and a large number of professionals realized and recognized the obvious fact that rural people were knowledgeable on subjects related and important to their lives. ITK became the source of information and to tap that cost-effective and time-effective PRA approaches were realized. PRAs grew over and above the structured and un-structured questionnaire format and helped professionals to restrict the type, quality and quantity of information. It also created situations and circumstances for the outsiders to come physically in close contact with the rural people who created amenable free flow of information. PRAs made formal surveys a part of history. The basic fundamental merits of PRAs were:

(i) It made flexible, exploratory, interactive and innovative progressive learning possible;

(ii) It created two-way communication situation where free flow of ITK, attitudes, information, etc., became possible;

(iii) It also created a new perspective to credibility, validity and repeatability of the information;

(iv) It allowed for information to be collected using batteries of techniques to cover different informants, places and also created cross-checking methods to get closer to the truth through successive approximations; and

(v) It created direct contact relationship between the investigators and the local people.

Community Participatory Institution-Building

Participatory development is a new socio-economic force aiming for sustained development at the village level. There is a close link between resources land, water, forest, mineral, etc. and community. Resources are used by the community, with a great deal of interaction among individuals. Allocation of resources based on a community approach, rather than on an individualized one, adds an element of sustenance to the development process. Participatory development is a non-conventional approach. It requires and encompasses evolution of non-market, non-governmental people's organization in the management of CPRs, changes in systems of property rights, methods of resource allocation etc. Participation as a process relates to increasing adherence to a set of rules. Adherence results in the emergence of an institution which is a recurrent situation either self-policed or policed by some external authority. As a process, participation has dynamics of conflicts, understanding, persuasion, prohibition, violation (of rules), etc. The participatory process, depending upon the strength of social decision system, can be classified as conflict-resolving, problem-solving, welfare-oriented, equity-oriented or development oriented. Careful attention is required in formation of groups or institutions in micro-watershed villages. The idea of forming village institutions does not create a new and conflicting power structure. The planners and implementors should ensure fulfillment of following points:

1. Have villagers understood the need for collective action? It should be based on concrete and objective criteria like RRAs and PRAs findings. Is it that the group formation is taking place to get some benefits from the project? Is it that until and unless groups are formed they cannot get to the problem and solve them? Are the villagers motivated to form a group? What has been the perceived role of each beneficiary into the group?
2. Do we have adequate and authentic information on prevailing local social systems? Who participate in existing institutions? How they function and how the decisions are arrived at? How has been the functioning of the group—satisfactory/un-satisfactory? Reasons? Who is the level of participation in existing institutions? What are the strengths and weaknesses? Who was involved in taking decisions for an activity that has/had come to the village? Were women,

landless, minorities and backwards involved in the process of decision-making? Will the formation of a village institutions sharpen the factions in the village or sharpen the leadership struggle among individuals, households, social groups, etc.?

3. Has it been ensured that the proposed village institution would allow for a wider participation among the relevant population including the women? Do the groups take the women into confidence? Are the women participating in the activities and in the decision-making? Are gender-based issues a priority goal or objective of the group?
4. Is the proposed village institution-building on any existing institution? If so, then how can the restrengthening of the weaknesses of the existing groups be ascertained? If new institutions are built, then what are the differences from the existing institutions?
5. Cooperation among villagers and decision-making capacity and management abilities of the beneficiaries should be tested and analysed through the implementation of small activities.
6. The project should start with small, single and simple organisations at hamlet or clan level. Activities and responsibilities to the people should only be given when the participation of poor and gender is assured, capacity-building in the members is ascertained and intended results are already achieved. Processes like meetings, accounts management, operations, etc. should be institutionalised.
7. Start with formal procedures (e.g., regular meetings) but do not give formal titles like president, secretary etc. New formally structured organizations should not be created unless there is an immediate pressing need to do so. Ensure that all the members have been trained in cooperation, participation, accountability, etc. Rotation of the responsibilities should periodically take place. Two-way communication among members should be encouraged.

Sustainable development involves various aspects. Sustainable development project should encompass appropriate technology, supportive policies, differences in ethics, changes in individual behaviour, local institution and participation, etc. Local institutions perform multiplicity of functions in a watershed area, such as:

1. Local institutions are important for mobilising resources and regulating their use with a view to maintain a long-term base for productive activity.
2. Available resources can be put to their most efficient and sustainable use with location specific knowledge, which is best generated and interpreted locally.
3. Monitoring changes can be quick and less costly. Adaptive changes made in resource use gets accelerated by institutionalised local decision-making.
4. Community norms and consensus condition people's behaviour. Preservation or institutional practices, which are environmentally sound, may require more than just individual incentives and persuasion. Community wisdom is more practical and sustainable.
5. In the absence of local institutions, all conflicts are dealt with at higher levels, yielding slower and often, less appropriate outcomes. Local institutions help in resolution of most of the local conflicts. It becomes a mechanism in conflict resolution.
6. Local institutions encourage people to take a long-term view by creating common expectations and a basis for cooperation that goes beyond individual interests. Local institutions carry a legitimacy, so people comply without inducements and sanctions. Local institutions have their own rules and pattern of management. They should be appropriate to the resource to be developed and maintained and they should impose sanctions which they can enforce in their own areas of operation. Such institutions must also have access to and control of resources to meet urgent needs and future operations.

Local institutions can produce practices that do not favour sustainability. Factionalism within the institution or among the groups may induce them to exploit local resources to their short-term advantages at the loss and peril of others. Local institutions regulating natural resources and common property resources are easiest to breakdown. This may further vitiate environment for existing institutions and probable ones. Local institutions by and large depend on, and are reinforced by, existing structures of authority. If tradition and authority uphold conservation or preservation, then it is accepted. The management and ownership of CPRs in Rajasthan was in the hands of feudal class, a focal point of traditional authority (Jodha, 1991). Informal protection groups/ Van Panchayats have been traditional source of authority in Madhya Pradesh and hence could manage forests, effectively. Panchayats, all over India have been a centre of traditional authority for centuries thereby enabling to effectively direct and lead the community and to manage and administer resources with authority. Individuals cooperate and follow the rules set down by the community only if the use of resources to be managed satisfies some of their very significantly felt-needs.

The local institutions consists of institutions at three tiers:

(a) *Group level:* Includes self-identified set of persons with some common interests. It may be persons in a small residential area like neighbourhood or an occupational, age, gender, ethic or other grouping. User groups, self-help groups, etc. a micro-watershed level are the lowest tier of local institutions.

(b) *Community level:* Includes relatively self-contained socio-economic residential unit. Watershed Development Committee and Watershed Association are second tier of local institutions in watershed areas.

(c) *Locality level:* The Local institutions having social and economic relations are included. It may be extended to block (sub-district) levels. Project Implementing Agency (PIA) or multidisciplinary team (MDT) in watershed come in the third tier. There is more prevalence of face-to-face interpersonal relationship which are often more frequent, intense and meaningful than within locality level (block level) institutions.

The fact that people know each other (especially in group level and community level institutions), creates opportunities for collective and mutual assistance for mobilising and managing resources on a self-directed and self-sustaining basis. People feel more mutual rapport and sense of obligation at these levels. Since, these institutions exist as social entities, decisions and activities are based on consensus, which grow out of discussion and mutual understanding. The individual and household level institutions are the smallest units of decision-making and activity. Decisions taken by them regarding sustainability of watershed project and sustainable utilisation of natural resources are not likely to be very effective or long lasting. Such decisions should be meshed with decisions by other individuals and households. Local institutions provide a basis for collective action for building consensus, for undertaking coordination and management responsibilities, for collecting, analysing and evaluating information energised by a degree of interpersonal solidarity. There are many types of institutions, some of which are also organisations, e.g., Gram Panchayats and other. An institution is a complex of norms and behaviour that persists over time by serving some socially valued purposes while an organization is a structure of recognized and accepted roles (Uphoff, 1992). Institutions can be organisations and vice-versa. Marriage is an institution but not an orgnisation, while family is both. Local institutions in the present context, are meant by institutions with organisational basis. The vitality of institutions at different levels depend to a large extent on the degree to which they meet the expectations of the members whose resource contributions (money or kind) are needed to keep them operating. Many institutions are vulnerable to the withdrawal of support by members. Institutions which fail to mobilise their resources due to the loss of support, loose their sustainability and start depending on outside resources.

Participatory Approach for Empowerment of Community

People's participation will be the key to watershed development programmes. Their participation alone will ensure long-term sustainability of the watershed development process through ownership of the programme by local communities, but also empower the watershed communities to initiate activities on their own and take optimal advantage of the watershed development project.

Implementation through Watershed Community

The empowerment of the local community will ensure their active participation in the planning and execution of development works. They should be aware of the availability of finance and mode of expenditure to reduce the conflicts in future.

Projects to be Demand Driven and Felt Needs of the Community

The project proposals have to be prepared by the community and that have to be prepared by bottom up process reflecting the felt needs of the community. Local indigenous technologies have to be utilized will preparing the proposals for easy replication.

Replication of Successful Watershed Development Projects

The members of the community would have created new technologies based on their exposure visits and local knowledge is innovative. As they are created by the local community they are easily sustainable and replicable.

Development of Common Property Resources

The development of common property resources of a village especially the contribution of the community in the form of cash or labour, will depend upon the sharing of the usufruct likely to accrue as a result. The usufructs should be made available to the beneficiaries.

Development of Forest Lands

Some watersheds may cover arable land of private owners and forest land owned by the State Forest Department. Such watersheds should be treated in an integrated manner.

Linkages with Panchayat Raj Institutions

The activities of watershed development should be implemented with the full involvement of the Panchayati Raj Institutions (PRIs). This linkage will help the community to sustain the project structures. Wherever possible the watershed projects can also be implemented by the PRIs.

Linkages with Credit Institutions

Linkages with the credit institutions particularly NABARD, Regional Rural flanks, Cooperative Banks etc. will ensure free flow funds for short-term crop loans, medium term loans for dairy animals, credit support to Self Help Groups etc.

Promoting Social Equity

Thrust of the approach should be on promoting social equity between all sections and caste groups by taking special efforts at strengthening their socio-economic status.

Means of Community Mobilization

The most observable situations in which participation emerges is the existence of common problems, which forces the people to come together to take decisions regarding common action. Threat of soil erosion to the agricultural plots, paucity of fodder and fuelwood, scarcity of water for drinking and domestic use, loss of vegetation, etc., are the commonly perceived problems which resulted in high level of community participation in watershed management programme. Participation may emerge either as a consequence of the conscious, collective action of rational economic agents or evolving organically out of individual behaviour. Self-enforced societal rules such as stall—feeding or social fencing by institutions regulate individual behaviour and social responsibility with respect to resources. The participatory development process, based on the creation of links between CPRs and PPRs in the watershed area, is found to be stable and sustainable. Apparently, under employed could be mobilised easily for participation. Participatory institutions own up added organisational responsibility of maintenance and repairs in watershed. They are better equipped to bridge the communication gap between the government and the people. Community participation is essential for successful implementation as well as for the maintenance of community assets created under the project. Community mobilisation could also be viewed as an important mechanism through which the responsibilities of common property resources management could be transferred back effectively to the people, so that, more productive, sustainable and equitable development is possible. The level of envisaged motivation and mobilisation could be possible by using various social processes:

1. *Awareness:* Use of promotional material, sharing information, attending topic-specific workshops, focussed awareness creation, and exposure visits to other projects.
2. *Involvement:* Participating in the planning process (PRA), giving opinions, ideas and alternatives, raising doubts, problems and options, and promising contribution and involvement.
3. *Learning:* Improvement of knowledge and skills through training, application of innovations, and developing a sense of self-appraisal.
4. *Organizing:* Attending community meetings, resolving conflicts, developing attitude to work or decide with consensus, establishing group norms and group dynamism, developing a feeling of solidarity, and arriving at group decisions.

Local Institutions' Effectiveness in Resource Management

Generally, around 50 per cent of the watershed community, that is, those villagers who are directly or indirectly dependent on the watershed are enrolled as members of at least one self-help group. Participatory or self-help institutions are more viable and effective in watershed areas. Separate self-help groups (SHGs) are organised for women, scheduled castes/tribes, agricultural labourers, shepherds, etc. SHGs should meet regularly at least once in a month and take all their decisions by common consensus amongst the members. The size of the SHG should be of about 10-20 members to enable effective individual participation in the group deliberations and working. The group may not necessarily be registered. The SHGs so created should have homogeneity regarding age, class, occupation, residence, etc., in the group. They should have an experience of about 6 months before effectively taking up large-scale activity. There should be culture of democratic working in the group and they should be well versed with maintenance of proper accounts/records. The project implementing agency should be convinced that the group has not come into existence only for the sake of participation in the project and availing benefits thereunder. There should be a genuine need to help each other and work together among the members. The SHGs should be restrengthened to take up active role in planning and implementation of WDP. Self-help groups of landless labourers, rural artisans, fishermen, etc. have been instrumental in initiating community mobilization and participation in watershed activities.

User groups have been more effective as they are related to the benefit sharing in the watershed areas. User groups should be groups of 10-20 homogeneous and common resource users in the village. Nearly 50 per cent of the families in the watershed community are represented in at least one user group. About 80 per cent of the watershed development activities should be carried out through the concerned user group. If the user groups are strong, the productivity, sustainability and equity concerns in the watershed areas are taken care of. They should meet regularly, at least once in a month, and take all decisions through common consensus amongst the members. The members should be able to give voluntary donations/ contributions for the related project activity in terms of cash, kind or labour as per the prescribed norms. The user groups like water utilization committee, dairy groups, farmer groups, etc., may play pivotal role in not only implementing watershed activities in an integrated fashion but also can actually take over the operations, and maintenance of the completed community works or activities on common property resources and personal property resources.

The characteristics of the natural resource in question, as well as of the persons who would use it, condition the feasibility of managing it beneficially through local institutions over time. Local institutions are more likely to be successful in natural resource management, when the resource is known and predictable rather than shifting and variable and where the users themselves are unidentifiable groups or community with its own authority structure. In watershed areas irrigation of water from water harvesting structures and fodder and fuelwood from socially fenced degraded forest patches are found to be most predictable and assessable resource. Institutional arrangements are more successful where the users are a socially cohesive group. Even in as predictable resource system as irrigation, there may be less solidarity among farmers in large systems. This may happen due to difference in size of land holdings, position of the fields (upstream/downstream), etc. The most irregular pattern was found in grass land management by migratory population. In such a condition, local institutions may find it difficult to control access and regular resource use. User management is another option, i.e., management by individuals who use the resource within certain cultural and social norms. Such institutions are based on shared values and expectations.

The potential of local institutions for natural resources management can be improved by investing in gathering information on resource and making it available to local people. Formulation of user groups, in the long run is a good investment for promoting local resource management. Social technological interventions like deployment of catalysts, like community organizers or social organizers to overcome barriers to resource, user cooperation may prove vital. The nature and distribution of costs and benefits from local management of natural resources will also affect the feasibility of local institutions taking responsibility. Cost and benefits from/on natural resources management can vary in:

1. *Space* : Costs/benefits accrued locally rather than remotely.
2. *Time*: Costs/benefits accrued immediately or in short time frame rather than after a long time.
3. *Tangibility:* Cost/benefits are quite evident rather than hard to identify.
4. *Distribution:* Benefits accrued to the same persons who boar the cost of management rather than to those who don't.

Quite evidently, local people take responsibility for natural resource management where the benefit accrue more quickly, locally, visibly and to those who bear the cost. The relative magnitude of costs and benefits from natural resource management are important, but these are often hard to measure and compare. Management will be more sustainable where benefits can be made more definite and immediate, or conversely, where costs are more ambiguous and deferred. The first step, in establishing participatory development, should be determine the unit for decision-making and activity above the household, whether a group, a community, a locality or some larger unit. This should not be decided unilaterally but on the basis of discussions with persons in the area concerned. Generally, it is most effective to start by talking with people in a household, then in small groups of households. The purpose of the discussions is to find a match between perceived difficulties (natural resource, health, education, agriculture, etc.), and areas or arenas of action to resolve them. The process of mobilising local participation for sustainable development initiatives depends very much on a consultative, problem-solving approach. Approaches like participatory or rapid rural appraisal carried out with communities and groups are a good starting point.

Success of Participatory Bari-Badhori Watershed Project

After ten years of intense interaction and *Paryavaran Yatras* of the whole Jammu and Kashmir state including 150 km long "Save the Siwaliks (Shivaliks)" *Padyaha*, it was decided to create a model for emulation to save the Siwaliks turning into a mountain desert like Aravallies by an NGO. It was felt that the people of foothill region would not just plant trees as they would not provide any income immediately as was seen under Social Forestry Schemes. Thus, an integrated watershed project based on conservation and development was adopted under which the beneficiaries had to contribute only 5 to 10 per cent (Jamwal and Gupta, 2006).

The watershed management project at Bari-Badhori, first of its kind, was sanctioned by the CAPART for Siwalik or Shivalik region of Jammu, Jammu and Kashmir State. It was undertaken with the objective to reverse the waste/degraded land of the area lying in the *Kandi* (drought prone) belt of low hill Siwaliks, which had occurred due to massive deforestation and denudation accompanied with heavy soil erosion. The project was started in December, 1998 by an

NGO, covering six villages, *viz.*, Bari, Badhori, Patti, Rahya, Suchani and Mahin Charkan with an area of 2500 ha. Despite the occurrence of perpetual droughts from 1999 every year upto July, 2003 and massive loss of plantation, the project area has withstood the vagaries of nature.

Soil and Water Conservation Work

The work done in the area comprises preparation of soil and water conservation working plans and implementation of these measures on watershed basis. Such working plans mainly consist of constructing the earthen check dams, digging of the trenches for planting trees, renovation of ponds and *baulies* and *'annasar'*-pond (named after Anna Hazare after his visit to the pond). The purpose behind constructing check dams was to stabilize the grade and harvest run-off water from large catchments. By constructing check dams the water, which previously used to go waste in small rivulets and cause flash floods and heavy soil erosion, is now being utilized for producing crops including forest/horticultural trees and vegetables. Roof water harvesting which is the need of the hour, has also been built-up with the objective for meeting the water needs of the area especially during droughts. Taking up of the abovesaid soil and water conservation measures have changed the attitude of the farmers. They are participating in watershed management programme and are adopting new technologies.

The unemployed youths are engaged in digging and renovating the prevailing dry ponds and constructing new check dams in Gurah and Mahin Charkan villages and, thus, earning their livelihood through development programmes.

Raising of Small Nurseries

The seeds of most of the forest tree species, fruit plants and vegetables are first sown in nursery beds and later on, when the seedlings get ready, they are transplanted in the main fields at proper spacing. As there is scarcity of well-known nurseries in Jammu region in general and in Siwalik belt in particular, so small nurseries were established in villages for catering the needs of the villagers, especially for growing indigenous species like *phalsa* (*Grewia asiatic*), *jaman* (*Syzygium cumini*), *dhiu* (*Atrocarpus lakoocha*) etc. Apart from these species, plants of grafted mango (*Mangifera indica*) and citrus fruits were also planted.

Setting up of Agroforestry

The agriculture is the main occupation of the people dwelling in *Kandi* belt as 70 per cent of its population is dependent for its living on land. Majority of the farmers are small and marginal, having their holdings scattered here and there. Despite these facts, the yield of the crops like maize, wheat, barley, pulses and oilseeds (mustard and sesame) was optimum before 1947. But owing to massive deforestation, denudation and heavy grazing of the grasslands, the soils of the area have now become very much eroded and unproductive. As a result, now the yield of the crops has considerably reduced. Sometimes, the yield of the crops is so low that even the peasants do not get the cost of the invested inputs they have applied in various agricultural enterprises (Gupta and Banerjee, 1991). It is because now the soils of *Kandi* have not only become "thirsty but are hungry too."

In light of the above facts as cited above, it becomes imperative to think about evolving certain alternative land-use system for such lands. Adoption of agroforestry is one such system which constitutes the need of the day for the *Kandi* dwellers. Briefly, agroforestry comprises a set of interacting biological and physical components (Gupta, 2005). It enhances the overall productivity of the land in respect of fuelwood, fodder, food, fertilizer and fibre *i.e.* '5 F'. It is the practice of combining agricultural, horticultural and forest activities *vis-a-vis* animal husbandry and fishery. Accordingly, five main kinds of agroforestry systems having great potential for *Kandi* areas of Jammu, have been proposed (Gupta and Raina, 1994). These are: agronomy-forestry, horticulture-forestry, agronomy-animal husbandry-forestry, agronomy-forestry-fishery and agronomy-animal husbandry-forestry-fishery. Recently, introduction of medicinal plants have been introduced in this farming system. Aforesaid concept of agroforestry has been very much followed by the peasants of the area under CAPART Watershed Management Project in the form of agriculture-silviculture, agriculture-horticulture, agriculture-sericulture-olericulture and agriculture-horticulture-fish culture.

We encouraged the farmers to take to plantations both of fruit, forest trees for fuelwood and timber, medicinal plants etc., so that the Siwaliks could be saved by regreening them. Among the various tree species, *dhaman* (*Grewia optiva*), *subabul* (*Leucaena leucocephala*), poplar (*Populus* spp.) have proved useful in agroforestry system. Among the fruit trees, *Umran* variety of *ber* (*Ziziphus jujuba*), seedling mango (*Mangifera indica*), papaya (*Carca papaya*), guava (*Psidium guajava*), citrus fruits like *kinnow*, orange, lime and *galgal*, pomegranate (*Punica granatum*) and aonla or *amla*, are the most promising ones.

Setting-up of Herbal Gardens

In order to get rid of the side-effects of allopathic medicines, the need now has again risen to boost the production of medicinal plants belonging to the Ayurvedic system of medicines which have little or no side-effects. Keeping in view the importance of medicinal plants a number of herbal gardens were setup. In these herbal gardens, medicinal plants like *harar* (*Terminalia chebula*), *bahera* (*Terminalia belerica*), aonla (*Phyllanthus emblica*), *ashwagandha* (*Withania somnifera*), *neem* or *nim* (*Azadirachta indica*) have been planted. Although these are still not in the bearing stage yet they are growing very well. In addition to these plants, Jatropha has also been grown. It is commonly known as Physic nut, *Ratanjot*, *Jamalghota*, *Jangali arandi* or *Kala-aranda* (*Jatropha curcas*), is a multipurpose, deciduous, large 3-4 m high shrub. Although it is a native of Mexico and tropical South America yet is now naturalized throughout tropical to sub-tropical Asia and Africa. The plant is reported to have been introduced into Asia and Africa by Portuguese as an oil yielding plant.

Nowadays, *Jatropha curcas* is occurring almost throughout India and Andaman Islands in semi-wild conditions. It is found to be cultivated in central and western parts of India like Madhya Pradesh, Rajasthan, Maharashtra, Gujarat and in southern states like Andhra Pradesh and Tamil Nadu.

"In *Kandi* belt of Jammu it is also known to grow naturally since long as the elders say." They further say, "*Ratanjot* naturally grows not only in *Kandi* belt of Jammu but in Siwalik hills of Kathua, Udhampur, Rajouri in addition to Jammu as well." Its seeds are used for making Jatropha bio-diesel – an alternative fuel in the global market. Compared to diesel emissions, it reduces emissions of carbon monoxide by 44 per cent, sulphates by 100 per cent, unburnt hydrocarbon by 68 per cent and particulate matter by 40 per cent (Kumar *et al.*, 2004). Shatabadi train was run from Delhi to Amritsar using B5 (5% biodiesel) blend. No problem was observed during the run.

In view of immense importance of *Ratanjot*, it is now growing in the *Kandi* belt under CAPART watershed management project in number of sites and is showing its performance nicely. Now we have taken-up the cultivation of *Ratanjot* in a big way like *amla, harar* and *bahera*.

Avenue Plantation

The studied area is now under pressure by the increasing population not only of human beings but also of livestock. Likewise there is considerable increase in the growth of cattle population, thus leading to overgrazing and consequent drying up of rich pasture lands in a way that chances of natural regeneration are totally eliminated. Apart from this there is shortage of drinking water and deterioration of the scrub forests. All these factors have affected the environment badly in spite of the social forestry and afforestation programmes taken up. Hence avenue plantation was initiated under watershed management project of CAPART with an aim to ameliorate the environment through planting quick growing tree species like poplar (*Populus nigra*), teak (*Tectona grandis*) etc., on the roads, parks, playgrounds.

Innovative Income Generating Schemes

After acquiring trainings in mushroom cultivation, bee-keeping, rearing of Jersey cows and rearing of silk worms, leaf cups making and, sissal and its crafts, many of the farmers including farm women, have started their own units for income generation. Many of the farmers especially unemployed youths both boys and girls, as well as dropouts, have now started their own income generated units after adopting some of these innovative agro-vocations. In this way, the watershed management project has proved a boon in solving unemployment problems, though partially. Fish culture in the ponds is a great success.

Conclusions

The needs of the growing population of our country may be fulfilled by increasing the agricultural production through increasing best use of existing resources. It has become necessary at this junction to stop any further deterioration of the natural land resources and to restore the agricultural productivity. Participatory watershed management approach should be adopted as a strategy for increasing the overall agricultural production of the country try which will be helpful for eradicating poverty and eliminating unemployment among the poor rural masses of the country.

REFERENCES

A booklet on Common Principles for Watershed Development (2000) Working group, Government of India.

Brookes, K.N., Folliot, P.F., Gregersen, H.M. and DeBano, L.F. (1997) Hydrology and the Management of Watersheds. 2nd Edition, Iowa University Press, Amsterdam, p. 502.

Choudhury, R. C. *et al.* (2002) (eds.), Field Manual on Planning and Management of Watershed Projects, National Institute of Rural Development, Hyderabad, p. 11.

GOI (1996) *Guidelines for watershed Development,* New Delhi.

GOI (2001) *Guidelines for watershed Development* (Revised), New Delhi.

Gupta, R.D. (2005) Agriculture production constraints in Kandi belt of Jammu district. In : Interaction Workshop on Water Management, NIH -Western Himalayan Regional Centre, Jammu, April 29-30, 2005.

Gupta, R.D. and Banerjee, S.K. (1991) Problems and Management of Soils and Forest Resources of North-West Himalayas, Mahajan Book Centre, Jammu, J&K (India).

Gupta, R.D. and Raina, J.L. (1994) Opportunities for agroforestry in the Dryland Belt of Jammu Region. In : Dryland Farming in India – Constraints and Challenges (Edited by J.L. Raina). Pointer Publishers, Jaipur, Rajasthan (India).

Jamwal, G.S. and Gupta, R.D. (2007) Watershed Management Project: A case study of Bari-Bandhori (J&K). In : Natural Resource Management for Sustainable Hill Agriculture (Arora, S., Kukal, S.S. and Sharma, V.; eds.), SCSI, Jammu Chapter, pp. 226-231.

Jodha, N.S. (1991) Rural Common Property Resource: A growing crisis, Gatekeeper series No. 24, IIED, London.

Kumar, R.V., Ahlawat, S.P., Nanda, A.K., Gupta, V.K. (2004). *Jatropha curcas* – the fuel of the future. Employment News, 39 (34) : 32-33, New Delhi.

Mahnot, S.C. and Singh, P.K. (1993) Soil and Water Conservation, Intercooperation Cordination Office, Jaipur, pp. 90.

Mani, N.D. (2005) Watershed Management: Principles, Parameters and Programmes, Dominant Publishers & Distributors, New Delhi.

McGuen, R.H. (1989) Hydrologic Analysis and Design, Prentice Hall, New Jersey, p. 867.

Murty, J.V.S. (1995) Watershed Management in India, Wiley Eastern Limited, Delhi, pp. 23-24.

Rajora, Rajesh (2002) Integrated Watershed Management – A field manual for equitable, productive and sustainable development, Rawat Publishers, Jaipur.

Rao, S.B., Kumari, Y.I. and Rao, R.V.V. (2005) Watershed Management – An approach for sustainable development. In : Watershed Management for Sustainable Development with reference to drought prone area, Mittal Publications, New Delhi, pp. 161-169.

Reddy Ranga A. (2005) Watershed—A blueprint for the development of agriculture of drought prone areas. In: Watershed Management for Sustainable Development with reference to drought prone area, Mittal Publications, New Delhi, pp. 109-120.

Reddy, Ranga A. (2005) Watershed Management for Sustainable Development with reference to drought prone area, Mittal Publications, New Delhi.

Reddy, B.R., Sakunthala, B. and Reddy, S. (2005) Role of the farmers and the government in water management. In: Watershed Management for Sustainable Development with reference to drought prone area, Mittal Publications, New Delhi, pp. 239-245.

Remote Sensing Centre (2000) Department of Agricultural Engineering, Government of Tamil Nadu, Chennai.

Sheng, T.C. (1990) Watershed management field manual: Watershed survey and planning. FAO Conservation Guide 13/6, FAO, Rome, p. 170.

Singh, Raj Vir (2002) Watershed Planning and Management, Yash Publishing House, Bikaner.

The Hindu, Watershed Management: Peoples Matter, Sunday, Jun 02, 2002.

Tideman, E.M. (1996) Watershed Management: Guidelines for Indian Conditions: Omega Scientific Publishers, New Delhi, p. 372.

Uphoff, N. (1992) Local institutions and participation for sustainable development, Gatekeeper series No. 31, IIED, London.

4

Sustainable Rural Development and Panchayat Raj in the Era of Globalization

Dr. M.R. Biju

Since an overwhelming majority of India's population lives in villages, a holistic development of its rural life is a requisite for the acceleration of the pace of overall economic development of the country. Rural development programmes are designed to facilitate a multi-faceted growth of the rural poor by extending the benefits development to them. Its aims at the improvement of their living standards by providing them opportunities for the fullest utilization of their potential through their active participation in the process of goal-oriented change. Rural development also tends to reduce migrational pressure on cities and towns. It also enables the use of human and national resources in the rural areas and to reduce area-wise differences. Evidence indicates that in India, public and governmental interest in rural development has been growing rapidly and a strong and various commitment towards it on the part of our polity-makers is clearly visible. The government has initiated a number of programmes to resolve the chronic problems facing village in India. In fact efforts to improve the rural economy were initiated soon after independence, particularly after the constitution came into force. Notably, in the early phases, despite some efforts at involving the people though democratic decentralization community development and panchayati raj rural development programmes were virtually synonymies with agricultural development. This followed the prevailing worldwide thinking and India's excessive concern especially till the green revolution in the late 1960s with food sufficiency. In the seventies, however, it came to be realized that rural development is much broader in scope than nearly agricultural development. Besides it was recognized that development in agriculture was not a panacea for all ills and that development should not be confined to a single area of change, however significance it may be. Therefore, it the strategy for rural development had to be made effective, a multi-pronged approach to rural problems was imperative. A package programme of rural development had to be devised, a multi-dimensional approach taken up and multi-institutional efforts had to be initiated.

In the Era of Globalization

As we have adopted policies of liberalization and globalization since 1991, we will have to look at the rural development from a holistic angle rather than from the angle of compartmentalization of between the urban development and rural development, particularly became of fast changes which are taking place in all spheres of life with market driven economy. In view of this position we will have a comprehensive outlook encompassing both the rural areas as well as the urban areas. Some of the important aspects of the rural development are discussed under.

Aspects of Rural Development

Broadly speaking there are four major aspects of rural development—Economic, Agricultural, Industrial, Infrastructure and Management.

Economic Aspects

The macroeconomics policies of our country will have to be formulated with certain specific consideration that, at macro level the economic growth is reflected. This economic growth at village level will not only be in terms of statistics but it will have to be in terms of physical achievement including better standard of living, health facilitates, education and housing facilitates as also availability of electricity, drinking water, roads etc.—in which government's macroeconomic policies will play important role from the point of view of distribution of resources. Integrated rural development will be one of the important dimensions of economic aspects. In our successive Five Year Plans, we have given considerable thrust on this aspect. Land in rural areas is the primary means of production to generate wealth. Although at the time of attaining our independence, the productivity of land was very low. But later we have been able to increase the productivity with the application of latest technology in agriculture and horticulture. Attention has now been drawn to top the rural market for industrial production to utilize the disposable income generated from agriculture and horticulture produces and also from the dairy industry. This will increase the trade and sincere in rural areas and villages. All these measures together will help in increasing the per capita income of rural people, which will give them a sort of social security. An important component of economic aspect is rural credit facilitates for different sectors such as agriculture, industry; individual trades and services as well as infrastructural facilities. These credit requirements are available from indigenous sector, scheduled banks with their lead bank branches, co-operative banks, regional rural banks and NABARD.

Agriculture Aspects

Agriculture is the backbone of Indian economy. When we became independent in 1947 the agricultural output was very low, the soil productivity was also very low and our agriculture was too much dependent on rains. After independence we build up high dams such as Bhakhra Nangal, Damodar Valley, etc. giant fertilizer plants such as IFFCO, KRIBHACO, GSFC, GNFC etc. we could make green revolution and today we are self-sufficient on food front with mechanized farming and using improved varieties of seeds and adoption of related technologies.

A glaring example is that of potato farming in the rural areas of a border town Deesa, situated in the district Banaskantha in Gujarat State. This area is a traditionally potato growing area. The town Deesa has now become a 'Vegetable City'. The total annual turnover is Rs. 1000 crore out of which 65 per cent share is that of potato. This is completely a matter of good variety of seed quality, timely, credit facility and improved technology. Potato farming has brought prosperity for Deesa.

Agriculture is one of the important means of production and much still remains to be done in this field, so that we can export our agriculture products such as wheat, rice, sugar, cotton, and horticultural product such as mango, apple etc. in sufficient quantity with world class quality by establishing research centers and agro-industrial complexes with latest technologies for green house which can be established on large scale in different rural areas by forming cooperative societies of farmers, traders and agro-industrial services, for longer shelf life. With India taking a very strong stand and WTO, we will be in a very good position to export our agri-horti products to member countries of WTO in very large quantities and we will be earning a good amount of foreign exchange by establishing necessary mechanism for the same.

As this policy would get momentum it would generate income for rural people and would make our villages and rural areas prosper at a faster rate than what it is today.

Industrial Aspect

The forgoing agricultural aspect is limited by the total availability of land. However in view of fast increase in population, supplementary means of production for rural development obviously is inevitable to generate the either the part time employment during lean season or fulltime employment when there is no work in the fields to supplement the income of farmers and agricultural labour.

Although considerable rural industrialization has taken place in the last two decades it is still necessary to develop on a vast scale, cottage, small and medium scale industries. Also where other resources like minerals, agro products etc. are available in a particular rural area, large scale industries such as cement manufacturing industrial unit, salt based industrial undertakings in coastal areas etc. too will have to be established. Down to the line, trades and other services too will have to come up in consonance with other developments taking place in rural areas.

Another important point to consider in industrial development is that, it would require to local entrepreneurs as well as those from outside he can invest money on a big scale. They will have to be invited even from outside the country what is now known as foreign direct investment. The technologies of production of different products and consumer items are fast changing. It is therefore necessary to have unskilled, semiskilled and highly skilled manpower in giving boost to rural industrialization. This leads us to develop human resources for various types of manufacturing industries as well as trades and service industries, hence the requirement of training institutes in rural areas appropriate to the types of rural development. This is one of the important factors for rural industrialization.

Infrastructural Aspects

As we go for rural industrialization and other socio-economic and agro developments they will demand infrastructural requirements. These requirements are, good motorable all weather roads. Extension of railway lines wherever possible, power, water, telecommunication facilities, housing facilities, education facilities, etc.

We have already embarked upon Quadrangular Highway project together with other roads linking big cities, towns and rural areas to move fast the traffic of all categories which would reduce the time of transportation. Railways too are moving thousands of tonnes of goods across the country's different cities, towns, village and rural areas. Now whenever the economic development takes place in rural areas they too will have to be connected by railways.

Today power requirements is one of our biggest requirement. Power is at the centerstage of our living. We are utilizing all resources, such as, thermal, hydro, nuclear, solar and wind energy to generate electricity. We will have to increase our efforts to give more power to rural areas which we want to develop at a faster rate. The economics of power is a complex matter which covers generation, transmission and distribution. Considerable efforts have made to improve the management of power sector in our economy by creating central and State Electricity Regulatory Authorities, to improve the working of state electricity boards, so that rural areas would get power of as much time as possible at reasonable tariff.

Management Aspect

When we take a comprehensive view of the forgoing different aspects of rural development it is imperative that it will require modern concept of management in all the aspects. If we go by the definition of management, it can be said that management of any organization, is to take work from others. For this matter certain clear objective will have to be formulated for development of rural areas. This will involve planning and the implementing machinery for the goals determined. The organization will require expert in the field of management. Subsequent to establishing this organization the rural people for whom the development is indented, will have to be involved to create an awareness for the need of development by educating them about the opportunities being created for their welfare, through the process of development. Once the development process states it will require monitoring by the concerned managers about the physical achievements within the stipulated time and corrections will have to be made whenever necessary. It is equally necessary to update the knowledge of managers in rural development for which institute such as IRMA for imparting education in rural management, established at Anand city in Gujarat State be taken as model for the same.

Rural Development, Democratic Decentralization and Mahatma Gandhi

Mahatma Gandhi underlined the significance of rural India by saying that India lives in villages. Since then successive governments have been trying to develop the rural areas, it has been one of the most abiding concerns. Gandhiji wrote in Harijan on 29 August, 1936: "I would say that if the villages perish, India will perish too. It will be no more India. Her own vision in the world will be lost. The revival of the village life is possible only when it is no more exploited."

Gandhiji's Views on Rural Development

Relationship between City and Villages

It was Gandhiji who first understood the importance, role and place of Indian villages in the whole country. His objective assessment of villages in overall Indian economic and political sphere was the key which helped him to bring them to the mainstream and ultimately win the freedom. The rural character of the economy and the need for regeneration of rural life was stressed by Mahatma Gandhi. He wrote in Harijan (4 April, 1936).

"India is to be found not in few cities but in its 700,000 villages. But we town dwellers have believed that India is to be found in its towns and the villages were created to minister to our needs. We have hardly paused to inquire if those poor get sufficient to eat and cloth themselves with and whether they have a roof to shelter themselves from sun and rain." He was thus critical of the role of the urban setups as they did not share proportionate resources with their counterparts living in villages. He considered urbanization as an evil insofar as (1) it is based on the exploitation of the countryside, and (2) is totally divorced from the rural way of life rooted in nature.

He said (in 1946):

"I regard the growth of the cities as an evil thing, unfortunate for mankind and the world, unfortunate for England and certainly unfortunate for India. The British have exploited India through its cities. The letter have exploited the villages. The blood of the villages is the cement with which the edifice of the cities is built." He has asked whether it was possible to retrace the steps and, if this was possible, whether this would not be incompatible with progress.

Gandhi gave a remarkably balanced answer to this question in the form of the following proportions: (1) "I want the blood that is inflating the arteries of the cities to run once again in the blood-vessels of the villages"; (2) "I do not want to depopulate the cities and send the city folk back to the villages. All I want is that they should re-adjust their lives so as to cease to sponge upon the poor village folk and make to the letter what reparation is possible, even this later hour, by helping to resuscitate their ruined economy"; (3) "In my picture of the rural economy the cities would take their natural place and not appear as unnatural, congested spots or boils on the body-politic, as they are today."

The views of Gandhiji on urbanization and its relationship with that of the villages are still evading us as we find the ballooning of the cities as population due to migration is increasing day by day, pollution, famines, shortage of soft drinking water etc., as ringing problems today. In addition as size is increasing their share in the proportion of the total funds at disposal is also increasing disproportionately.

Co-operative From of Enterprise

In the East man has relied on his group – family, clan, caste, guide or the village community. Gandhiji thought that if the Indian economy as well as the Indian policy, if it has to be restructured from the bottom outwards (rather than upwards in a pyramidal structure) it would be necessary to refashion the village communities as an 'ideal type' and readapt them to the modern methods of "cooperative" operations.

Gandhiji did not think that the village communities in future India would be a replica of the old village communities. In answer to Louid Fisher's suggestions of the nature of the new order in India after the British left, Gandhi said in 1942: "I admit that the future society of India is largely beyond my grasp." But he took care to explain (1) that power concentrated now in New Delhi or in Culcutta and Bombay, in the cities, would have to be distributed among the 7,00,000 villages of India; and (2) that "voluntary cooperation will produce real freedom and a new order".

An Ideal Village

In 1919 Gandhi wrote for the Navjivan a series of article on the condition of Indian peasants and the means of ameliorating it. The English translation appeared in the Young India. Gandhiji said:

"Mr. Lionel Curstis' description of an Indian village as a collection of insanitary dwellings constructed in a dunghill is not much exaggerated. There should be some system about the structure of a well ordered village, there should be some ordered about the village lanes, and the roads should be so scrupulously clean in this land of crores of barefooted pedestrians that nobody need not hesitate in walking or even sleeping in the streets. The lanes should be mechanized and have gutters for letting out water. The temples and mosques should be kept so beautifully clean that the visitors should feel an air of tranquil holiness about them. The village should, as far as possible, be full of shade giving trees and fruit bearing trees in and around them. It should have a dharmashala, a school and a small dispensary. Washing and privy arrangement should be such as may not contaminate the air, water and roads of the village. There was time when the Indian village satisfied most of these conditions. Every village should be self-sufficient, so far as its needs for food and clothing are concerned and should be capable of defending itself against robbers or wild animals. An ideal village should approximate to the description I have given for. Only such village could be called self-governing, and if all Indian villages should come up to that ideal, India should be free from most of its worries... it is my firm belief that these small units are easily capable of being well ordered and organized."

Gandhiji thought of a casteless egalitarian rural society against the stark background of a caste ridden village community. This was a contradiction. He not only faced it, but also tried to resolve it by means of a progressive interpretation of the ancient differentiation of social functions, which, in the course of social decay, and in his view, degenerated in to a hide-bound, caste-ridden social order.

"Village Republic" – A Vision of Gandhiji

This picture of a new India which Gandhiji presented in Harijan article must be delineated in his own words as follows:

1. "Indian independence must begin at the bottom. Thus every village will be a republic or panchayat having powers. It follows, therefore, that every village has to be self-sustained and capable of managing its own affairs, even to the extent of defending itself against the whole world. It will be trained and prepared to perish in the attempt to defend itself against any onslaught from without."

2. "Ultimately, it is individual who is the unit. But this does not exclude dependence on the willing help from neighbours or from the world. It will be free and voluntary play of mutual forces."
3. "Such a society is necessarily highly cultured in which every man or women knows what he or she wants, and what is more, knows that no one should want anything that the others cannot have with equal labour."
4. "In this structure composed of innumerable villages there will be ever-widening, never-ascending circles. Life will not be a pyramid with the apex sustained by the bottom. But it will be an oceanic circle whose center will be the individual, always ready to perish for village, the latter ready to perish for the circle of villages till at last the whole becomes one life composed in individuals, never aggressive in their arrogance, but ever humble, sharing the majesty of the oceanic circle of which they are integral units. Therefore, the outermost circumference will not wield power to crush the inner circle, but will give strength to all within and will derive its own strength from it."
5. "In it there is no room for machines that would displace human labour and that would concentrate power in a few hands. Labour has its unique place in a cultured human family. Every machine that helps every individual has a place."

Gandhiji was aware that by presenting a picture of republican village India he was exposing himself to ridicule in political atmosphere in which politicians of the urban classes were dreaming of power-politics and power-structure of the usual run of democracies, while reflecting on the content of independence in conventional terms.

Democratic Decentralization and Gandhiji

A democratic policy involves decentralization of power in such a way that the affairs of the local people are managed by means of their positive participation. It implies the extension of democracy at the grassroots level in view of the fact that the people's participation signifies the constitution of a democratic government not merely at the top but also at the foundation level of the political system.

Mahatma Gandhi made reference to democratic decentralization for the first time in February 1916. While appreciating the working of the ancient Indian Panchayat System. He said, India is really a republican country as it is because it has survived every shock hitherto delivered. He was sure that the problem of village sanitation would have been solved long ago and India would have been enjoying self-government suited to its requirements had village panchayats been acting as a living force.

In his presidential address at the Belgaum Congress, Gandhiji referred to the panchayat system as the right medium for securing cheap justice as well as for avoiding reliance of the government on the settlement of mutual disputes. During his term of office as president of the Indian National Congress he extensively toured the country, that reinforced his conviction that India would be benefited a great deal if the villages were governed by the village panchayats. However, he felt that, the reorganization of the village administration could not be taken in isolation. He was sure that Indian village life had great vitality and character. It was because of this that it has persisted all these long years and had weathered many a storm. Gandhiji's view of democratic decentralization developed over the years. He laid emphasis on PR or democratic decentralization till the last moment of his life. Simple living and high thinking is the ideal, the very foundation and essence of the Gandhian approach to decentralization.

Gandhiji opposed all types of concentration of power. Since to him, centralization is a menace and a danger to democracy. Concentration of power in his view distorts all democratic values. So he argues, possession of power makes men blind and deaf; they cannot see things which are under their very nose and cannot hear things which invade their cars. In other words centralization is a system inconsistent with non-violent structure of society.

Moreover, he was convinced that moral progress was possible only in a decentralized set-up in a nutshell, he argues that without decentralization it is impossible to ensure individual liberty and mental and moral growth of man. Similarly it is equally essential for the realization of the ideal democracy, for the rule of the people; which it stands for, is not possible without adequate opportunities to individuals to participate in the management of their own affairs.

Gandhiji rather pleads for decentralization of economic and political power. For the success of political decentralization, in his view depends upon economic decentralization. This follows from his conviction that a highly centralized political set-up is likely to bring dictatorship of one kind or another by a self-increased and power-hungry minority imposing itself on a deluded and subservient majority. While elaborating his ideas on decentralization, Gandhiji keeps in mind two different structures. First, the power state structure of the west. Basically he rejects it on the ground that it leads to centralization of power, exploitation of the weak denial of individual freedom and moral degradation. It is democratic in its external framework but dictatorial in actual practice.

Second is the panchayati raj – building up from below. In other words, it can be called democratic decentralization. Basically Gandhiji is drawn towards this model. One important feature of this model is economic self-sufficiency at the grassroots level. To him this is the only way to eliminate exploitation of the weaker sections in society and to bring happiness to the millions. Further this decentralization implies the fundamental principle of self-sufficiency. But it is not absolute sufficiency. It is mostly confined to the basic needs such as food, clothing and shelter. He reiterated that if a new democratic egalitarian social, political order free from exploitation had to be established on firm foundations. Decentralization in economics must go side by side with decentralization in politics. Even success of political decentralization depends upon decentralization. In other words without economic decentralization, political decentralization would be meaningless. The manifesto of the Congress parliamentary board 29 July, 1934 which was drafted by Gandhiji declared. In order to end the exploitation of the masses political freedom must include real economic freedom of the starving millions. Similarly his advocacy of charkha and village industries only demonstrate his living faith in decentralization of economic power.

Gandhiji was not against the modern science and technology. His attitude is entirely rational and scientific his main thrust is that science and technology instead of becoming masters should function as the servants of the people. Basically he has no objection to machines as such. But he argues that, it is wrong to carry the process of mechanization of industry so far as to kill the cottage industries and concentrate them within a narrow field. Accordingly, he wants villages to be production centers and towns to be clearing houses for such product instead of being the reverse as it is today.

Therefore, Gandhiji's concept of democratic decentralization bears the stamp of his passionate belief in non-violence, truth and individual freedom. He calls it PR village swaraj. He wants to see each village as a little republic self-sufficient in its vital wants, organically linked with the higher bodies and enjoying the maximum freedom of deciding the affairs of the locality. According to Gandhiji, real India lives in its villages. So villages held an important place in Gandhiji's scheme of life and social organization. He was a strong and ardent supporter of moral atmosphere, rural life and rural development. For him Indian villages were the backbone of India or real India. He believed that if village perished, India would perish too. It will be no more India. Her own mission in the world will get lost.

Till 1936 Gandhiji had not made up his mind or he was not clear about the character of the structure of Indian polity. At the Faizpur Congress Session in 1936 he expressed the opinion that India must have a polity suited to her genius. But he could not give its blueprint. This shows that he was clear about the spirit but not of the form of Indian polity. He only indicated that the western mechanism of democracy was not suitable for India. This meant that India must seek its own institutional framework to realize the values of democracy. He made some loud thinking in this connection. The institution of the village panchayat which had provided a democratic structure at the grassroots level for centuries in India showed him direction. The institution of panchayat, for him, was the fundamental unit of democratic decentralization.

Further in 1942, during the course of an interview with Louis Fisher, he remarked that voluntary co-operation and cooperation induced by Nazi methods was the essence of the panchayat system. He again pleaded for the distribution of power among the villagers. He said ,"You see, the center of power now is in New Delhi or in Culcutta and Bombay in the big cities. I would have it distributed among the seven hundred thousand villages of India. That will mean that there is not power. In other words, I want the seven hundred thousand dollars now invested in the Imperial Bank of England, withdrawn and distributed among the seven hundred thousand villages. Then each village would have it dollar which cannot be lost." Emphasizing this point he said the seven hundred thousand dollars invested in the Imperial Bank of India could be swept away by a bomb from a Japanese plane. Whereas if they were distributed among the seven hundred thousand shareholders nobody could deprive them of their assets. This will then be a voluntary co-operation will produce real freedom and a new order vastly superior to the new order in Soviet Russia.

The above mentioned interview reveals Gandhiji's deep faith in decentralized democracy based on village panchayat drawing their powers from the initiative and willing cooperation of the people and it must belong to the people. He fully subscribed to the principle that power resides in the people and it must belong to the people. It seeks expression through democratic decentralization or panchayati raj. Again in the 1946 Gandhiji while rejecting western political institution of parliamentary democracy laid stress on the concept of decentralized democracy consisting of concentric village republics. He elaborated his plan for independent India at the time of transfer of power. He asserted that independence must begin at the bottom. Thus every village would be a republic or panchayat having full powers. It follows, that every village had to be self-sustained and capable of managing its affairs even to the extent of defending itself against the whole world. It would be trained and prepared to perish in the attempt to defend itself against any onslaught from without. Thus ultimately, it is the individual who is the unit. But Gandhi points out that this does not exclude dependence on and willing help from neighbours or from the world.

Under the Gandhian constitution, the scheme of Government was briefly as follows:

1. First, the primary political unit was to be the village panchayat, whose member would be elected by the audits of the village. The panchayat would control chowkidars, patwaris, police and schools. It would also assess and collect land revenue, supervise cooperative farming irrigation and interest rate as well as khadi and other village industries.
2. Secondly, above the village panchayat came a hierarchy of indirectly elected bodies. First came taluka and district panchayat, each comprised the sarpanches of the next lower panchayats and having only advisory power over them. Members from the district and municipal panchayat would form the provincial panchayat, which would elect president to serve as head of the provincial government. Presidents of

a provincial panchayat would comprise the all India panchayat whose president would be the head of the State and of the Government, which would be ministerial in character. Among the responsibilities of provincial panchayat would be transport, irrigation, natural resources and co-operative bank.

The national panchayat would be responsible for such things as defence, currency, customs, the running of key industries of national importance and the coordination of provincial economic development plants.

Functions and Powers of Village Panchayat

One of the most important functions, according to him, under the jurisdiction of institution of democratic decentralization, was the settlement of disputes between individuals. Its object was to make justice available to be village without incurring much cost or inconvenience. So he said in his presidential address at the Belgaum Congress, administration of justice should be cheapened and with that end in view, the final court of appeals should be not in London, but in Delhi. Parties to civil suits must be compelled in the majority cases to refer their dispute arbitration, the decisions of these panchayats is to be final expect in cases of corruption or obvious misapplication of law. Municipaiity of intermediate courts should be avoided.

However, its jurisdiction was based on the voluntary principle. Thus in his instruction to the village panchayat of Nainital, he laid down that the panchayat might try civil suits if the parties to the suit referred their disputes to the panchayats.

To him every panchayat will be expected to attend to education of boys and girls in its village, its sanitation, its medical needs, the upkeep and cleanliness of village wells or ponds and the uplift of and the daily wants of the so-called untouchable.

Gandhiji pleads for decentralization of both economic and political power. He staunchly believes in political decentralization. Gandhiji visualize a social and political order passed on decentralization of both economic and political power. He wants to create convenient regions not only to manage their political affairs but also their economic and political power. He wants to create convenient regions not only to manage their political affairs but their economic affairs too. Thus he wants to transform every region into a small republic or a panchayat. For, the real freedom, to Gandhi, is the management of one's own affairs by oneself. And it can function effectively only in small units.

Conclusively, Gandhi's approach to democratic decentralization is based on the principles of non-violence, truth, individual freedom, non exploitation and morality suited to the genius of the Indian masses. Conversely, his approach incompatible with compulsion, force, strict control from above and centralization of power. It does not begin from the top but has to grow from below.

As regards the implementation of Gandhiji's view not much seems to have been achieved. However, some efforts were made at both the official level. After his death some of his followers made efforts to give shape to his views. In this context, a reference may be made to such loadable attempts as the Bhoodan movement, reconstruction of Indian polity through communication approach, total revolution etc.

However, they failed in their mission to realize or develop Gandhi's dreams of decentralized social, political order or Gram Swaraj or Panchayati Raj or rural democracy. He could neither fill up the gap nor develop his scheme of democratic decentralization, due to various shortcomings, as the structure of local government was systematically destroyed out of political consideration. There was a lack of commitment of democratic decentralization, rather they created confusion in their approach by introducing in it certain extraneous factors; the principle of unanimity as advocate by them failed to produce any fruitful thing. Jana Shakti (people's power) was hardly generated and Raj Niti (power politics) dominate the gramdan villages. Lack of team work was notable and workers who finally showed their skin deep differences and even Jayaprakash Narayan and Vinoba Bhave, parted with each other in the long run.

To come to the efforts made at the official level; we find that while the institutional fabric of the country was radically reshaped, little was done to build it according to Gandian principles. The Indian Constitution bears witness to this fact. The people were quite hopeful that the new construction would definitely reflect the Gandian spirit, but surprisingly the draft constitution that appeared immediately after the independence did not make a mention of democratic decentralization or PR of Gandhiji's conception.

Thus, the neglect of Gandian concept of decentralization in Indian Constitution was not an accident of history; rather it was the end result of a chain of events and thought which had been secretly working at the back of the minds of most of those who mattered at the time of constitution-making.

While reviewing and evaluating in Gandian terms the functional competence of PRI in different parts of the country, it has been found that except in a few states like West Bangal, Karnataka and Andhra Pradesh, these institutions have been rarely given a change to perform their functions on a sizable scale.

Regarding the financial position of PRIs, it can be said that the financial resources are not adequate and satisfactory and as a result these do not fit into the scheme of Gandhian approach to democratic decentralization as Gandhiji wanted the local bodies to be self-reliant and self-sufficient so far as the basic or daily requirements of these bodies were concerned. Similarly, they must be provided with adequate and independent financial resources to discharge their duties properly.

Further PRIs do not possess absolute autonomy as these are created as well as controlled by Central/State Government.

Thus, the PRIs failed to become a part of the whole democratic system of the country. There has been a lack of organic linkage among these institutions and these were kept aloof from the democratic setup at the state as well as the national level.

The irregularity of elections to its various institutions constitute another distortion of the system. In fact, the State Government never realized the growing importance and urgency of holding the timely and regular elections to these institutions.

In the end, the history democratic decentralization. In India repeats its own pages that the subject remained a controversial one ever since the independence. All politicians exploited it as much as possible in the name of Gandhiji, intellectuals gave it a different colour by interpreting according to their own mental make up; peoples showed their apathy and lacked interest, initiative and cooperation and participation in its operational process; the officials and representatives showed their indifference towards it and misused their power too. The government both at the center and the state levels have also spread no efforts to make a capital out of it, without doing any tangible efforts either to strengthen it or to improve its image. It would therefore be futile to suggest any remedy. For, the ills or distortion or lapses themselves speak of the remedy.

Rural Development Programmes in India – An Overview

The ministry of rural development is implementing a number of programmes aimed at sustainable development of rural areas with a focus on weaker and vulnerable section. In order to catalyze development in rural area, top priority has been accorded to rural development, not only in terms of allocation of funds and resources but also through introduction of new programmes and restructuring of the existing ones. Development should be participatory, tapping the local talent and resources in order to be sustainable. Stress is being given to make the Gram Sabha as pillar of Panchayati Raj Institutions as an effective unit of local self-government and an effective and vibrant forum for decentralized planning and implementation of rural development programmes.

To ensure sustainable development of rural areas, the allocation for rural development was increased substantially. As against a budgetary allocation of Rs. 12,265 crore during 2001-02 the allocation in the year 2002-03 were Rs. 13,670 crore, which was further enhanced to Rs. 14,070 crore for the year 2003-04 and to Rs. 15,998 crore for the current financial year, 2004-05.

Anti-poverty programmes are a dominant feature of government initiatives in the rural areas. The programmes were reviewed and strengthened in successive year in order to sharpen their focus on reduction of rural poverty. The results achieved are worth noting. In percentage terms, rural poverty has reduced from 56.44 per cent of the country's population in 1973-74 to 37.27 in 1993-94 and again to 27.09 per cent in 1999-00. However, the cause for concern is that the estimated number of rural poor is still about 19.30 crore which has led to further review and restructuring of the anti-poverty programmes. The Swarnjayanti Gram Swarojgar Yojana (SGSY) is the result of such latest review and restructuring of programmes. Launched on 1 April, 1999, the SGSY is different from the earlier programmes in terms of strategy envisaged for implementation has been conceived as a holistic Programme of Self-Employment, viz., organization of rural poor into Self-Help Groups and their capacity building, training, planning for activity clusters, infrastructure build up, technology and marketing support.

Gainful employment, food security and strengthening of infrastructure in rural areas is a must for national renewal for a resurgent India. On 25 September, 2001, the Sampoorna Grameen Rozgar Yojana was launched to attain these objectives. The scheme envisages an annual expenditure of Rs. 10,000 crore. Under the scheme, 50 lakhs tonnes of foodgrain amounting to Rs. 5,700 crore (at economic cost) are to be provided every year to State/UTs free of cost. About Rs. 5,000 crore is to be utilized to meet the cash component of wage and material costs. About 100 crore man days of employment is likely to be generated every year, besides creation of durable assets in rural areas as per the felt needs of Gram Panchayats. In order to ensure people's participation, the programme would be implemented through PRIs.

Notwithstanding the efforts made over the years at the state and central levels through different programmes, about 40 per cent of habitations are still without road connectivity. Even where the connectivity has been provided, the roads constructed are not all-whether roads. There is close link between rural connectivity and growth, be it in the area of trade, employment, education to health care. Keeping this in view the government launched a major initiative—Pradhan Mantri Gram Sadak Yojana on 25 December, 2000 with the objective of providing connectivity to all unconnected habitations with the population of more than 1,000 within three years and similar such villages with a population of 500 by the year 2007 through good all-whether roads.

Considerable success has been achieved in meeting the drinking water needs of the rural population. With an investment of more than Rs. 45,000 crore or rural drinking water supply by central and state governments since independence, 94.37 per cent partially covered. The programme has been revamped to usher reforms by institutionalizing community participation in rural water supply sector with a view to gradually replace the government oriented, centralized, supply-driven and non-people participating Rural Water Supply Programme by people oriented, decentralized, demand driven and community based Rural Water Supply Programme.

Since land is a critically important national resource among the natural resources, the efficient management of which is vital for economic growth and development of rural areas. Around 20 per cent (63.85 million hectare) of the country's geographical area is wastelands/degraded land. To meet the imperative need to put in place an integrated mechanism capable of responding effectively to the challenges of managing country's scarce land resources, a separate Department of Land Resources came into being in April 1999 under the Ministry of Rural Development. All the land-based area development programmes are being implemented through the watershed development approach since April 1995, in accordance with the recommendations of the Hanumantha Rao Committee.

Empowerment has to be an essential ingredient in planning and implementation of the programmes. Accordingly, under the programmes of the ministry, a predominant role for Panchayati Raj Institution (PRIs) in their implementation has been envisaged through a four-pronged strategy viz.,

(i) Enhancing the level of awareness about the schemes;
(ii) Promoting transparency in the implementation of programmes;
(iii) Encouraging people's partnership; and
(iv) Ensuring accountability/social audit.

Pradhan Mantri Gram Sadak Yojana

The Pradhan Mantri Gram Sadak Yojana (PMGSY), a 100 per cent centrally sponsored scheme was launched on 25 December, 2000. The prime objective of the PMGSY is to provide connectivity, by way of an all-weather roads to the unconnected habitations in the rural areas in such a way that habitations with a population of 1,000 persons and above are covered in three years (2000-03) and all unconnected habitations with a population of 500 persons and above by the end of the tenth plan, i.e., 2007. In respect of the Hill States (North-East, Sikkim, Himachal Pradesh, Jammu and Kashmir, Uttaranchal), Tribal and Desert Areas, the objective would be to connect habitations with a population of 250 persons and above.

As on 1 April, 2000, about 8.25 lakh habitations in the country, about 3.30 lakh habitations were not connected by all-weather roads. The PMGSY seeks to provide connectivity to about 1.70 lakh unconnected habitations besides upgradation of some existing rural roads to prescribed standards by the end of the tenth plan. According to estimates based on a survey, about 3.70 lakh kilometers of roads will be constructed under the programme. The total cost of the construction and upgradation of other rural roads is likely to be of the order of Rs. 1,30,000 roads estimated to cost Rs. 14,377 crore have been cleared up to the end of March 2004 and 20,651 road works have since been completed. The remaining works are in various stages of execution. A cumulative expenditure of Rs. 6,559 crore was incurred till March 2004.

Rural Water Supply Programme

Drinking water facility to rural habitations are provided under state sector programme. The central government endeavours to supplement the efforts of the states by providing assistance under the Centrally-Sponsored Accelerated Rural Water Supply Programme. Powers have been delegated to the states to plan, sanction and implement the rural water supply schemes.

The government envisages provision of safe drinking water to all rural habitations. The strategy to achieve the objective revolves around the following issues to accelerate the coverage of remaining "not covered and partially covered" habitations with safe drinking water systems; to tackle the problem of water quality in affected habitations and to institutionalize water quality monitoring and surveillance system and; to promote sustainability both of systems and sources, to ensure continuous supply of safe drinking water in "covered" habitations.

An investment of more than Rs. 45,000 crore has been made in the water supply sector so far. Status of coverage of rural habitations, as per information received from states till 28 May, 2004 is 5,936 not covered and 71,463 partially covered rural habitations. During 2003-04, as per information received upto rural development 28 May, 2004, 3,716 not covered and 30,540 partially covered habitations have been covered with drinking water facilities. Ninety-nine per cent of rural habitations have access to drinking water facility.

The government has revamped the Rural Water Supply Programme, which, inter-alia, envisages institutionalization of community-based rural water supply system by incorporating the following basic principles for ensuring peoples participations:

(i) Adoption of demand-driven, responsive and adaptable approach of villages to ensure their full participation in the arrangements;
(ii) Shifting the role of Government from direct service delivery to that of facilitator; and
(iii) Partial cost sharing either in cash or kind or both and 100 per cent responsibility of operations and maintenance by

end-users. Sixty-seven districts all over the country have been identified for implementing the reform projects on a pilot basis. The reform initiative launched has now scaled to Swajaldhara to cover the entire country.

Central Rural Sanitation Programme

Rural sanitation is a state subject. The efforts of the state are supplemented by the central government through technical and financial assistance under the Central Rural Sanitation Programme (CRSP)

The programme was launched in 1986 with the objective of improving the quality of life of rural people and providing privacy and dignity to women. The concept of sanitation was expanded in 1993 to include personal hygiene, home sanitation, safe water, and disposal of garbage, human excreta and waste water. The components of the programme included construction of individual sanitary toilets for households below poverty-line (BPL), conversion of dry latrines of water-pour flush toilets, construction of village sanitary complexes of women, setting up of sanitary marts and production centers, intensive campaign for creating awareness and health education, etc.

Keeping in view the experiences of the central and state governments, NGOs and other implementing agencies and the recommendations of the Second National Seminar on Rural Sanitation, the strategy for the Ninth Five Year Plan was revised by the programme was restructured from 1 April, 1999. The restructured programme moves away from the principle of statewise allocation of funds, primarily based on poverty criteria, to a demand driven approach in a phased manner. Total Sanitation Campaign (TSC) was introduced and the allocation-based programme was phased put by 31 March, 2002. TSC is community-led and people-centred. There was a shift from a high subsidy to a low subsidy regime. The TSC approach emphasis awareness-building component and meets the demand through alternate delivery mechanism. School sanitation has been introduced as a major component to encourage wider acceptance of sanitation among rural masses. The State/UTs are required to formulate project proposals under the TSC in order to claim central government assistance.

Under the TSC, so far 398 projects in 29 States/UTs have been sanctioned with the total project outlay of about Rs. 3,744.24 crore.

The central, state and beneficiary panchayat contributions are about Rs. 2,213.81 crore, Rs. 826 crore and Rs. 703 crore respectively. The components sanctioned in the 398 projects are *(a)* construction of 323 lakh individual household latrines; *(b)* 3,53,041 lakh toilets for schools; *(c)* 25,236 community sanitary complexes; *(d)* 59,562 toilets for Balwadis/Anganwadis; and *(e)* 2,942 Rural Sanitary Marts/Production centers. Besides, funds have been earmarked for start-up activities, Information, Education and Communication (IEC) and administrative charges.

The total number of household toilets constructed upto 2003-04 are 80,87,130 (provisional).

Rural Housing

Rural housing meets the shortage of housing in rural areas, the India Awaas Yojana (IAY) was launched in May 1985 as a sub-scheme of Jawahar Rozgar Yojana (JRY). It is being implemented as an independent scheme since 1 January, 1996. The Indira Awaas Yojana aims at providing assistance to rural people below the poverty-line belonging to Scheduled Castes/Scheduled Tribes, freed bonded labourers and non-Scheduled Castes/Scheduled Tribes categories in construction of dwelling units and up-gradation of existing unserviceable kutcha houses by providing grants-in-aid. From 1995-1996, the IAY benefits have been extended to windows or next of kin of defense personnel killed in action. Benefits have also been extended to ex-servicemen and retired members of the paramilitary forces as long as they fulfill the normal eligibility conditions of the IAY. Three per cent of funds are reserved for the disabled persons living below the poverty line in rural areas.

The District Panchayat/District Rural Development Agency (DRDA) on the basis of allocation made and targets fixed decide the number of houses to be constructed/upgraded panchayat-wise under IAY, during a particular financial year. Accordingly, the targets are intimated to the Gram Panchayat concerned. Thereafter, the Gram Sabha selects the beneficiaries from the list of eligible BPL households, restricting this number to the target allotted as per the Programme Guideline. Selection by the Gram Sabha is final. No approval by a higher body is required. Zilla Parishads/DRDAs and Block Development Office are informed accordingly to provide assistance to selected beneficiaries.

Under the scheme, allotment of the house is done in the name of the female members of the households or in the joint names of husband and wife. A minimum of 60 per cent of funds is to be utilized for construction of houses for the SC/ST. Sanitary latrines and smokeless chulhas should also be provided to beneficiaries. Selection of construction technology, materials and design is left entirely to the choice of beneficiaries. The ceiling on assistance for construction of new houses has been increased from Rs. 20,000 to Rs. 27,500 per unit for the plain areas and from Rs. 22,000 to Rs. 27,500 per unit for the hilly/difficult areas from 1 April, 2004. The upper limit in respect of conversion of kutcha houses into semi-pucca houses (upgradation) and subsidy under credit-cum-subsidy scheme has increased from Rs. 10,000 to Rs. 12,500 per unit. Upto 20 per cent of the IAY funds are allocated for upgradations and assistance under credit-cum-subsidy scheme. A household having annual income of Rs. 32,000 is eligible to get loan upto Rs. 50,000 under credit-cum-subsidy scheme.

Undet the Indira Awaas Yojana, since its inception and upto March 2004 about 114.78 houses have been constructed with an expenditure of about Rs. 20,023 crore.

Swarnjayanti Gram Swarozgar Yojana (SGSY)

The Swarnjayanti Gram Swarozgar Yojana (SGSY) has been launched as an integrated programme for self-employment of the rural poor on 1 April, 1999. The objective of the scheme is to bring assisted poor families above the poverty line by organizing them in to Self-Help Groups (SHGs) through the process of social mobilization training, capacity building and provision of income generating assets through a mix of bank credit and Government subsidy. The scheme emphasizes on process approach and building the capacity of the rural poor. Therefore, it provides for involvement of NGOs/CBOs/individuals/banks as facilitators/Self-Help promoting institutions in nurturing and developing SHGs. The scheme provides for the cost of social intermediation and skill development training based on the local requirement.

The focus of the programme is on establishing a large number of micro enterprises in rural areas based on the ability of the poor and potential of each area, both land-based and otherwise, for a sustainable income generation. Due emphasis is being laid on different components such as capacity building of the poor, skill development, training, credit training, technology transfer, marketing and infrastructure. The subsidy allowed under SGSY is 30 per cent of the total project cost, subject to a ceiling of Rs. 7,500 (for SCs/STs and disabled persons subsidy limit is 50 per cent of the project cost subject to ceiling of Rs. 10,000). For Self-Help Groups (SHGs), subsidy would be 50 per cent of the project cost subject to a ceiling of Rs.1.25 lakh or per capita subsidy of Rs. 10,000, whichever is less. There is no monetary ceiling on subsidy for minor irrigation projects for SHGs as well as individual swarozgaris.

The SGSY has special focus on the vulnerable groups among the rural poor. Accordingly, the SCs/STs would account for at least 50 per cent of the swarozgaris, women for 40 per cent and the disabled for three per cent. The SGSY seeks to promote multiple credit rather than a one-time credit injection.

The SHGs may consist of 10-20 members and in case of minor irrigation and in case of disabled persons and in case of people living in difficult area, i.e., hilly, desert and sparsely populated areas, this number may be minimum of five. The Self-Help Groups should be also be drawn from the BPL list approved by the Gram Sabha. The SHGs broadly go through three stages of evolution such as group formation, capital formation through the revolving fund are skill development and taking up of economic activity for income generation.

Selection could be made upto 10 key activities per block based on local resources, occupational skills of the people and availability of market so that the swarozgaris can draw suitable incomes from their investment. The SGSY emphasis on cluster approach, i.e., each block should concentrate on four to five selected key activities and attend to all aspects of these activities, so that the Swarozgaris can draw suitable incomes from their investments. The SGSY lays special emphasis on development of Swarozgaris through well-designed training courses tailored to the activities selected and the requirement of each swarozgaris.

The SGSY is being implemented through the District Rural Development Agencies (DRDAs). with the active involvement of Panchayati Raj Institutions (PRIs), Bank and the NGOs. It is financed on 75:25 cost-sharing basis between the center and the state.

Sampoorna Grameen Rozgar Yojana (SGRY)

The Sampoorna Grameen Rozgar Yojana (SGRY) was launched on 25 September, 2001 by merging the non-going schemes of EAS and the JGSY with the objective of providing additional wage employment in the rural area as also food security, alongside the creation of durable-community assets in the rural areas. The programme is self-targeting in nature with special emphasis on women, scheduled castes, scheduled tribes and parents of children withdrawn from hazardous occupations. While preference will be given to BPL families for providing wage employment under SGRY, poor families above the poverty line can also be offered employment under the programme. The annual outlay is Rs. 10,000 crore which includes 50 lakh tonnes on foodgrains. The cash component is shared between the center and the state in the ratio of 75:25 foodgrains are provided free of cost to the States/UTs. The payment of foodgrains is made directly to FCI at economic cost by the center. However the cost of the transportation of foodgrains from the FCI godown to the work-site/PDS and its distribution are the responsibility of the state governments. Minimum wages are paid to the workers through a mix of minimum five kg of foodgrains and at least 25 per cent in cash.

The programme is implemented by all the three tiers of PRIs. Each level of panchayat is an independent unit for formulation of Action Plan and executing the scheme. The resources are distributed among District Panchayat, Intermediate Panchayats and the Gram Panchayats in the ratio of 20:30:50.

The Gram Panchayat can take up any work with the approval of the Gram Sabha as per their felt need and within available funds. Fifty per cent of the funds earmarked to the Gram Panchayat are to be utilized for infrastructure development works in SC/ST localities. 22.5 per cent resources must be spend on individual beneficiary schemes meant for SCs/STs out of Zilla Parishads and Panchayat Samiti's share of resources. Contractors are not permitted to be engaged for execution of any of the works and no middlemen/intermediate agencies can be employed for executing works under the scheme. Evaluated through impact studies conducted by reputed institutions and organizations sponsored by the central/state government.

CAPART

In order to encourage, promote and assist voluntary action in rural development with focus on injecting new technology inputs for enhancement of rural prosperity, the government setup the Council for Advancement of People's Action and Rural Technology (CAPART) in 1986.

CAPART has nine Regional Committees/Centres at Jaipur, Lucknow, Ahmedabad, Bhubaneswar, Patna, Chandigarh, Hyderabad, Guwahati and Dharwad. The Regional Committees are empowered to sanction project proposals to voluntary agencies upto an outlay of Rs. 20 lakh in their respective regions. Since inception and upto June 2003, CAPART has sanctioned 21,621 projects involving an amount of Rs. 701.63 crore and has released Rs. 545.5 crore.

Wastershed Development Programmes

The Department of Land Resources is implementing three area based watershed programmes for development of wastelands/degraded land namely Drought Prone Areas Programmes (DPAP) Desert Development Programme (DDP) and Integrated Wasteland Development programme (IWDP). DPAP was launched in 1973-1974 to tackle the special problems faced by those areas that are constantly affected by drought conditions. Presently, 972 blocks of 182 districts in 16 states are covered under the programmes. DDP was launched in 1977-78 to mitigate the adverse effects of desertification. Presently, 235 blocks of 40 districts in seven states are covered under the programme. IWDP has been under implementation since 1989-90. The projects under the IWDP are generally sanctioned in areas that are not covered under DDP or DPAP.

Since 1 April, 1995, the three programmes are being implemented on the basis of a Common Guidelines for Watershed Development. Details of projects sanctioned and fund released from 1995-86 to 2003-04 are as under:

Name Scheme	*No. of projects sanctioned*	*Area covered (in lakh ha.)*	*Total fund released by the center (Rs. in crore)*
DPAP	18803	94.01	1442.21
DDP	9876	49.38	1085.82
IWDP	662	50.79	977.49
Grand Total		**194.18**	**3505.52**

The cost norm for all the three schemes is Rs. 6,000 per ha. Under DPAP and DDP, it is shared between the center and states in the ratio of 75:25 in case of IWDP, the cost sharing between the center and state is in the ratio of 11:1.

Funds are released in seven installments - six installments at the rate of 15 per cent and the last installment at the rate of 10 per cent. The first installment is released along with the initial sanction-order and subsequent installments on receipt of reports of utilization of 50 per cent of the available funds as well as the following documents: *(a)* Quarterly progress reports *(b)* Utilization certificates; *(c)* The audited statement of accounts for the previous year; and *(d)* Evidence of satisfactory completion of institutional arrangements.

Implementation

Projects are implemented by District Rural Development Agencies/ Zilla Parishads (DRDAs/ZPs) through Project Implementing Agencies (PIAs); PIAs could be a line Department (of the state government), Panchayati Raj Institutions or a reputed NGOs; one PIA normally handles 10-12 watershed projects covering an area of about 5,000-6,000 hectares. The PIA is required to maintain a technical team of 4 experts called Watershed Development Team (WDT), and Individual Projects (500 hectares) are planned and executed by the local people living in the watershed area called the Watershed Association (IWA) through an elected body called Watershed Committee (WC).

Hariyali

Department of Land Resources launched a new initiative called, Hariyali with the objective of empowering PRIs both financially and administratively in implementation of Watershed Developemnt Programme namely, Integrated Watershed Development Programme (IWDP), Drought Prone Areas programme (DPAP) and Desert Development Programme (DDP) would be implemented through the PRIs. New projects under the ongoing area development programmes shall be implemented in accordance with the guidelines for Hariyali from 1 April, 2003. Projects sanctioned prior to this date shall continue to be implemented as per the Watershed Development Guidelines of 2001.

In the new arrangements, the Gram Panchayat shall implement the projets under the overall supervision and guidance of Project Implementation Agencies (PIAs). An intermediate panchayat may be the PIA for all the projects sanctioned to a particular Block/Taluka. In case, these panchayats are not adequately empowered, then the zilla panchayat can either act as PIA itself or may appoint a suitable Line Department like Agriculture, Forestry/Social Forestry, Soil Conservation, etc., or an agency of the state Government/University/Institute as PIA. Failing these option, the ZP/DRDA may consider appointing a reputed Non-Government Organization (NGO) in the district with adequate experience and expertise in the implementation of watershed projects or related area development works as the PIA after thoroughly examining their credentials.

The Project Implementation Agency (PIA) will provide necessary technical guidance to the Gram Panchayat for preparation of development plans for the watershed through Participatory Rural Appraisal (PRA) exercise, undertake community organization and training for the village communities, supervise watershed development activities, inspect and authentic project accounts, encourage adoption of low-cost technologies and build up on indigenous technical knowledge, monitor and review the overall project implementation and set up institutional arrangements for post-project operations and maintenance and further development of the assets creating during the project period.

Land Reforms

Two Centrally Sponsored Schemes viz, (i) Computerization of Land Records (CLR) was started in 1988-89 with 100 per cent financial assistance as a pilot project in eight districts, viz., Rengareddy (A.P.), Sonitpur (Assam), Singhbhum (Bihar), Gandhinagar (Gujarat), Morena (M.P.), Wardha (Maharashtra), Mayurbhanj (Orissa) and Dungarpur (Rajasthan) to remove the problems inherent the manual system of maintenance and updating of Land Records and to meet the requirements of various groups of users. It was decided that efforts should be made to Computerize Core data contained in land records, so as to assist development planning and to make records, peoples/planners and administrators.

During the Eighth Five Year Plan, the scheme was approved as a separate Centrally Sponsored Scheme on Computerization of Land Records. The total expenditure under the scheme during the eighth plan period was Rs. 59.42 crore.

During the Ninth Five Year Plan, the Ministry of Rural Development released a sum of Rs. 169.13 crore for covering 259 more districts under the scheme. At present, the scheme is being implemented in 582 districts of the country leaving those districts where there are no land records. A decision has been taken during 1997-98 for operationalization of the scheme at the tehsil/taluk level for facilitating delivery of computerized land records to users and public at large. Under this programme, funds are released to the state government to purchase of hardware, software and other peripherals. 3,142 tehsil/taluks have been covered under the programme. Since inception of the scheme, the ministry has released Rs. 300.51 crore till 31 March, 2004. The utilization of funds reported by the States/UTs is Rs. 203.01 crore, which is approximately 68 per cent of the total funds released.

Strengthening of Revenue Administration and Updating of Land Records

With a view to assist the State/UTs in the task of updating of land records, Centrally Sponsored Scheme for Strengthening of Revenue Administration and Updating of Land Records (SRA & ULR) was started in 1987. Initially the scheme was approved for the state of Bihar and Orissa in 1987-88 and extended to other States/UTs during 1989-90. The scheme is being implemented by the state governments through their revenue/Land Records Departments. It is financed by the center and the state on 50:50 funds sharing basis. However, Union Territories are provided full Central Assistance.

Under the scheme, financial assistance is given for purchase of Modern Survey Equipments like Global Positioning System (GPS), EDM, Total Stations, Theodolites, Work Stations, Aerial Survey, Office equipments like photocopies, laminating machines and basic facilities to improve work efficiency of lower staff of the Revenue Departments, construction of Office-cum-residence of Patwaris construction/repair/renovation of Training Institutes and equipments for training, etc. Financial assistance of Rs. 265.97 crore has been provided to the State Governments/UTs upto 31 March, 2004 towards central share under the scheme. The utilization of the funds reported by the state/UTs is Rs. 170.31 crore which is approximately 64 per cent of the total funds released.

Monitoring and Evaluation

The government lays great emphasis on monitoring and evaluation of all rural development programmes being implemented in various States/UTs. The monitoring mechanism includes; inter-alia, the Performance Review Committee, the Area Officer Scheme, Periodic Progress Reports, Audit and Utilization Certificates, Video

Conferencing and Field Visits. The government conducts quick evaluation/concurrent evaluation of all major programmes. States/UTs have been advised to reconstitute Vigilance and Monitoring Committee at state and district—levels to monitor the implementation of programmes and introduce greater transparency in the same. These committees, inter-alia, include MPs/MLA, representatives of Panchayati Raj Institutions and NGOs.

In order to strengthen the monitoring mechanism, the government has prepared a panel of National Level Monitors by involving ex-serviceman and retired civil servants to monitor and furnish periodic reports on the implementation of programmes in selected districts.

A system of District Level Monitoring also has been put in place in selected districts of the country through independent locally based institutions for physical verification of assets created under various rural development programmes and ensuring transparency in programme implementation.

Social Structure and Rural Development in the Context of Globalization

Rural India now contains 72 per cent of the population, and some 70 per cent of the labour force is engaged in agriculture. Despite the land reforms of late 1940s and early 1980s, the distribution of land ownership in rural India has been grossly unequal. In the early 1970s, over 96 per cent of India's household owned less than 20 acres of land; 43 per cent owned less than 5 acres; and 24 per cent owned no land at all with the percentage of landless labour increasing. The disparities in land ownership are revealed in the fact that 10 per cent of the rural families hold 70 per cent of the cultivable land.

As has been indicated earlier, the social structure in India consists of powerful status groups based on religions, castes and language. Although a class system has also begun to emerge in India, it still remains tenuous. The slow process of industrialization and urbanization had led to a highly uneven pattern of class-growth. Status group continues to cut across class lines. As a result, the development of class identities and political mobilization based upon class appeals has been securely inhibited. India's urban based class structure is small compared to the rural society. The 15 million industrial workers in the organized sector of the economy make up only 10 per cent of the total work force of 150 million. Of these, only 3 per cent, or 5 million work in large modern factories. The industrial work force moreover is not only small, but its portion of the total labour force has also remained remarkably stable over the past several decades.

In comparison to this the size of the urban population represents a consumer market larger than the entire European Union. These changes in the rural/urban population and the merging class structure have meant the evolution of new administrative policies, strategies and institutions. In the past forty years, there has been a proliferation of a number of administrative institutions, authorities and agencies both at the center as well as states to cater to the strategies of integrated rural development, and the needs of growing urban metropolises, incredibly crowded, lacking in adequate housing, transportation, water and electricity sewage and sanitation facilities. The administrative strategies evolved have ranged from technological and scientific innovations in the field of agriculture production to the establishment of institutions of democratic decentralization and a host of specified agencies for regulating industrial development, large, medium and small scale and a host of institutions for providing a number of services for good urban life have come into operation. Because of a growing concern for environmental degradation a number of regulatory agencies have come into being to protect the environment from further degradation, although with little success. All these developments have further meant a keen political competitions among various segmented social groups and cultural communities based on language, religion, region and caste, creating additional pressures on the administrative systems. The existence of a number of multifarious agencies with conflicting and overlapping jurisdiction have not only highlighted the problems of unified direction, control and coordination, but have also raised afresh the basic issue of centralization and the relative autonomy of various units of administration.

In the Era of Liberalization

The Government of India has adopted policies of globalization, liberalization and market economy in the wake of the serious economic crisis owing to a steady decline in exports, negative growth rates in industry and agriculture, and 0.3 per cent decline in the domestic production of crude oil. Among the long-term domestic factors contributing to high cost and low productivity were: *(a)* the inadequate returns and continuing losses from the massive investments in the public sector undertaking, and *(b)* economic populism resulting in increasing state subsidies, especially in fertilizers and writing off loans to farmers and hidden payments incurred through lower tariff rates of state undertakings in power and transport sectors.

India's adoption of a programme of globalization, market economy and competitiveness came after more than six months of negotiations with the World Bank starting in January 1991. The package of reform measures announced by the newly installed Narasimha Rao Government in July 1991 consisted of two separate economic policies: *(a)* a macro-economic stabilization programme (IMF inspired) essentially focus on reducing the twin deficits on the balance of payment and on the state budget, and *(b)* a comprehensive programme for structural change of the economy (World Bank inspired) in the fields of trade, industry, foreign investments, public sector and the financial sector among others.

'Globalization', 'competitiveness' and liberalization' come to India as a booster, and through the backdoor of "economic reforms". The sanctity of economic reforms had been derived from it. It was argued that progress is taking place through globalization, and economic reforms are the only means to join in this process. Hence economic reforms are the only alternative for human security and India's future. Globalization as a phenomenon involves two different entites *(a)* finance capital through multinational corporations; and *(b)* new technologies such as computers and telecommunications. It was argued that the growth and internationalization of finance capital is good and desirable for projects because it promotes growth of technology. Globalization provides a useful means to develop technology necessary for the production of goods and services that improve our well-being.

The post-1991 economic reforms were initially launched under compelling balance of payments crisis. At the same time it was felt that by adopted market-oriented and globally competitive restructuring policies somewhat similar to those of Southeast Asian countries, the Indian economy could grow much faster and become more self-reliant in managing its balance of payments and could at the same time speedily accelerate growth and reduce the level of poverty, thus contributing to human security including freedom from hunger, disease, ignorance, unemployment and homelessness.

The Pre-Reform (1991) Scenario

The structural adjustment policy and economic reforms were introduced in the Indian polity at a time when the domestic inflation raged at an annual rate of 17 per cent. The growth rate of gross domestic product (GDP) in 1991-92 stood at 0.6 per cent. The industrial sector also showed the same growth rate, while the index number of agricultural production had declined from 148.4 in 1990-91 to 145.5 in 1991-92 with foodgrains production declining from 176.4 million tonnes in the previous year to 168.4 million tonnes. In the view of the fast deteriorating economic situation the fight of capital had started from the country. This resulted in a severe balance of payment (BOP) crisis, the foreign exchange reserve touching the bottom line of $ 1 billion from 4.4 months of inputs to 1.1 months in 1990-91. To attain that growth and to reduce poverty on a sustainable basis, a series of measures have since been undertaken to bring back the macro-economic balance of the economic and to initiate the necessary structure adjustment programme for improving efficiency in resource use. In this perspective, the emphasis in policy objectives has shifted to higher 'growth', with the expectation that higher growth will automatically percolate as benefits to the poor.

Reform Package

The New Industrial Policy of 24 July, 1991 spelled out the process of liberalization. It stated that foreign investment and technology collaboration was welcomed to obtain higher technology to increase export and to expand the production base. The number of industries reserved for the public sector was reduced to only eight, and compulsory industrial licensing was restricted for only eighteen industries. The policy indicated the need for more dynamic relationship between domestic and foreign industry than before in terms of technology and investment. The direct approval of investment upto 51 per cent of foreign equity in high priority industries was made without any bottleneck. Liberalized Exchange Rate Management System was evolved to help in the free working in the foreign exchange market and secure convertibility of the rupee. Coupled with changes in industrial licensing, the financial and banking sectors were also revamped. The directional paper of the Planning Commission (1991) had clearly indicated that the public sector should make investments of an infrastructural nature in areas were private participation is not likely to come quickly, but it should withdraw from areas were no public purpose is served by its presence. The paper stated that in large part of public sector operations, where commodities or services are produced and distributed, unless it is necessarily for protecting the poorest in society, the main operating principle should be that of the market economy.

The Role of the State

In the context of the new economic policy in operation since mid-1991, a controversial question that has often been raised is about the role of the state. State is not only required to achieve a balance between the functions of security, equity, ecology, development and safety, but also to provide an equilibrium between stability and growth. It is wrong to assume that under liberalization, the state folds up. The rolling back of the state on the economic issues necessitates a re-defining of its new role and a re-examination of its structures and process it may no longer remains to be the owner of strategic industries, but it is still a regulator – a pro-consumer regulator that oversees and prevents the abuse of the market and to provide the legal, physical and human infrastructure. It has to concentrate on 'Development dynamics' that would benefit primarily the poor and the disadvantaged.

The Protect the Living Standard of Poor

In order to protect the living standards of the poor during the transition period and provide for human society, the complimentary social measure reflecting india's commitment to good governance were also conceived to ensure equitable distribution of both the gains and costs of economic reforms. Since over half of India's population continued to live below the poverty line. A number of direct attacks on poverty were launched during 1980's. Prominent among these were special programme for backward areas, such as subsidized food supplies though a Public Distribution System (PDS), concessional loan schemes for marginal farmers and agricultural labourers, employment-oriented programmes sponsoring different employment schemes like Jawahar Rozgar Yojana (JRY), Nehru Rozgar Yojana (NRY), that are geared mainly towards urban housing improvement. After the introduction of the policy of globalization, market economy and liberalization, and despite the fiscal austerity, the government committed itself to increased outlay for clearly targeted social sector expenditure and rural development during the overall plan period 1992-97. In particular, employment creation and human capital development in rural India through (both Poverty Alleviation Programme [PAP] and Social Services, such as primary health care, elementary education and rural water supply-cum sanitation) were to be expanded and broadened. However constraints on budgetary resources forced the government to postpone the provision of extra-funds for those programmes, and on the contrary to curtail them along with all other public expenditures. However, in February 1992, a National Renewal Fund (NRF), meant to provide assistance to workers who would become redundant as a result of the adjustment programme was created. Together with the rural development and social sector programmes, NRF was intended to constitute a comprehensive and permanent social safety net, providing adequate shelter for those who would be temporarily affected by India's SAP.

Employment Generation for Poverty Alleviation

During the last one and a half decade, poverty alleviation and employment generation programmes which have been in operation of several years have been redesigned for generation of self-employment and wage employment of rural areas and restructured to improve their efficacy and impact on the poor. An outlay of Rs. 9650 crore has been provided in 1999-00 (BE) as against 9345 crore in 1998-99 (BE). The former Integrated Rural development Programme (IRDP) and allied programmes such as training of rural youth for self-employment, Development of Women and Children in Rural Areas (DWCRA) and Million Wells Scheme (MWS) have been restructured into a single self-employment programme called the Swarnajayanthi Gram Swarozgar Yojana (SSGY) from April 1999. Simultaneously, Jawahar Rozgar Yojana (JRY) has been restructured and streamlined with effect from April 1999 and has been renamed as Jawahar Gram Samridhi Yojana (JGSY). The other ongoing programmes include, National Social Assistance Programme (NSAP), Urban Employment and Anti-Poverty Programme (UEPP). The Swarna Jayanti Shahari Rozgar Yojana (SJSRY) has subsumed the earlier three urban poverty programmes viz. Nehru Rozgar Yojana (NRY), Urban Basic Service for the Poor (UBSP) and Prime Minister's Integrated Urban Poverty Alleviation Programme (PMIUPEP) and has become operative from December 1997.

Conclusion

The forgoing analysis provides a summary of the various measures taken by the government in the field of rural development. Despite the serious commitment on the part of the government, the benefits of the programmes do not seem to reach the indented targets and they fail to serve fully the purpose for which they were launched. It has been observed that, more often than not, the rural development programmes are implemented without testing their local suitability. Theoretical perfection of a scheme is regarded as the criterion for the soundness of a programme, which should not be the case. Factors such as psychological receptivity, local conditions and constraints and lifestyle are often ignored while designing the rural development programmes.

Most of the rural development programmes though indented for the poorest of the poor, have not fully helped in alleviating their problems. There is a lacuna in the identification of the really poor, with the result that the rich farmers have benefited much more from these programmes. The programmes have, no doubt, generated a ray of hope for the underprivileged sections of society, byt they have, as yet, not brought about a perceptible rise in the income of these sections. Further, some other programmes have succeeded only partially because of the low motivation level among the villages. The basic problem of being unable to arouse popular participation has plagued most of these programmes. Little wonder, most of the programmes did not affect the rural poor substantially. It was found that the village level workers, who ought to have worked as the rural animators, did not truly accomplish their role satisfactory. An impression exists that a VLW is of greater help to the rural elite than to the rural poor. A look at the rural development programmes will also show that some of them have been launched by various political leaders with only an inadequate understanding of the complexity of the problems faced by the rural poor. It appears that, sometimes, they were simply forcing the programmes down the villagers' throats. Programmes with catchy slogans have also been launched in a haphazard manner just before elections and, hence, have been implemented in a half-hearted way.

A number of programmes, such as the TRYSEM, JRY, DWCRA, etc., are employment-oriented. Yet, they hold little or no interest for the rural youth who perhaps feel that there is little future for traditional cottage industry. These programmes offer only manual jobs, where as the youth today want opportunities that are gainful and yet decent. Some programmes also suffer because of lack of adequate trainers. The involvement of the rural poor in the process of rural development is low, particularly in the planning and implementation of such programmes. On the other hand, top-level planners and administrators, generally, have not held a 'correct' perspective of the values of traditional Indian society and, very often, they offer solution which do not have much bearing on the holistic development process in rural areas. For instance, a beneficiary may be supplied with a buffalo, but due to the poor water resources in the village or absence of a veterinary doctor, the animal may die. Or else, the villager may be forced to sell it. Involvement of beneficiaries can help in making programmes more realistic.

There are several cases of default on the part of the beneficiaries also. There have been cases when the beneficiaries, financed by a bank for buying an oil engine, sold the engine off without the permission of the bank. The concerned banks do not have adequate staff to monitor and provide after-case service to the beneficiaries. Hence, the process of recovery by banks, including taking legal action against the defaulter, must be made for effective.

A number of voluntary agencies are also involved in rural development. They are mostly dependent for their funds on the government. Those procedures are often slow and time-consuming, or on foreign donor agencies, whose grants may not be available on a regular basis. There is also lack of communication between the government and these agencies. As a result, the government funds may lapse because the agencies sometimes have no knowledge of these funds and when to avail themselves of them.

Financial institutions, chiefly the banks and cooperatives have a very crucial role to play in the success of the rural development programmes. It has been found in many cases that the loan sanctioned by the bank was inadequate and not timely, resulting in the diversion of funds for some other non-productive purposes. It was also found that some cooperative societies were charging the farmer more than the authorized interest rate. The banks also do not actively participate in the identification of the beneficiaries. They do not carry out pre-sanction inspection of the village before financing an activity. For instance, it has been found that, sometimes, an electric motor pumpset was financed without consideration of availability of electric power.

Regarding the involvement of the rural poor, all experiments in rural development including most of the present-day rural development schemes, emanate at the top. It is necessary that emphasis is laid on planning from the bottom and the exclusive reliance placed on the pyramidal structure approach has to be given up. Because of this approach to planning, the programmes also tend to have very high administrative costs. New technology, such as high yielding seeds, tractors, oil engines, etc., has no doubt been introduced in the agricultural and irrigation sectors, but it has helped the already rich farmers rather than the small and marginal farmers and agricultural labourers who have very little land to begin with. Had the measures of agricultural growth been preceded by land reforms, this problem could have been tackled more rationally.

And, lastly, the organizational dimension needs a reappraisal. With a number of models of rural development administration experimented with and applied for over the last decades and more, it is time that the respective efficacy of each was intensely examined. Since the last one and a half decade, our general understanding of government and governance has been changing at a very fast pace. The forces of globalization, liberalization and the revolution in information technology have shattered many a myth hitherto held sacrosanct about the government and more specifically concerning its primary institution of governance the public administration. No longer can governments afford to support, rigid, bureaucratic, reactive, rules driven administrative organizations. Rather, today's administrative system must be flexible, consultative, result-oriented and proactive-encouraging and supporting creativity and innovation from the bottom to the top in order to govern and provide services to the citizens at large. There has been a considerable rethinking the way the governments now conduct their business, and they are looking more and more towards innovative solution to respond to an increasing number of complex new environmental and global problems and pressure, which are further accentuated in a developing, multi-linguistic, and a multi-cultural country like ours having diversity of social and religious systems.

REFERENCES

1. Robert Chambers, Rural Development: Putting the Last First, Longmans, London, 1983.
2. Iqbal Narain, Panchayati Raj Administration in India, Laxmi Narain, Agra, 1973.
3. C.M. Vijay, Rural Development Administration in India, Pratiksha, Jaipur, 1989.
4. Vasant Desai, Fundamentals of Rural Development: A Systems Approach, Himalaya, Bombay, 1991.
5. Hasnet A. Hye Integrated Approach to Rural Development, Sterling, New Delhi, 1986.
6. Sharma S.K. and Malhotra S.L., Integrated Rural Development, Abhinav, New Delhi, 1977.
7. Jaiswal N.K. and Kolte N.V., Development of Drought Prone Area Programmes, N.I.R.D, Hyderabad, 1981.
8. Rakesh Hooja, Administrative Intervention in Rural Development, Rawat, Jaipur, 1987.
9. Manmohan Singh, Rural Development Administration and Anti-Poverty Programme, Deep and Deep, New Delhi, 1988.
10. Maheswari S.R., Rural Development in India, Sage, New Delhi, 1985.
11. Jain R.B., Public Administration in India, Deep and Deep, New Delhi, 2002.
12. Haragopal G and Sudharshanan. G, Liberalization Policy: Implication for Hister Education, IJPA, July-Sept., 1996.
13. Ramesh K. Arora and Rajini Goyal, Indian Public Administration, Viswa Prakasham, Lucknow, 1996.
14. Vaidya B.V., Some Aspects of Rural Development, Kurukshetra, April 2002.
15. Yogesh Upadhyay and S.K. Singh, Rural Development—Gandian View, Kurukshetra, May 1999.
16. D. Sunder Raj, Peoples Participation in Rural Development, Kurukshetra, February 2000.
17. Mishra S.N., Decentralized Planning for Rural Development, Kurukshetra, February 2000.
18. L.K. Tyagi and Rajesh Kumar, Rural Development in the New Millennium, Kurukshetra, February 2000.
19. S.K. Varma, Rural Development Through Co-operatives, Kurukshetra, May 1999.
20. M.R. Biju, Gandhiji and Panchayati Raj, Indian Communicator, 5 October, 1995.
21. M.R. Biju, Gandhiji and Panchayati Raj II, Indian Communicator, 6 October, 1996.
22. Government of India, India: 2005, A Reference Annual, Publications Division, New Delhi, 2006.

5

Role of Panchayat Towards Sustainable Rural Development

Dr. Reepunjay Singh and Sonia Deoval

Concept and Historical Background of Panchayati Raj

Panchayati Raj implies the creation of local government institutions at the village, block and district levels. These bodies play a vital role in rural administration when more and more governments are carrying the banner of welfare state. The units of local self-government in rural areas are village panchayat, panchayat samiti's and zilla parishads. The village panchayats have been linked to the panchayat samiti at the block level and to the zilla parishad at the district level.

"Community development is a movement designed to promote better living for the whole community with the active participation and on the initiative of the community."

Community development denotes the processes by which the efforts of the people themselves are united with those of the governmental authorities to improve the economics, social and cultural conditions of the communities. It is a balanced programme for stimulating the local potential for growth in every direction. Community Development by promoting a measure of autonomy at the lowest level makes it feasible and practicable to provide the people a chance of thinking over their difficulties.

The National Extension Service Programme was formulated and put into operation on 2 October, 1953. It is a human movement that seeks to "instill in the people a will for a better life, create in them a passionate desire for improving their standard of living through their own efforts and in full cooperation with the neighbours.

The starting point of Local Self-Government at district and taluka level began by establishing district and taluka local fund committees in 1869. The next important landmark in the development of local self-government, was Lord Ripon's resolution on local self-government adopted by the British government in 1882.

The Constitution of India has guaranteed certain fundamental rights to the citizens of India and enunciated certain Directive Principles of State Policy, that the state shall strive to promote the welfare of the people by securing and protecting social order in which justice—social, economic and political—shall inform all the institutions of the national life.

The First Five Year Plan emphasized that the administration of the country has to provide for establishment and development at the village level and appropriate agencies which derive their authority from the people.

The Second Five Year Plan recommended that village panchayats should be organically linked with popular organizations at a higher level.

Implications of Panchayati Raj

Determinants and Structure of Panchayati Raj, District Boards, Village Panchayats, An Administrative Tool, An Agency of Local Self-Government, The Public Image of Panchayati Raj, The Operational Image of Panchayati Raj, Impact of Panchayati Raj on Socio-Economic Developments, Elections and Factions, Social Mobility Under the New Set-up, Rural Administration for Rural Development, Economic Development and Democratic Decentralization.

With the advent of freedom and the acceptance of the concept of welfare state, new challenges were posed with apparently conflicting aims. Economic growth and social justice within the framework of parliamentary democracy and secularism raised new issues, apart from giving new dimensions to the old problems. The governmental machinery was required to effect adjustments far beyond its inherent capacity. To face the needs of development, it was felt necessary that people's participation should be secured in carrying out various programmes.

Demand for An Egalitarian Society

A demand of an egalitarian society in which the 'elite', not only traditional but the newly emergent too, wish to participate. There is a feeling that the developments that have taken place so far—both on the socio-economic front as well as the political—have not kept pace with time. In this context, democratic decentralization is regarded by some as an important milestone in the progress of democracy in our country. There is another group which feels that Panchayati Raj has introduced a new dimension in the body politic which has helped the traditional leaders and vested interests in creating and promoting factionalism.

Politicization of Rural Life

The basic concept behind establishing Panchayati Raj was to create rural, local government agencies responsible for discharging certain select functions pertaining to development. It is not merely a state agency but a self-propelling institution which could mobilize its own resources, both human and material, so that development could be energized. Apart from the scope it give to people at various levels, for effective participation the realization of their local goals. This also leads to a certain amount of social responsibility.

Statutory Bodies at the Local Level

Gram Sabha

The constitution of gram sabhas is based on the assumption that the village is and could be a self-sufficient unity consisting of a homogenous community. It is essential to activise the gram sabha, which can move the people and bring them together, these could be a concrete programme based on their real needs, the acceptance and image of the local leader or a crisis facing them.

Gram Panchayat

The panchayat should be located at potential growth centres, covering a group of villages which could serve awards and act as its hinterland. The functions of the gram panchayat should essentially be the maintenance of institution established by higher tiers and to serve as a feedback to the levels above in the process of planning.

Panchayat Samiti

The Panchayat Samiti could consist of representatives of various gram panchayats by indirect elections so that they could be responsible and accountable to the panchayats and to the village people. The samiti should be entrusted with the responsibility of mobilization of local resources and implementation of various schemes, depending upon the capability in terms of staff and resources that are available.

Zilla Parishad

The Zilla Parishads should have some regulatory and advisory functions enjoined on them by stature and they should be in a position to match schemes with resources and be responsible for their enforcement. The Zilla Parishad will have a crucial role to play in galvanizing the lower tiers into activity and in sustained the tempo of development.

The Committee System

An important recommendation relating to the structural and functional designs of Panchayati Raj Institutions in general, and the Zilla Parishad in particular is the introduction of the committee system. It is envisaged that the Zilla Parishad will function through a number of committee like an agriculture, education, small industries, finance, public works and social justice. The committees are to be constituted on the basis of proportional representation with a view to have all shades of opinion represented on them.

The Collector's Role in the District

The District Collector will continue to play an important role in the district setup notwithstanding the transfer of all developmental functions to the Zilla Parishad. It has been recommended that the regulatory functions will remain with the Collector, as, far some time to come, he will continue to exercise the regulatory revenue and other functions assigned to him by the State Government.

Relation with the Cooperatives

The relationship between the Panchayati Raj Institutions and the cooperatives will broadly be of five types:

(i) Functions which could more appropriately and effectively be discharged by cooperative institutions.

(ii) Functions requiring concurrent and conjoint action of Panchayati Raj and cooperative institutions.

(iii) Cooperative functioning agents and Panchayati Raj Institutions.

(iv) Functions in respect of which cooperatives require facilities from the Panchayati Raj Institutions.

(v) Where cooperative participate in functions which are essentially the responsibility of Panchayati Raj Institutions.

Role of Nyaya Panchayats

Nyaya Panchayats try petty cases arising out of civil and criminal law and have no representational or development role to play as far as the Panchayati Raj Institutions are concerned.

Training of Panchayati Raj Non-Officials

The Panchayati Raj non-officials being elected representatives tend to regard all training as formal and textbookish while the state governments are reluctant to spend large sums upon training people who are not likely to remain in office for a long time to make use of the training imparted to them. The State Governments should continue to make arrangements for training a large number of Panchayati Raj non-officials overcoming their propensity to put off summons from the Panchayati Raj training colleges on one ground or the other.

Sustainable Development

The concept of Sustainable Development emerged as an important theme in 1987. The Brundtland Commission on Environment and Development in its report. Our Common Future called for application of sustainability as a criterion for all development initiatives. "In order for development to be sustainable, it must meet the needs of the present without compromising the ability of future generation to meet their own needs," said the Commission.

Goals of Sustainability

Sustainability Development has a fixed set of goals. These are:

(i) Basic needs of all human beings i.e. food, clothing, shelter, education, health and security.

(ii) Development processes should be so articulated that ecological balance and environmental purity is least disturbed if at all.

(iii) All nations and people must join hands to support each other and work with each other to create a world in which the above two goals are optimized.

Environmental Sustainability

1. *Man-Nature Relationship:* Environmental Sustainability aims at ensuring the protection, conservation and better management of earth's natural resources. It aims at such a pattern of use, that resources, are neither exhausted nor polluted nor destroyed.
2. *Ecosystem Integrated:* All natural ecosystems are characterized by four qualities. These are complexity, stability, diversity

and resilience. If any of these characteristics are weakened, the system collapses.

3. *Biodiversity:* It has to be seen from three perspectives – genetic diversity, species diversity, ecosystem diversity.
   Genetic Diversity : Sum of chromosomal information carried by genes of individual plants and animals.
   Species Diversity: Each of the plant and animal species is interdependent and contains gene pool of great importance.
   Ecosystem Diversity: Natural as well as man-made ecosystems should be planned.
4. *Man-Land Ratio :* "The quality of human life is inseparable from the quality of the environment. Both are inseparable from the questions of human members and concentrations", says UNEPA (1990).
5. *Environmental Planning:* Its aim is four-fold:
   - Environmental protection.
   - Rehabilitation and restoration of degraded ecosystems.
   - Augmentation of the carrying capacity of both natural and human managed ecosystems.
   - Creation, expansion and development of new ecosystem, both minor and major.

Integrating Ecosystems Approach into Rural Development

The Eco Development Concept

Eco development is a development process which stresses, specific solutions for a particular problem in each eco region, taking into account, ecological and cultural contexts as well as present and long-term needs.

(a) *Environmental Regeneration:* It includes reclaiming degraded land and making it productive through a mix of measures, ensuring a perennial supply of potable water, water for cattle and for irrigation.

(b) *Forest Protection and Enhancement:* It includes planting trees in degraded areas wastelands, growing fuel wood and fodder vegetation in community lands and involving the community in planning and management tasks.

(c) *Sustainable Livelihood Security:* Livelihood is maintaining adequate stocks and flow of food and cash to meet basic needs. Security refers to secure ownership of, or access to resources and assets to offset risk ease shocks and meet contingencies. Sustainability refers to the maintenance of resources productivity on a long-term basis.

(d) *Equity:* It indicates the degree to which the poor benefit from development in absolute terms.

Eco-development: Planning Steps at Village Level.

Environmental planning process would consist of three major steps:

1. Analytical Process.
2. Plan Preparation Process.
3. Implementation and Planning Process.

The various steps, methods, outputs and results are indicated below:

Steps	*Method*	*Output*	*End result*
Setting up the baseline of parameters	Survey of state of environment critical information	A quantified statement of the available natural resources in the area	Knowledge of potentials
Analysis of current use/ consumption	Quantitative and qualitative methods for assessment of the rate of utilization of the resources	Identification of stresses	Identification of broad strategy
Plan preparation	Prioritization assessment of thresholds to development	Identification of problems (how to)	Objectives (programme abstract)
Implementation and plan modification process	Functional linkage matrix, identification of logs, gaps and mismatches	Activity schedule	Impact measurement and plan modification
Monitoring	Identification of critical environ-mental indicators (in relation to data collected at 1 above)	Observation of the trends of degradation	Replanning

The data requirement for a village farm ecosystem development plan would pertain to:

- Land resource inventory, Nature and extent of land degradation, Land classification and optimal land use, Biological potential of the land, Physical, chemical, microbiological and erodability characteristics of soil, water quality and availability, Impact of irrigation and crop intensification on the water resources of an area, Rate of exhaustion of aquifer, quality of ground water, increase in salinity etc., Cropping practices (data, density and manner of sowing), Genetic erosion of Flora and Fauna, Biomass (adequacy, availability and potentials).

The areas that need management attention to promote agricultural production on an economically and ecologically sustainable basis at a village level area:

- Land and water management, Crop management, Energy management, Post harvest management, Farming systems management, Technology options, Delivery systems, Participation.

Resource Evaluation for Sustainable Rural Development

Historical Background of Indian Rural Sustainability

In rural areas, the pressure of population increased in relation to growth population. Moreover, due to lack of enough employment and farming opportunities, selective migration of young male workers to large cities takes place. As a result, many villages in India, having 70 per cent of total population, cannot sustain themselves today with food, employment and basic amenities. However, the Post-Independence period has experienced a tremendous growth in food production in India with green revolution. In spite of that, nearly 50 per cent of population in India is under the poverty line with severe economic stress in the midst of plenty.

Objectives

Need for Reviving Sustainable Rural Development: It is essentail to evaluate resources in each region to find out whether:

(*a*) The major landuse pattern is matching with carrying capacity of land.

(*b*) Whether present land utilization of each landuse zone is matching with its potential level of output in relation to its ecosystem.

(*c*) Whether the process of land utilization has improved or degraded physical resources.

(*d*) Whether there has been distinct improvement in backward regions in terms of health, education and employment of people.

(*e*) Micro-level planning has to be evolved, based on local ecosystem, on one hand and socio-eco background of the people, on the other, with appropriate, implementable technology, organized by the people themselves in each village.

Methodological Framework

(*a*) There is a need of a detailed survey of physical human resources at a village level within an ecological region. Geographic Information System (GIS), is used for spatial and temporal analysis for the purpose of planning.

(*b*) Broad classification of land resources, mainly based on physical variables like relief, slope, climate variables, soil fertility, texture, erosion, vegetative cover, quality and quantity of surface and underground water.

(*c*) An evaluation of land resources of regions can be done by matching the current utilization of land with that of the land capability as given by land classification.

(*d*) Present output per unit area and farm income per person should be compared with those of potential figures.

Micro-Level Planning

Micro-level planning has various facets which need to be coordinated and implemented:

(*a*) Positive promotion of environmental change.

(*b*) Coordination of different government and non-government agencies.

(*c*) Participation of villagers in all programmes.

(*d*) Management of physical and human resources.

The basic physical resources like land, water and vegetation can be easily maintained and protected individually as well as through community approach. Water harvesting and conservation of soil can be done with the help of water collecting wells, check dams, plantation of trees, drip-irrigation and appropriate use of land. Use of non-conventional energy like bio-gas, wind and solar energy can certainly raise the standard of living in villages without creating any problem to environmental resources. In this regard, development of human resources is extremely essential to train the local people so that they will be able to harness the local existing resources and will be able to find out alternative ways of using resources. Management of resources should include not only environmental conservation but also production of items with proper design and quality so as to capture market with proper price. Marketing of products requires a combined effort of all farmers in the form of a cooperative system. Self-help and individual training along with participation of all communities can bring prosperity to rural people.

Approach and Recommendations

The institutional, structural and functional specifics of Panchayati Raj would vary over time as well as space, we can do no more than indicate the spectrum of possibilities while the various State Government would have to work out the actual details keeping in view their changing requirements. Whatever be the variations, they have to be round the crucial theme of linking institutions of democratic decentralization with motivated sustainable economic development.

When State Government delegate the responsibilities for implementation to lower levels, they can concentrate on refinement of strategies and higher level policy making in the management of challenges of development administration in areas such as rural land structural deficiencies, agricultural modernization, rural industrialization, credit universalisation and planning for fuller utilization of natural resources.

Structure

The institutional design for Panchayati Raj should take into account the functional necessity of propelling the ongoing developmental thrusts, build upon the intricacies at the appropriate levels and transmit the impulse to the people through location specific involvement.

The emerging scenario of the dynamics of development necessitates that the technical expertise of a high order be made available at levels below the state to sustain the momentum of rural development, which in many cases, has been already administratively decentralized at the district level. The inescapable compulsion, is that the district should be the first point of decentralization, under popular supervision below the state level.

Functions

The entrustment of development functions to Panchayati Raj Institutions would remain incomplete unless all the Panchayati Raj Institutions are vested with the authority to take their own decisions and plan according to their own requirements. Planning would, therefore, be an important function to be discharged by the Zilla Parishads.

They would have to play a promotional role in activating community action build up organization and project formulation. They would continue to perform the functions conventionally assigned to them under various statutes. They would have increasing role to play in the sphere of municipal and welfare functions.

The Panchayati Raj Institutions in general and the Mandal Panchayat in particular can play an important role in the sphere of municipal and welfare functions by supplementing the state plan outlays in this regard. Many of these requirements might be so local that even such comprehensive programmes as the Revised Minimum Needs Programme (R.M.N.P.), may not be able to cover them but the Mandal Panchayats are most intimately concerned about such items.

Planning

With the district as the strategic level for economic planning, the Zilla Parishad should be made responsible for planning at the district level. The appreciation of the total resources, the credit availability and the necessary strategy formulation covering several blocks would be feasible at the district level. An elected Zilla Parishad would also provide the much needed corrective to the techno-economic plans. The state government would have to provide continuous assistance in the process of district planning . It would have to ensure that the national objectives relating to weaker sections are pursued by the Panchayati Raj Institutions. They will also have to provide the financial and physical parameters as well as technical expertise to the technical group. It should also ensure equitable allocation of resources and fixation of long-range priorities.

The total credit inflow for agriculture development is expected to rise significantly in the years to come. The Panchayati Raj Institutions should therefore, pay greater attention to the institutional finance rather than concentrating on budgeting sources as in the past. This would be possible only if the Panchayati Raj Institutions pay due attention to ensuring greater responsiveness in project implementation by ascertainable people's participations like the Revised Minimum Needs Programme. The Panchayati Raj Institutions should not only be regarded as a forum for obtaining the views of people's representatives but, in due course, they should become capable of planning for themselves within the resources available to them.

Weaker Sections

Panchayati Raj Institutions as people's institutions can provide the field level support to Finance/Development corporations for SC/ST providing financial and technical assistance for various programmes beamed at SC and ST.

It should be the special responsibility of the State Government to ensure, through purposeful administrative measures (both protective as well as developmental), that the scale-neutrality of the new technology is maintained, credit flow is made accessible to the poorer sections of society for credi-worthy programmes and development of their skills is continuously fostered. A number of physical resources are still available under the control of Panchayats and Panchayat Samities which are not being fully realized for the benefit of the poorer sections of the community. The State Government should undertake necessary eviction proceedings and launch a vigorous drive to restore these to the Panchayati Raj Institutions, it is also necessary that the relevant regulatory functions, should be placed under the Panchayati Raj Institutions as part of their developmental functions.

Administration

Even after the decentralization of district level functions to Panchayati Raj Institutions, the State Government would continue to maintain some district level staff for the execution of its schemes but the extent of dualism of staff would be restricted to State functions which would be determined at the time of decentralizing the powers to the Zilla Parishad.

On account of increase in the volume of development work and their growing complexity, it would be necessary to constantly study the developmental requirements and mould the structures and functions of the state level departments looking after the Panchayati Raj Institutions. There should be a Minister for Panchayati Raj whose main tasks would be as follows:

(*a*) Enactment of Panchayati Raj legislation;

(*b*) Elections to Panchayati Raj Institutions;

(*c*) Training of elected office-bearers and executive officers and administration of all training centres meant for the Panchayati Raj system as a whole;

(*d*) Promotion of Audit of Panchayati Raj Accounts;

(*e*) Review of Panchayati Raj activities for report of the State Legislature; and

(*f*) Promotion of camp training of elected members of Panchayati Raj.

Financial Resources

The pattern of budgeting followed by the Panchayati Raj Institutions, should be simple. The State Government also will have to evolve a budgetary procedure which will indicate the transfers of different types to the Panchayati Raj Institutions. Each State Government may, taking into account the local circumstances, prepare comprehensive guidelines for the use of their officers and Panchayati Raj Institution for preparation as well as for approval of budgets. As important element to be emphasized both in the preparation of the budget as also in its format is the emphasis to be placed on sufficient allocation and earmarking of the funds for the project for the weaker sections.The quantum provided and the appropriate utilization for the target groups would be within the jurisdiction of the social audit.

Approval of budget by a higher authority seems to be a desirable practice, as it provides a linkage and also enables the higher level tiers of Panchayati Raj to know what is happening at lower tiers and also to make suggestions for better utilization of such funds. A sufficiently high ranking finance officer should be placed at the district level as the entire plan and non-plan funds would be under his supervision. The State Government should consider the establishment of a committee of the Legislature to be specifically concerned in the financial and physical performance of Panchayati Raj bodies. Along with the consolidated finance accounts, the State

Government should also lay on the table of the Legislature, an administrative Report on Panchayati Raj Institutions.

Human Resource Development

The human factor is not only a component of growth but also shapes the texture of the society. In many ways, therefore, the human resources is more vital than the financial. Development of human resources should be, therefore, a primary feature of Panchayati Raj Institutions. There should be an evaluation for each of the training programmes so that it will be possible to make necessary modulations from time to time. Importance should be attached to the programmes for adult education to develop the latest civic consciousness in all the people and thus strengthen the faith in the working of the Panchayati Raj Institutions. The Panchayati Raj Institutions should have a major role in organizing such programmes.

As a large segment contributing the successful operation of a democratic system, special attention is paid to the role of women in Panchayati Raj Institutions. Their role should be strengthened in two ways: by allowing them to participate in the election processes more actively and also by giving them opportunities for decision making. There should be a committee of women to operate and look after specific programmes which largely concern women and children. The present and the future success of the democratic process through Panchayati Raj Institutions lies with the rural youth. Young farmers clubs can be formed to activate the interest of the rural youth both in Panchayati Raj Institutions and rural development. The role of voluntary agencies in mobilizing people's support for Panchayati Raj will be crucial. They should be strengthened and encouraged to supplement the efforts of Panchayati Raj Institutions. The motivational and promotional role of the Panchayati Raj Institutions should be clearly spelt to build up and facilitate the work of voluntary agencies and women's organizations. Voluntary agencies with requisite expertise proven standing and well equipped organization can assist the Panchayati Raj Institutions in the planning process. They can be involved in formulation of projects and schemes and to create strong opinion in support of measures aimed at sustainable rural development.

Relationship with Other Institutions

The Panchayati Raj Institutions are expected to take up the overall view of the economic and social well-being of the people, while the cooperatives have to meet the economic requirements. The relationship between the Panchayati Raj Institutions and cooperatives has thus to be coordinated rather than of a subordinate character. The pattern of functional relationship between the Panchayati Raj Institutions and the cooperatives will broadly be:

(i) Functions which could more appropriately and effectively discharged by cooperative institutions;

(ii) Functions requiring concurrent and conjoint action of Panchayati Raj and cooperative institutions;

(iii) Cooperatives functioning as agents of Panchayati Raj Institutions;

(iv) Functions in respect of which cooperatives require facilities from the Panchayati Raj Institutions; and

(v) Where cooperatives participate in functions which are essentially the responsibility of Panchayati Raj Institutions.

Representation form the cooperatives on the Panchayati Raj Institutions will be helpful in providing on institutional dialogue between the Panchayati Raj Institutions and the cooperatives. A reciprocity of representation of Panchayati Raj Institutions on the cooperatives does not appear to be necessary. Panchayati Raj Institutions can assist the center and state sector corporations and boards established particularly for commercial activities with promotional and marketing components. In this context, the role of Panchayati Raj Institutions would consist of creating the local organization and locating the area wise specialities. Zilla Parishad will be responsible for assessing the overall credit requirements and arranging for its inflow by localizing the needs and locating the areas. The lower tiers should follow this up. Mandal Panchayats should assist in the establishment of Regional Rural Banks by providing necessary infrastructure and also help the banks in verification procedures or in the analysis of the viability of loan proposals.

REFERENCES

Archer A.A.: Man's Dependence on the Earth.

Bhatnagar S.: *Rural Local Government in India,* Life and Light Publishers, New Delhi, 1978, p. 27.

Dey S.K.: *Community Development Through Panchayati Raj,* p. 4.

Dubey S.N.: *Organizational Analysis of Panchayati Raj Institutions in India Indian Journal of Public Administration,* Vol. XVIII, No. 2, 1972, p. 254.

Dutt Vijay Ranjan: *Dynamics of Panchayati Raj.*

Fadia B.L.: *Indian Government and Politics.*

Henry Maddick: *Panchayati Raj – A Study of Rural Local Government in India,* (London : Longmans, 1970).

Inamdar N.R.: *Functioning of Village Panchayats, in George Jacob.*

Majumdar A.K.: Singh Bhanwar: *Historical and Conceptual Development of Panchayati Raj.*

Maheshwari S.R.: *Rural Development in India.*

Mathur P.C.: *Performance of Panchayati Raj Institutions in Rajasthan.*

Mehta Balvantray : Some Recent Trends in Panchayati Raj in India, *The Indian Journal of Public Administration,* Vol., VIII, No. 4, 1962, p. 458.

Sharma H.S.; Chattopdhyay Sri Kumar : *Sustainable Development.*

Sharma H.S.; Sharma M.L.; Bhalla L.R.: *Geography of Rajasthan.*

Singh Reepunjaya (Dr.); Devel Sonia: *Role of Panchayati Towards Sustainable Rural Development Case Study Silora Village* (Kishangarh Panchayat Samiti), Dissertation, M.A. Final Geography, M.D.S. University, Ajmer 2004.

Singh S.K.: *Role of Panchayati Raj in India.*

Yojana: 2003, June issue, 1997, November issue.

6

Role of Panchayats in Sustainable Social Development

Dr. G. Palanithurai

Introduction

It is an irony that in India core development issues are not brought to light either in public debate or among political classes. Social development issues are being discussed and deliberated upon only among the academic community and the administrators who draft policy papers and are being intensely researched. As a result neither the political class nor the public evince keen interest in the issues of social development.[1] Hence, on human development, India is lagging behind many of the poor nations in the world. Even after six decades of democratic governance and planned administration we are not sensitive towards sanitation.[2] We do not seriously discuss malnutrition. Nearly half of the women population in India are anemic and of them women from rural areas are mostly affected.[3] There are many serious issues on which the Indian public has to be sensitive. But they are not so. The UNDP has made the political class wake up from its deep slumber and has alerted a segment of our personnel in administration to the importance of social development through its Human Development Reports.[4]

Even though we talk much about development administration, we never bother to discuss development politics as if development administration brings everything needed to the society in the absence of development politics. Despite our plans, programmes and schemes for development through our systematic government efforts by our centralized top down approach we could not state that people are provided with needed facilities and services to lead a decent and dignified human living in Indian society. One can judge that in

India in any village half of the people or more than that are living in sub-human living conditions. They lead such a life without knowing what a decent, dignified honourable human life is, irrespective of their social and economic status.

Our spending has not been reduced on the issues of development. It keeps on increasing many folds through schemes and programmes carried out by a plethora of departments and agencies.[5] Reports are being made of out how much they have spent and what they have done. The output is perfectly explained leaving the outcome unexplored and unexplained.[6] The activities carried out in the rural areas are always not demand based. The supply determines the activities. As a result the demands continue to grow on unchecked.[7]

There is yet another issue which has been forgotten for long in the sphere of development activities, namely, outcome. When a programme is launched, it is not evaluated from the perspective of the outcome. They are all evaluated in terms of their output. A large number of rural development programmes are being carried out and they are not being evaluated from the perspective of the outcome. School buildings are constructed, furniture have been provided, and teachers have been appointed. These are all the facilities but nobody bothers whether these facilities have been used to achieve the results as expected. A number of health schemes such as Anti-Natal Care (ANC) and Post-Natal Care (PNC) have been provided to pregnant women. But nobody bothers whether the number of newborn underweight babies is reduced. There are many schemes for children too but nobody bothers whether the number of malnourished children is reduced. Our spending on schemes is increasing while the problems are also increasing.

After the establishment of the Panchayat Raj System both the Centre and State Governments have fixed targets for social development through the 11th Schedule for Panchayats. How Panchayats have responded to the challenges is the focus of this study. In the absence of sensitivity on the part of politicians at higher level and the people in general on social development issues, how can Panchayat leaders evince keen interest in social development? This study attempts to analyse the role performed by the Panchayat leaders in achieving social development. Further it analyses the processes of achieving such social development.

Generally observations are made about the Panchayat leaders as they are also politicians and they will also have the same traits as politicians. They are also drawn from the same social milieu. The Panchayat is the third tier of governance in the orbit of governance in India. It is not isolated from the general system of governance. Then how can the governing institutions at the grassroots be free from corrupt practices? When the politicians of the state and federal level are not sensitive to social development issues how can one expect the Panchayat leaders at the grassroots to be sensitive to issues of social development? Having got the institutions positioned and elections conducted, leaders are in position with a set of roles and responsibilities to be discharged in the community. How those responsibilities are discharged is the major focus of this study.

Expectations

Decentralization of powers is a global phenomenon which has been effected through Constitutional Amendments in many countries and operationalized according to their own conditions and needs. There are some common expectations that are to be met in the process. These expectations are not uniform in all the countries and societies.[8] Decentralization can address poverty, gender inequality, environmental concerns, improvement of health care, education and access to technology. Decentralization brings decision-making closer to the people and therefore yields programmes and services that better address local needs. Decentralization will alter the mode of activities for development from a supply driven one to a demand driven one. It helps to include the marginalized and excluded segments of the society into the decision-making process. It enables the community to deepen democracy and evolve micro plans from below with the active participation of the people to achieve development and social justice. It helps the voiceless and powerless groups to raise their voice in the public to decide their course of action to achieve their development. It alters the position of the people from that of beneficiaries and petitioners to that of development participants, citizens and stakeholders, with responsibility and commitment. To fulfill the above expectations, local body institutions have been created statutorily by the respective state governments based on the Constitutional Amendment in India. The legal framework has created such a space in the local body system to fulfill the above expectations.

Methodology

To analyse the relationship between the functioning of local bodies and the social development activities in the communities, cases have been drawn from Gram Panchayats of different districts. This study has been conducted through case study method. Cases were drawn from the action research project of The Hunger Project.[9]

List of Panchayats that Developed Micro Plan with the Participation of People Supported by The Hunger Project

Sivagangai District

Sl. No:	*Gram Panchayat*	*Block Panchayat*
1.	Veppangulam	Kallal
2.	Nerpugapatti	Kallal
3.	Kalipuli	Kallal
4.	Velangudi	Tirupathoor
5.	Vaduvanpatti	Singampunari
6.	Sevalpatti	Singampunari
7.	Kozhikudipatti	Singampunari
8.	Urathupatti	S.Pudur
9.	Manaloor	S.Pudur
10.	Keelavayal	S.Pudur

Pudukkottai District

Sl. No.	*Gram Panchayat*	*Block Panchayat*
11.	Parambur	Annavasal
12.	Melapudhuvayal	Gunnandarkoil
13.	Neunjikudi	Ponnamaravathi
14.	Mookkampatti	Pudukkottai
15.	Veerasilai	Thirumayam
16.	Meenaveli	Viralimalai
17.	Merpanaikadu	Aranthangi
18.	Poovalur	Avudaiyarkoil
19.	Pudhukulam	Kandarvakottai
20.	Izhakadividuthi	Karambakudi
21.	Idayathimangalam	Manamelkudi
22.	Melathur	Thiruvarankulam
23.	K. Rayavaram	Arimalam

Dindigul District

Sl. No.	Gram Panchayat	Block Panchayat
24.	Sithargalnatham	Nilakkottai
25.	Kodanginaickenpatti	Nilakkottai
26.	Noothulapuram	Nilakkottai
27.	Karisalpatti	Reddiarchatram
28.	Pannaipatti	Reddiarchatram
29.	Kamatchipuram	Reddiarchatram
30.	Silvarpatti	Reddiarchatram
31.	Athoor	Athoor
32.	N.Panjampatty	Athoor
33.	Thevarappanpatty	Athoor
34.	Kallikkampatty	Athoor
35.	Anaipatty	Dindigul
36.	M.M.Koviloor	Dindigul
37.	Balakrishnapuram	Dindigul
38.	Mullipadi	Dindigul
39.	Thottanoothu	Dindigul

Tuticorin District

Sl. No.	Gram Panchayat	Block Panchayat
40.	Ottanatham	Ottapidaram
41.	Puthiamputhur	Ottapidaram
42.	Kodiyankulam	Ottapidaram
43.	Pattinamaruthur	Ottapidaram
44.	Tharuvaikulam	Ottapidaram
45.	Sriparangusanallur	Srivaikundam
46.	Siruthondanallur	Srivaikundam
47.	Thirupani Chettikulam	Srivaikundam
48.	Parakiramapandi	Srivaikundam
49.	Mukkani	Srivaikundam
50.	Mettilpatti	Puthur
51.	Mathalapuram	Puthur
52.	Kadalkudi	Puthur
53.	Thappathy	Puthur
54.	Iyanrajapatti	Puthur

For this article data have been collected from the respective Panchayats and secondary data from the documents prepared from the other action research projects of the Rajiv Gandhi Chair. With the help of The Hunger Project, New Delhi, fifty-four Gram Panchayats have been selected in four districts to demonstrate the evolution of devolution through preparing a micro plan with the active participation of the people and the support of the government machinery. The focus will be on the efforts of Panchayats on social development issues with the active participation of the community. The fifty-four Panchayats are taken for their exercise based on our previous project outcome. Since we gained rich experience operating a small project in ten villages with the support of the Population Foundation of India, New Delhi, on social development activities,[10] we have extended the project with a different approach of evolving a micro plan for the holistic development of the villages with the participation of the people and the support of the government departments. In the previous pilot project, funded by the Population Foundation of India, by announcing and giving incentives to reach the target on certain issues of social development by the Panchayat the project activities were carried out very effectively. But, in the micro plan preparation, we prepared the entire team of Panchayat representatives and representatives of the community. The leaders were sensitized on the social development issues and made to realize the implications of social development. Through training they have been made to understand the development process. How to transform the process of development activities from supply driven to demand driven mode? Through preparing micro plan based on the need of community, the Gram Panchayat Presidents have been counselled. Further they have been oriented to the methods to be adopted to prepare a plan with the participation of the people. How to collaborate and to make alliance and partnership with the government departments has been explained to them clearly. Thus the Panchayat team has been geared up for the new exercise which is the constitutional mandate and, to help them, we have a few staff members from Gandhigram Rural Institute. Two things are made clear: that the Panchayat and people are the owners of the plan; and that, to carry out the activities planned in the plan document, the Panchayat and the members of various groups should negotiate with the respective departments, which Gandhigram Rural Institute will facilitate. On the above conditions, the people have been geared up for the plan exercise. The following are the steps followed in the preparation of the perspective plan for Gram Panchayat.[11]

A. Environment Building

1. *Meetings with district administration*—Right at the outset, prior to commencing the process of plan creation a meeting with the district administration explaining the objectives of the process and outlining the nature of the support required from the administration is necessary. Through out the process of creation of the plan regular meetings with the administration are critical to ensuring their commitment to the process and their interest. In Pudukottai, the administration provided the physical space and the basic infrastructure in the District Rural Development Agency (DRDA) for a spearheading team to be located in. Regular meetings and interaction and the commitment of the District Administration to the process, as well as to the Panchayats, ensured that existing schemes and projects were dovetailed into the thirteen Panchayats where the plans were being created.
2. *Identification of Gram Panchayats (GPs)*—Inputs from the administration can aid the process of identifying Gram Panchayats. If the exercise were to be undertaken on a pilot basis in select Panchayats, then it might be prudent to ensure that the geographical spread of the Panchayats across the district is limited to reduce the time as well as recurring costs.
3. *Memorandum with GPs*—Once the GPs are identified, a preliminary discussion with representatives of the Panchayat is necessary outlining the objectives of the planning process and clarifying the respective roles of the facilitating agency and the Gram Panchayat. The GP should subsequently pass a resolution committing its willingness to create a Panchayat level plan for the Panchayat.
4. *Orientation*—A day-long orientation for GP members, representatives from SHGs, youth groups, and other opinion makers at the village level should be held within the Panchayat. The orientation should emphasise the importance of planning, the steps to be taken and the importance of the Panchayat owning the process.

5. *Gram Sabha meetings*—At the outset the Gram Sabha should be appraised of the activity. There are seven statutory committees that a Gram Panchayat must establish (see Annexure). If these committees have not been established then they must be set up in consultation with the Gram Sabha. The Appointment Committee does not have any specific relevance to the planning process. However, there is a need to create a Planning Committee to oversee the entire process of creation of the Panchayat Plan. If the number of committees at the Panchayat level is to be kept within manageable limits the Panchayat Council can take on the responsibilities of the Planning Committee with one co-opted non-elected member from each of the six statutory committees. Periodic updates presented to the Gram Sabha will assist in a broad based participation in the process and ensure that there is constant direction.
6. *Capacity building*—A five-day workshop for elected representatives of these Panchayats - inclusive of Council members—can serve as the foundation. The workshop should consist of a vision exercise as well as sessions on planning. Once the Planning Committee of the Panchayat has been created, a three-day workshop on "Planning for social development" will ensure that the focus of planning does not remain limited to infrastructure creation.
7. *Orientation of committee members*—The members of the Committees will require orientation and role clarification to take forward the plan creation process.
8. *Interface between elected representatives and the district administration*—At regular intervals from the inception onwards there should be regular interactions between the elected representatives and the district administration. In the long run, this will develop the capacity of the elected representatives to deal with the administration and the interest and commitment of the administration will add value and lend credence to the plan creation exercise.
9. *Exposure*—Organising brief exposure visits to witness innovations undertaken by other Panchayats in the State will enable the Panchayats to "think out of the box". The fact that they do not have to limit themselves necessarily to only scheme based activities but they can plan their own interventions will be reinforced.

10. *Ward/Hamlet level meetings*—To generate interest amongst all sections, ideally meetings must be held at the ward/ hamlet level about the need for plans, the steps to be taken, committees and the roles.
11. *Village level officials*—An opportunity for a meeting between members of the statutory committees, the Gram Panchayat and village level officials should be created. This will ensure the inputs of village level officials and can facilitate their participation in the plan creation process.

B. *Information Collection*

12. *Identification of information needs*—In consultation with the members of the statutory committees and the Gram Panchayat, an identification of the information that needs to be collected to develop the plan must be undertaken. The sources of the information and the processes by which the information can be verified must be explored. Each committee must take on the responsibility to collect the information pertaining to its area of work.
13. *Finalization of tool to collect the information*—The tool to collect the information must be finalized.
14. *Identification and orientation of investigators*—The committees might need to enroll additional village level volunteers to assist in the collection of information. An orientation for those undertaking the responsibility to collect the information must be organized to facilitate information collection.
15. *Review of information and collation*—Once the information has been received, it should be reviewed with the committee members and investigators if any, to identify gaps and to establish the veracity of the information being collected. Once this step is completed, the information should be compiled and consolidated.
16. *Presentation of information*—The information that is collected should be presented to the Gram Panchayat and the Gram Sabha. An analysis must accompany the presentation of the information. Feedback, comments at both forums are important and will need to be incorporated into the information.

C. Community Based Planning

17. *Hamlet level development conferences*—Comprehensive hamlet level development conferences should be held. At the hamlet level a series of activities need to be undertaken with an emphasis on enhancing the participation of families. *(a)* Identification of the most vulnerable—Poor families, women headed families, landless families, homeless families, families headed by a person with disability and no other/inadequate wage earners, families headed by the aged and infirm. An attempt must be made to explore the extent of benefits these families receive from existing social security and employment schemes to try and verify the accuracy of the targeting. This information is also useful inasmuch as the Panchayat can use it to monitor the extent of benefits that it is able to make available to the most vulnerable on a regular basis. *(b)* Identification and prioritization of needs—The needs emerging from each hamlet and the priorities should be identified. *(c)* Solutions, possible costs and a realistic re-prioritisation—For each of the needs that have been identified, potential solutions and the estimated costs should be identified. Once this information is available, it is possible that the hamlet may choose to re-prioritise its needs. *(d)* Information sharing and review—The Information collected and a brief analysis of it should be shared with the members present at the hamlet meeting since it could aid discussions and assist in identifying needs and priorities.

In the past, Venn diagrams, ranking of priorities, resource maps, and wealth ranking have been used as tools. Even in the absence of any PRA technique being utilized, a sensitive and focused facilitator with an inquisitive mind can in a group situation cull out a wide variety of responses and achieve all of the above. The role of the facilitator for the group meetings is absolutely critical.

D. Approval, Ratification and Pre-Implementation

18. *Consolidation of Hamlet plans*—The inputs emerging from the hamlet level meetings need to be consolidated by the Committees.
19. *Presentation and approval of Gram Sabha*—The consolidated plans must be presented to a special Gram Sabha for inputs,

comments, feedback and approval. The plan should be finalized only after approval of a special Gram Sabha. The costs for each component and the possibility of internal financing from the community should be definitely discussed. Future operation and maintenance costs of assets and the financial implications must also be raised and planned for.

20. *Panchayat meeting*—The GP should incorporate the suggestions made by the Gram Sabha and then prepare an action plan with the next steps to be taken and allocate responsibilities for each. The plan should ideally be broken up into realistic annual plans to make it more realistic for follow-up and monitoring.
21. *Identification of potential support institutions /departments*—The Gram Panchayat could try and identify potential sources of support both monetary or otherwise for specific components of the plan. These could include sectoral departments, DRDA, MP-LAD, MLA-LAD, local NGO's, Banks etc.
22. *Proposal creation*—Several components might require to be converted into specific proposals that are then presented to either sectoral departments or the DRDA for support. Technical details wherever necessary might need to be added to the proposals prior to their acceptance by departments.

E. *Implementation, Monitoring and Review*

23. The statutory committees and the Gram Sabha must play a key role in the implementation, monitoring and review of the process of transforming the plan into reality. The easiest way to guarantee this is by ensuring the ownership of each of these critical stakeholders in the Plan. In the plan document itself they have indicated what they are going to achieve. They are:
    - Enrolling all the children who have completed five years of age in school.
    - Ensuring that the enrolled children continue their studies without dropping out.
    - Conducting school annual day celebration to enable the students to display their creative potential.
    - Providing basic amenities like drinking water, toilet, playing ground and vegetable garden in the school.

- Creating a sanitation and toilet culture among the students.
- Establishing reading rooms to encourage the desire to learn among the villagers and putting to use the Ayyan Thiruvalluvar Library.
- Providing toilet facility and playthings for children in the anganwadi and trimming their nails to ensure hygiene.
- Enrolling all the children who have completed two and a half years of age in the anganwadi and helping them to learn the habit of attending to their personal cleanliness.
- Ensuring the age-specific weight and the general health of children by providing them with appropriate balanced nutritious meal and ensuring the proper conduct of activities such as providing nutritious flour and noon meal under the integrated child welfare scheme.
- Preventing female infanticide by creating awareness among the villagers.
- Ensuring that all the children receive fully and properly the benefits of the immunization programme.
- Creating an environment free of child labour.
- Adopting measures to prevent child mortality.
- Creating awareness among the people about gender equality.
- Ensuring that all deliveries take place only in hospitals.
- Creating awareness among women about prenatal and postnatal care.
- Helping women to fully receive the benefits of the activities under the postnatal child welfare schemes.
- Helping pregnant women to properly receive benefits such as prenatal care, medical examination, immunization vaccines, nutritious flour and pregnancy assistance money.
- Providing the required minimum basic facilities in the sub-health centre.
- Helping the village health nurse to discharge her welfare functions well.

- Taking steps to ensure optimum utilization of the women's sanitary complexes.
- Ensuring that all the people get safe drinking water.
- Completely eradicating open air defecation.
- Arranging for common public toilets and their proper use.
- Removing waste in order to create a sanitary village.
- Creating awareness among the people about the dangers to the village from non-degradable substances like plastics and polythene and taking steps for their prohibition.
- Augmenting finances by converting public wastes into fertilizer.
- Planting, rearing and protecting saplings in public places to transform the village into a green village.
- Ensuring minimum basic amenities to all the habitations in the village.
- Installing solar lights on streets.
- Ensuring that all eligible families get ration cards.
- Arranging to issue pattas to those who own no house sites.
- Ensuring that essential commodities are properly available under the public distribution system.
- Building houses for houseless people.
- Eradicating untouchability and creating social harmony.
- Ensuring that the Adi Dravidar community gets all the benefits it is eligible for.
- Organizing poor women into self help groups and helping them to achieve social and economic upliftment.
- Making all the arrangements required to enable the self help groups to produce articles and to market them.
- Bringing together the village artisans into a federation, enhancing their manual skills and arranging for employment opportunities for them.
- Creating awareness to ensure that girls are married only after they complete twenty-one years of age.
- Observing the families of weak, destitute, elderly people, poor widows, poverty-stricken artisans and guaranteeing their livelihood.

- Identifying the disabled and reaching to them benefits that ought to reach them.
- Showing the way for male as well as female self help groups to function robustly.
- Motivating and guiding self help groups participating fully in public welfare activities and in Gram Sabha meetings.
- Repairing and maintaining water sources such as ponds, tanks, ooranis and kanmois, collecting rainwater in them and using them properly.
- Creating the right perspective among the people regarding the importance of water, water management and utilization of water.
- Developing natural resources and protecting them from damage and degradation.
- Creating awareness among the people to cultivate medicinal plans in public places in the village and in habitations and to use them.
- Creating awareness among the people to effect changes in agriculture to suit circumstances.
- Reclaiming common property resources from encroachment.
- Regulating common property resources and taking steps to augment the Panchayat income through them.
- Reorienting the Panchayat activities to a people-centred mode and carrying them out with people's participation.
- Transforming the Panchayat into an arena for people's action.
- Transforming the people into social citizens and making them participate in all Panchayat activities.
- Transforming the Gram Sabha into a forum for social upliftment instead of a forum for collecting grievances.
- Involving women and Dalits in a big way in all the activities of the village.
- Synergising the different organizations functioning in the village for development activities.[12]

After indicating the activities, how these activities would be carried out are being explained. They are:

GRAM PANCHAYAT AND SOCIAL DEVELOPMENT

Activity Chart

INDICATORS

Sl. No.	*Activities*	*Responsibility*	*Outcome*	*Verification*
1	2	3	4	5
1.	100% enrolment of eligible children	President, Vice-President, Ward Members, PTA, SHG Members, Youth Clubs, NGO, Retired Officials, Education Committee	Level of literacy increased	School records
2.	Reduction of dropouts	President, Vice-President, Ward Members, PTA, SHG Members, Youth Clubs, NGO, Retired Officials	Increase in educational standard	School records
3.	Ensuring protected drinking water supply to school	President, Vice-President, Ward Members, School Teachers	Improvement of students health, reduction of ill health of students	Physical verification
4.	Providing toilets to school	President, Vice-President, Ward Members, School Teachers	Increase in health of children	Physical verification
5.	Utilizing the toilets by the school students	President, other members of the Panchayat Council Teachers, PTA, Parents	Toilet culture developed	Physical verification
6.	Cutting the nails of the students every Monday in Balwadi and School	Youth Club, SHG, Panchayat Ward Members, School Teachers	Health education, reduction of diseases, improvement of health	Physical verification

Contd....

1	2	3	4	5
7.	Planting of saplings in the school premises	President, teachers, agriculture departments	Environment awareness eco development	Physical verification
8.	Creating a school garden	President, teachers PTA, Youth Clubs, Agriculture Department	Increase in nutrition as the vegetables are given to noon mean centers	Physical verification
9.	Keeping the Balwadi clean and neat	Balwadi teacher, President, Vice-President, Ward Members	Health education, increase in status of health, culture of cleanliness is cultivated	Physical verification
10.	Providing a toilet in the Balwadi	President, Vice-President, Ward Members	Education, increase in health status	Physical verification
11.	Bringing a toilet culture among the kids	Balwadi teacher	Health education, increase in health status	Physical verification
12.	Adding vegetables to the noon meal by getting donations and getting the vegetables from the school garden	President, Vice-President, Balwadi teacher, School teachers	Nutritive food for students	Physical verification
13.	Taking steps to prevent the practice of child labour	President, Vice-President, Ward Members, School teachers, PTA, NGO, SHG, Youth Club	School enrolment, literacy, HRD	Physical verification
14.	Cleaning overhead tanks	OHT operators, under the instruction of Panchayat regularly	Health status, productivity	Verifying the records

Contd....

1	2	3	4	5
15.	Creating awareness among the people about the consequence of alcohol and stop brewing and selling the same in the Panchayat premises	President, Vice-President, Ward Member, Health Committee, SHG, Youth Club, NGO	Economic status of poor, status of women and children, health of individuals and reduction of social problems	Physical verification
16.	Creating awareness among the people about family welfare	PHC Staff, President, Vice-President, Ward Members, Health Committee, SHG, Youth Club	Livelihood security ensured	Verifying the records of small family
17.	Identify the vulnerable families and ensure food security to them and constantly monitor them with the help of government schemes	President, Vice-President, Ward Members, SHGs	Income generation, reduction of poverty, status of women	Physical verification
18.	Building the skill of the women through training	Presidents, Vice-President, Ward Members, Training institution, Social Welfare Department at the District Women Development Corporation	Income generation, reduction of poverty, status of women	Physical verification
19.	Establish link between the skilled persons and banking sector for the establishment of business venture by the women	President, Vice-President, Ward Members, Planning Committee Members, NGO, Banks, SHG	Development of rural economy and increase of status of women	Panchayat profile
20.	Building the skills of the youth through training	President, Vice-President, Ward Members, Training institutions, NYK	Human Resource Development, Economic Development	NYK Report

Contd....

1	2	3	4	5
21.	Establish link between the skilled persons and Banking sector for the establishment of business venture by the youth	President, Vice-President, Ward Member, Planning Committee Members, NGOs, Banks, NYKs	Development of Rural Economy	Panchayat Profile
22.	Ensuring proper functioning of PDS	President, Vice-President, Ward Members and SHG, officials of Civil Supply	Food Security	Verifying the BPL List
23.	Prevent open defecation in the villages by creating awareness and constructing toilets in each and every house	President, Vice-President, Ward Members, SHG, Youth Club, NGO, Project Staff, TRSP, Retired Employees	Improvement in Health, Sanitation Environment	Physical verification
24.	Creating awareness about RCH by printing a card and giving it to every family	President, Vice-President, Ward Members, Health Committee, NGO, Staff of PHC	Improvement in women and children, health, economic status	PHC records
25.	Ensure the delivery of services from sub centre and PHC to the people through the schemes available for prenatal and post natal care	PHC Staff, President, Vice-President, Ward Members, SHG, NGO, Health Committee	Increase in health status and economic status	Verifying the PHC records
26.	Creating awareness about growing medicinal plants and make it a business by involving SHG and youth clubs	President, Vice-President, Ward Members, SHG, Planning Committee, Youth Club, NGO, NABARD Bank Staff	Income generation for improvement of rural economy	Physical verification

Contd....

1	2	3	4	5
27.	Creating awareness among the importance of water management	President, Vice-President, Ward Members, Community leaders, Planning Committee Members, NGO	Rational Utilization of Water	Physical verification
28.	Creating a common burial ground into graveyard in the villages	President, Vice-President, Ward Members, SHG, Youth Club	Social justice	Physical verification
29.	Taking steps to manage the solid waste and earn money from it for Panchayats	President, Vice-President, Ward Members, Planning Committee, NGO, SHG	Environment development, income generation, better agricultural practices	Panchayat records
30.	Organise workshop for pregnant women to disseminate the needed information akin to ANC and PNC	PHC Staff, SHG, President and Vice-President	Increase of health awareness, health status, economic status, Reduction of infant mortality and new born babies are in exact weight	Verifying with PHC records
31.	Conducting medical camps for poor and school children	President, Vice-President, Ward Members, NGOs, SHG, nearby Rotary and Lions Club	Improved health status	Verifying with PHC records
32.	Make the SHG and Youth Clubs to take up Panchayat works instead of employing contractor	President, Vice-President, Ward Members, SHG Youth Club, NGO	Employment opportunity, quality of work, reduction of expenditure, local needs	Panchayat records
33.	Regularly conducting Gram Sabha meetings	President, Vice-President, Ward Members	Peoples participation, Good Governance	Panchayat records

Contd....

1	2	3	4	5
34.	Ensuring 60 per cent attendance in Gram Sabha meeting	President, Vice-President, Ward Members, all eligible members, SHG members, NGOs working in the Panchayats	Transparency, accountability of Panchayats	Panchayat records
35.	Ensuring Women/Dalit participation 50 per cent of attendance	President, Vice-President, Ward Members, SHG, NGO	Social justice, status of weaker section	Panchayat records
36.	Information disseminations 1. Income/Expenditure display 2. Report on schemes implemented display 3. List of schemes proposed to be implemented 4. List of beneficiaries	President and Panchayat Clerk	Transparency, accountability credibility of Panchayat, Better participation	Seeing the Display Board of Panchayat
37.	Participatory decision making 1. Opportunities for discussion to all communities 2. Equal status to all in seating 3. Developing consensus	President, Ward Members, community leaders/retired government officials, school teachers, Planning Committee Members, Dalit Leaders, NGOs and other association members	Achieving communal harmony, evolution of social capital	Verifying the records of Panchayats
38.	Develop a system of communication to give information about Gram Sabha meeting	President, Clerk, Ward Member, SHG, Youth Clubs, NGOs	Transparency, accountability	Physical verification
39.	Provision of water supply to Dalit hamlets	President and the concerned Ward Members, Committee for water supply	Receiving the services continuously	Physical verification

Contd....

1	2	3	4	5
40.	Removal of untouchability by 1. Preventing the two tumbler system 2. Participating in temple festival	President, Ward Members, SHG, Youth Clubs, Community Leaders	Social justice, Communal harmony	Physical verification
41.	Training to Dalit Youths in skill development and availing THADCO schemes	President, Youth Clubs, NGOs, Education Institutions	Economic development, Social justice	Physical verification
42.	Identification of all CPR verifying the status of encroachment details	Panchayat President, Vice-President, Ward Members, Government Officials, Police Department	Environment development Social justice, income generation	Verifying Panchayat records
43.	Removal of encroachments	Panchayat President, Vice-President, Revenue and Police Department	Productive use of resources, equity, income generation for Panchayats	Verifying Panchayat records
44.	Utilizing the common properties and developing the same	Panchayat President, Ward Members, NGO, SHG, Youth groups	Environment development, income generation	Verifying Panchayat records
45.	100 per cent house tax collection	President, Clerk, Vice-President, Ward Members, SHG, Youth Club	Financial status of Panchayat, more government funds	Verifying Panchayat records
46.	Panchayat functioning as a system	President, Clerk, Vice-President, Ward Members	Accountable	Verifying Panchayat records

Contd....

1	2	3	4	5
47.	Records maintenance/transparency	President and Clerk	Good Governance	Verifying Panchayat records
48.	Preparing a perspective plan through village planning forum	President, Ward Members, Planning Committee, School Leaders, NGO, Youth, SHG	Planned development, better use of resources	Verifying Panchayat records
49.	Formation of Statutory Committees	President	Efficiency of Panchayats accountability	Verifying Panchayat records
50.	Old age, Physically and mentally disabled, destitute, orphan and other vulnerable sections	President, Ward Members, SHG, NGO, Government and Planning Committee	Social security, social harmony	Verifying Panchayat records

The above projected activities could be carried out easily if the Panchayat meets some key assumptions. They are:

Key Assumptions

- Harmony prevails in Panchayat.
- Panchayat is perceived as development space.
- Community supports the Panchayats.
- Panchayat leader has got commitment.
- Panchayat leader has vision.
- Panchayat leader has got skill and capacity.
- Panchayat is not leader centric.
- Panchayat is people and system centric.

Once the plan is prepared, it will be presented in the special Gram Sabha meeting and approved by the Gram Sabha. After obtaining the signatures of the Gram Sabha members, the document has to be shown to the District Collector for his approval. The Collector will affix his stamp on the plan document. The document is then published. The plan document is also been sent to various sectoral departments for their pursuance. Responsibilities are fixed for follow-up.

The planning exercise was done in a phased manner. In the first phase it was done in Sivaganga District. It was done in ten Gram Panchayats headed by women leaders, of whom four were Dalits. Knowing fully the problems they faced in society and in the Panchayat, a strong support structure was created through an NGO. The entire exercise was done by the staff of the NGO and PRA was done by another NGO drawn from Kerala. But people participated at all levels. The focus was on social development. But people were interested only in infrastructure. It was very difficult to change their mindset. But the Panchayat leaders were sensitive towards social development issues. To achieve the target in social development incentives were announced to Panchayats. The incentives worked very well.

In the second phase, planning was done in Pudukkottai District in 12 Gram Panchayats. In the next phase instead of an NGO, Gandhigram Rural Institute lent four staff members for a short period to help the Panchayats to prepare the plan and conduct PRA exercises in the villages. Officials were actively involved under the direction of the District Collector. It was not only for social development but for the overall development of the village. Once the planning was over Gandhigram Rural Institute withdrew from the scene.

In the third phase, the responsibility was given to Village Panchayat leaders and the committees to do all the exercises on their own. Initially an intensive training was given to the Presidents and other functionaries in the art of preparation of plans. Simultaneously it was carried out in 15 Panchayats each in Dindigul and Tuticorin. Gandhigram Rural Institute staff supervised the entire exercise. After the completion of the exercise dissemination was done at the district headquarters. Expenditure wise, the plan consumed more in Sivaganga than in Dindigul and Tuticorin. Now it has been demonstrated that people can do without the help of others if the format was designed.

Critical Analysis

In five decades of democratic governance and administering development for the first time people have looked back on their way of living scientifically and they have come to the conclusion that they cannot lead a decent human living in society and further they have understood for the first time what decent human living is. In their whole life, they have taken the responsibility and ownership for their development activities and turned the government officials into facilitators. Their position and status as beneficiaries and petitioners has been changed to citizens and development participants. They have started envisioning for their village. How should be their school? What are the facilities to be provided to the school to make it a good school? How to clean their water bodies? How to clean their village? How to make their village totally sanitized? How to achieve an anemia free village? How to achieve cent per cent exact weight new born babies? How to achieve cent per cent literacy? How to make the village as knowledge centre? The vision exercise has made them dream and chalk out activities. For the first time people have come to act upon data. The generated data have given the exact conditions of the village and the facilities available in the village. A collective decision-making culture has been developed through this plan. In this process the excluded groups have been included and their priorities have been included in the plan. A new democratic culture has been created by which the possibility has been created to democratize the society. During the entire period of Plans, for the first time in India a Gram Panchayat has developed a plan document. The issues of women and Dalits have drawn the attention of all segments and approved in the plan. Minute details of social development issues have found a place in the plan for operationalization. The existing framework of leadership has moved from rulership to democratic leadership to work collectively. For the first time the public have come to attack social development issues. A major breakthrough has been achieved in the domain of development activities by looking at the outcome instead of the output. In the process of developing the plan, the people have come to know of the plenty of rural development schemes available with various department and are making the departments responsible for success or failure. Accountability has been fixed on the department of government by the people. Through the plan preparation people have been put first from the last and government officials have been pushed back. People have realized that for many of the social development activities, money is not required but a new mindset is required on the part of the people. People have realized their worth and potential and as a result they have started believing the people. In this process their outlook towards the government as giver has gone. People have started negotiating with MLAs and MPs for funds. The District administration has evinced keen interest as their targets could also be achieved very easily. No government department can achieve its target without the cooperation of the Panchayats.

So far the officials have shown the target of activities completed by them. They would not show the results or outcome or implications. But the Panchayat Presidents are showing the way to officials. Officials quote the number of toilets constructed but the leaders show how toilet culture has been created and there is no open air defecation. Officials indicate the buildings constructed and facilities provided to the schools. Panchayat leaders indicate the total number of students admitted in the school and reduction of dropouts in the schools. Officials have projected how many tablets have been distributed to pregnant women, and how many children have been immunized. But Panchayat leaders show how the number of anemic patients, especially women, has been reduced and how malnutrition of children has been reduced. Officials talk about health care system. But the Panchayat leaders have talked about health governance.

Before the Government of Tamil Nadu announced and launched a massive scheme on sanitation, Mr. Paneer Selvam of Keerapalayam Panchayat made the entire Gram Panchayat fully sanitized with the support of DANIDA.[13] He got an award from the Government of Tamil Nadu. Rani Sathappan of K. Rayavaram Gram Panchayat in Pudukkottai District has banned the use of plastics and polythene through a Gram Sabha resolution.[14] Ponnusamy of Semmipalayam Gram Panchayat achieved 100 per cent school enrolment and completely put an end to child labour in his Panchayat.[15] Ms. Chinnammal of Orathupatti Gram Panchayat by providing nail cutter to the Balwadi and constructing baby toilets, providing mats to the Balwadis has introduced a new health behaviour among the children.[16] Ms. Kala of Nuthulapuram Panchayat by her active intervention and supervising at the PHC, has been benefitted the Dalits. They need not go to private hospitals. Providing assistance to the differently abled persons, destitutes and widows is the priority of Veerakalaiarasi of Veppankulam Gram Panchayat. With the active intervention of the Gram Panchayats Tamil Nadu has changed the index on sanitation from 14 to 40. Of the 39 awards Nirmal Puraskar given all over India Tamil Nadu alone received 13 awards. Thus the Panchayats proved their worth.

Conclusion

Social development is the exclusive domain of activities of officials and bureaucrats of the government departments. It has been neither the work of the political class nor the public. Why are we poor in Human Development? It is not because of the poor allocation of resources to the social development sector, but it is mainly because of the negligence of the political class and the public to play their due role. Further people's participation is essential to achieve social development goals. Further, when government officials perform their part and role in implementing schemes and programmes to achieve social development, they achieve targets. But the exact outcome is not evaluated. But now Panchayats have come and started sensitizing the people on social development after themselves are being sensitized.

By developing a micro plan for the overall development of the village and the community, people have been made to think about their living conditions and to envision for their development. People have realized that they are leading life in sub-human living conditions. People have realized in the process of planning that for many of the social development works people need no money. It has been demonstrated that Panchayats can work on social development. Panchayats activities could be seen in the outcome.

NOTES AND REFERENCES

1. Jean Dreze, "Democracy and Right to Food", *Economic and Political Weekly*, April 24, 2004.
2. Even after five decades of development activities, Government of India evolved a new scheme called Total Sanitation Programme. But it was conceived very seriously by M.K.Gandhi in his Constructive Programme.
3. PTI March 23, 2005 quoted by *Women's Link*, Vol.11, No.3, July-September, 2005, p. 47.
4. In all the District Planning meeting, vital statistics prepared by the State Planning Commission for State Development Report supported by UNDP are being discussed and fixed targets to improve the conditions by dovetailing the existing schemes.
5. G. Palanithurai, *Three Tier Panchayati Raj in Tamil Nadu: Act Rules and Schemes* (Tamil), Chennai: South Vision, 2005.
6. Every year Annual Reports are prepared for Rural Development. They are not evaluation of the outcome of the activities. They are compilation of the statistics on activities not the impact of activities. There is no such culture or practice developed in Government.
7. In every Gram Sabha one would the same document despite implementation of several programmes.
8. James Manor, *The Political Economy of Democratic Decentralization*, Washington DC: The World Bank, 1999.
9. In the context of no initiation from the State Government and District Planning Committee, The Hunger Project has initiated micro-plan at Gram Panchayat level in select districts of Tamil Nadu as pilots.
10. G.Palanithurai, *Panchayats, Communities and Social Development*, Gandhigram: Rajiv Gandhi Chair for Panchayati Raj Studies, 2003.
11. The action points are taken from Meenaveli Gram Panchayat in Pudukkottai District.
12. G.Palanithurai, M.A.Thirunavukkarasu and G.Uma, *Guidelines for Micro-Plan Preparation* (Tamil), Gandhigram: The Hunger Project, 2004.
13. G.Palanithurai, *Leadership Matters in Government at Grassroots*, Pathfinders, Vol.10, Gandhigram: Rajiv Gandhi Chair for Panchayati Raj Studies, 2005.
14. G.Palanithurai, *Leadership Matters in Government at Grassroots*, Pathfinders, Vol.4, Gandhigram: Rajiv Gandhi Chair for Panchayati Raj Studies, 2004.
15. G.Palanithurai, *Leadership Matters in Government at Grassroots*, Pathfinders, Vol.1, Gandhigram: Rajiv Gandhi Chair for Panchayati Raj Studies, 2004.
16. Ms.Chinnammal, *Perspective Plan of Orathupatti Gram Panchayat*, Gandhigram: Rajiv Gandhi Chair for Panchayati Raj Studies, 2002.

7

Rural Development, National Rural Employment Guarantee Act and Panchayati Raj Institutions: An Overview

Dr. Aditya Kumar Patra

Three-fourths of people of India live in rural areas. The rural India is characterized by high incidence of poverty, widespread unemployment and under-employment, fragile food security and lack of infrastructural facilities. This leads to exodus of rural masses to urban centers. Ever since independence 'Rural Development' occupies a prominent place in the government plan and policies. Over the years, rural development has emerged as a strategy designed to improve the economic and social life of a specific group of people–the rural poor. The twin major objectives of RD programme are: accelerated economic growth with wider participation and most equitable distribution of its gains. During the last six-decades of planning era a number of policies and programmes were launched to revitalize the rural economy. Beginning from the Community Development Programme, launched way back in 1952, to NREGA the latest one in this row, a series of programmes have been directed towards this and in the process, the most disadvantaged sections of the society receive high priority.

An attempt has been made in this chapter to examine how far the National Rural Employment Guarantee Act (NREGA), 2005 is able to achieve its desired objective. This write-up is organized as follow: Section–I details the rural set-up of Indian economy. Section–II gives a panoramic view of rural development initiatives. The anatomy of the new act is the theme of Section–III. Section–IV depicts the role of Panchayati Raj Institutions (PRIs) in implementing the scheme and Section–V concludes the chapter.

SECTION – I

Rural Set-up

India is predominantly a rural economy. According to 2001 census 72.22 per cent of Indian population is residing in rural area. Though the percentage of rural population shows a moderate decline over the years, the absolute figure shows a large rural base (Table–1).

Table–1
Rural Population of India (1951-2001)

Year	*Number in Crore*	*Percentage*
1951	29.86	82.71
1961	36.02	82.03
1971	43.90	80.09
1981	52.38	76.66
1991	62.88	74.30
2001	74.16	72.22

Source: Various Census Report, Government of India.

When one thinks of our country, the first impression one gets is the appalling poverty of our rural population. Poverty is the most critical problem confronting India. It is viewed both in absolute and relative sense. In the absolute sense it means the inability to obtain the minimum standard of consumption necessary for one's bare existence. Relative poverty is said to exist when the consumption standard of one person or a group falls behind the consumption standard of other person or groups. The most common measure of poverty is to count the number of persons below the poverty line (poverty line is defined for 2004-05 as per capita per month expenditure of Rs. 358.03 for rural areas and Rs. 540.40 for urban areas) and express it as a percentage of total population in the country. This is known as Headcount Ratio (HCR). 'Poverty Gap' and 'Squared Poverty Gap' indicate the 'Severity' and 'Depth of Poverty' respectively. On the contrary the 'Gini Coefficient' reflects inequality in the distribution of income.

Table–2 clearly indicates that poverty has declined over the period but still a large chunk of Indian population is suffering from absolute poverty. However, the inequality in the distribution of income as reflected by Gini Coefficient has worsened particularly during the post liberalization period, both in rural and in urban sectors.

In rural India another deplorable fact is the widespread unemployment and underemployment. Out of the total rural labour force cultivators and agricultural labourers accounted for 69.7 per cent of the rural male and 79.9 per cent of rural female labour force in 2001.

Table–2
Estimates of Poverty and Inequality (in per cent)

		1983	*1987-88*	*1993-94*	*2004-05*
Headcount Ratio	Rural	46.5	39.0	37.2	28.7
	Urban	43.6	38.7	32.6	25.9
Poverty Gap	Rural	12.36	9.29	8.5	5.8
	Urban	11.4	10.2	8.0	6.2
Squared Poverty Gap	Rural	4.87	3.23	2.84	1.76
	Urban	4.4	3.8	2.9	2.0
Gini Coefficient	Rural	30.4	29.9	28.6	30.5
	Urban	33.9	35.0	34.4	37.6

Source: Himansu, EPW, February 10, 2007, p. 498.

A typical feature of rural employment is that it is low income employment. Since the poor are so poor to remain unemployed, they take up any job no matter how much income they earn from such job. The chronic unemployment (or, open unemployment) is rarely found in rural areas. Bulk of the rural unemployment is basically under-employment or employment with low earnings. In rural areas, employed- and-poor is a much larger category than unemployed-and-poor. Another feature of rural employment is its growing 'casualisation' i.e., the rural labour force is seeking employment through 'daily wage labour' as distinct from self-employment or regular salaried employment. Further casualisation among female is more discernable than male workers.

'No work' and 'Low wages' for a longer period are the root causes for the distressing conditions of the poor. The majority of poor in India is living in rural areas and belongs to the categories of landless agricultural and casual labourers, marginal and small farmers, rural artisans etc. A large section of them are SC, ST and Backward Castes. Solving the problem of unemployment and underemployment among these sections is the only answer to mitigate the misery of these rural masses.

As is observed from NSSO 60th Round Survey (2004) unemployment rates on the basis of current daily status were much higher than those on the basis of usual status (unemployed on an average basis in the reference year) implying a high degree of intermittent unemployment. This is mainly because of the absence of regular employment for many workers. The rural unemployment rates were higher than in urban areas. (Table–3)

Table–3

Unemployment Rates (in per cent)

Status of Unemployment	*Rural*			*Urban*		
	Male	*Female*	*Total*	*Male*	*Female*	*Total*
Usual-Principal Status	24	22	23	46	89	53
Current Weekly Status	47	45	46	57	90	64
Current Daily Status	90	93	91	81	117	88

Source: NSSO Estimates (60th Round).

According to Dr. Swaminathan's "Food Insecurity Atlas", India has largest absolute number of undernourished people in the world. In India income poverty is 26 per cent. However, the nutritional poverty is 56 per cent. Poverty is a major threat of food insecurity and sustainable progress in poverty elimination is critical to improve access to food. It is necessary to target those people and areas suffering mostly from hunger and malnutrition and identify causes and remedial action to improve the situation.

The analysis of incidence of poverty across Indian states indicates that poverty is very closely linked to the absence of economic and social infrastructure. Investments in rural infrastructure have been reported to have a significant impact on increase in economic activities in the area and consequent reduction in poverty. Availability of infrastructure has also gone a long way in redressing the issues of regional imbalance.

The Eleventh Finance Commission had prepared an 'Index of infrastructure' by taking into account economic, social and administrative infrastructure. If we put the index of infrastructure vis-à-vis the incidence of poverty we find that states with high value of infrastructure index have low incidence of poverty. This is reflected from Table–4.

The rural youth are in dire need of appropriate and satisfying jobs within the villages. But unfortunately the process of displacement/marginalisation of Indian agriculture has led to increasing reliance on non-farm activities of urban centers. Hence, exodus of rural labourers to urban area. Higher man-land ratio, underemployment at the place of origin, pull of higher wages, opportunities for education and training and lack of infrastructural facilities are some of the reasons of migration.

Table–4
Index of Infrastructure and Incidence of Poverty
(1999-2000 in per cent)

State	*Index of Infrastructure*	*Incidence of Poverty*
Andhra Pradesh	103.30 (9)	15.77 (6)
Assam	77.72 (13)	36.09 (12)
Bihar	81.33 (11)	42.60 (14)
Gujarat	124.31 (5)	14.07 (4)
Haryana	137.54 (4)	8.74 (2)
Karnataka	104.88 (8)	20.04 (7)
Kerala	178.68 (2)	12.72 (3)
Madhya Pradesh	76.79 (14)	37.43 (13)
Maharashtra	112.80 (6)	25.02 (9)
Orissa	81.00 (12)	47.15 (15)
Punjab	187.57 (1)	6.16 (1)
Rajasthan	75.86 (15)	15.28 (5)
Tamil Nadu	149.10 (3)	21.12 (8)
Uttar Pradesh	101.23 (10)	31.15 (11)
West Bengal	111.25 (7)	27.02 (10)

Notes: Figure in parenthesis shows the rank.
Source: Eleventh Finance Commission Report, HCR– Planning Commission.

SECTION–II

Rural Development — A Birds' Eye View

The major schemes of the Rural Development could be grouped under five major heads viz., (1) Generation of Employment: Self and Wage, (2) Rural Infrastructure Development, (3) Area Development Programmes, (4) Programmes for Social Welfare and Social Security, and (5) Minimum Needs Programme. However, very often Government's concept of Rural Development is limited to Anti-Poverty Programmes implemented by the Ministry of Rural Development. Rural Development is a broader concept and Poverty Alleviation Programme is a major sub-set of it.

Time and again poverty alleviation and employment generation programmes in India have been re-structured and re-designed with a view to generate employment and income. The major schemes of poverty alleviation could be grouped under two heads viz.(1) Self-Employment and (2) Wage Employment.

Self-Employment Scheme

Lack of assets is a major source of poverty in rural areas. Since radical land redistribution has not been possible the second best solution was to transfer non-land productive assets that would generate incomes for the poor through self-employment programmes. Accordingly Integrated Rural Development Programme (IRDP) was started in 1980-81 in all the blocks of the country and continued as a major self-employment scheme. By way of providing subsidy accompanied with bank credit on soft terms to enable rural poor households to purchase/create income generating assets for supplementing their income. Subsequently TRYSEM, DWCRA, SITRA, etc., were introduced as special programmes of IRDP to take care of the specific needs of rural population.

The IRDP and allied programmes including the GKY were merged into a single programme known as SGSY (Swarna Jayanti Gram Swarozgar Yojana) on 1st April, 1999. The SGSY aims at bringing every assisted family (Swarozgari) above the poverty line in 3 years by organizing them into Self-Help Groups (SHGs) through a mix of bank credit and government subsidy. This aims at building the self-confidence of the poor through community action, collective decision-making, prioritisation of their needs and resources so as to improve their collective bargaining power and empowers them socially and economically. SGSY tries to integrate various agencies – District Rural Development Agencies (DRDA), banks, line departments, Panchayat Raj Institutions (PRIs), Non-Governmental Organisations (NGOs) and other semi-Governmental Organisations.

Wage Employment Programme

Another set of programmes known as wage employment schemes, form an important component of the anti-poverty strategy aimed at providing employment opportunities during lean agricultural season and also in times of flood and drought and natural calamities.

These programmes fulfill the twin objectives of creating rural infrastructure to support further economic activity and the generation of employment opportunity.

Wage employment programmes have in existence since 1977 when the Food for Work programme was taken up. This was replaced by NREP (National Rural Employment Programme) in 1980 and RLEGP (Rural Landless Employment Guarantee Programme) in 1983. These two programmes were later merged in 1989 with the JRY (Jawahar Rozgar Yojana). Initially the JRY also included the IAY (Indira Awas Yojana) and the MWS (Million Wells Scheme). Both these schemes were made two independent schemes in 1996. JRY has been strengthened and restructured as JGSY (Jawahar Gram Samridhi Yojana) with effect from 1st April, 1999. The primary objective of JGSY is creation of demand-driven durable community assets with employment generation as a secondary objective.

The Employment Assurance Scheme (EAS) was launched on 2nd October, 1993 in drought prone area and basically tribal and hill area blocks. It was later extended to all the blocks in 1997-98. It was designed to provide employment in the form of manual work in the lean agricultural season. The food for work programme was started in 2000-01 as a component of the EAS in 845 drought affected areas of the country. It aimed at augmenting food security through wage employment.

JGSY and its complimentary programmes EAS and FFW programme were revamped and merged under the new Sampoorna Grameen Rozgar Yojana (SGRY) w.e.f. September 2001. The basic aim of the scheme continued to be the generation of wage employment, creation of durable economic infrastructure in rural areas and the provision of food and nutrition security to the poor.

National Food for Work Programme (NFFWP) was launched on 14th November 2004 in 150 most backward districts of the country with the objective to intensify the generation of supplementary wage employment. The programme is open to all rural poor who are in need of wage employment and desire to do manual unskilled work.

The NFFW and SGRY has been merged with effect from 2nd February, 2006 under the name National Rural Employment Guarantee Programme (NREGP). Initially starting from 200 most backward districts of the country, it will be extended to the whole of India within a period of five years. The objective of the NREGP is to enhance the livelihood security of people in rural areas by generating wage employment through works that develop the infrastructure base of that area (Annexure-1).

SECTION-III

NREGA, 2005

National Rural Employment Guarantee Act (NREGA) 2005 is a historic Act, which provides 100 days guaranteed employment to adult persons of a rural household in each financial year. This Act helps the rural inhabitants to ensure their livelihood/food security by earning minimum Rs. 6000/- per year in all over the country (except J & K). This Act received the assent of President of India on 5th September, 2005 and has been implemented in 200 districts of India since 2nd February, 2006, which further extended to additional 130 districts from the fiscal year 2007-08. The present Act borrowed the idea of guaranteed employment from Maharashtra's Employment Guarantee Act, 1976 (which is still in force). The Act stipulates that every State Governments have to make an Employment Guarantee Scheme within 6 months from the date of commencement of this Act, in order to implement the work guarantee. The Act has enough relevance in providing livelihood security, creating durable community assets, preserving the environment, empowering women in rural areas, fostering more equitable social order, empowering PRIs and to offer sustainable solution to rural development.

The NREGP marks a paradigm shift in delivery of Government programmes in the country. It accepts a right-based approach to work. It makes the right to work a fundamental legal right for the first time. The State Governments have been given the responsibility to prepare, finalise and approve the annual action plans. State Governments to provide at least 100 days of guaranteed wage employment in every financial year to every household whose adult members volunteer to do unskilled manual work, failing which states would have to provide unemployment allowance @ 1/4th of the wage for first 30 days and @ 1/2 of the wage for remaining period of the financial year to the concerned family. The major responsibility for programme implementation has been given to Panchayati Raj Institutions. The cost of material component of works including wages to skilled and semi-skilled workers will be restricted to 40 per cent of the total project cost. The contractors are not allowed to be engaged in implementation of the NREGP projects. 1/3rd of the proposed jobs would be reserved for women. The funding of the scheme will be shared between center and state in the proportion of 90:10 basis.

The NREGP provides an indispensable lifeline to the poverty stricken rural masses. This Act aims at removing poverty in rural area with the generation of gainful employment. Besides employment generation, the objective of the scheme is to create durable community assets for sustainable development of rural sector and to have a dent on migration of local people to cities. The NREGP is critically linked to the Government's efforts to usher in 2nd green revolution in the rain fed areas. Keeping this in view the NRE Act gives emphasis on water harvesting and water conservation, drought proofing including aforestation and plantation, construction of irrigation canals, micro and minor irrigation works and provision of irrigation facilities to land owned by SCs and STs. Renovation of traditional water bodies, land reclamation and development and rural connectivity have also been given importance.

The wage rate is fixed by the State Governments as per the prevailing minimum wage rate in the state (for a period of seven hours per day). The disbursement of wage shall be made weekly but not later than a fortnight. The labour is entitled to get 10 per cent extra wage if the work site is beyond 5 km away from his/her place of residence.

The NREG Act sanctions a number of social security provisions like free medical facilities in case of injury on account of the work, half of the wage as daily allowance in case of hospitalization along with accommodation, treatment and medicines, a sum of ex-gratia payment of Rs. 25000/- in case of death or permanent disability. The facility of safe drinking water, childcare and first aid box shall be provided in the work site.

Central Government will establish a National Employment Guarantee Fund and State Governments will establish State Employment Guarantee Funds for implementation of the scheme. The Central Government has provided Rs.11300 and 12000 crore in 2006-07 and 2007-08 respectively. States would contribute their share Rs. 1130 and 1200 crore towards this.

As provision of employment for 100 days is a statutory commitment of the Government, fund allocation for the programme has to be increased in the event of a higher demand from the State

Governments. In this sense, NREGP is an open-ended scheme. The scheme to be self-selecting in the nature that those among the poor who need work at the minimum wage would report for work under the scheme. The employment seekers will submit the application along with their details to the Sarapanch of the Gram Panchayat (GP) / the Programme Officer (PO) at the block level. The registration will be done after a proper enquiry and a job card will be issued to the person.

The NREGP is based on the principle of decentralization of governance. Though from the central level to state, district, block and village administrations are entrusted with the task of joint responsibility to implement the scheme the PRIs have been assigned a pivotal role for its success. It adopts a bottom-up approach. The different actors that are involved for the implementation of the Act are: The State Council, The District Coordinator, The Programme Officer, The Intermediate Panchayat (IP), The Gram Panchayat (GP) and The Gram Sabha (GS).

BOX–1
Highlights of the NREG Act

1. Provision of livelihood security of rural households.
2. 200 districts in the first stage and rest in next 5 years.
3. 72 crores of people will be covered under NREGS.
4. Ensure 100 days of guaranteed wage employment to each rural household who are interested to do unskilled manual work.
5. Unemployment Allowance will be paid if employment is not provided within 15 days of receipt of application.
6. Minimum wage not less than Rs.60 per person per day.
7. Equal wage for men and women.
8. Employment (work) on demand.
9. 33 per cent work should be allocated to women.
10. Employment within 5 km radius, beyond additional payment of 10 per cent more.
11. Disbursement of daily wages shall be done on weekly basis. However, it should not take more than 15 days.
12. Payment of wages will be made in front of community.
13. Private contractors and labour replacing machines are banned.
14. The mandatory work sites facilities are drinking water, shade, medical aid, crèche (of more than 5 children below 6 years of age).
15. 50 per cent work will be done by GP and rest by other implementing agencies.

Gram Panchayat shall be responsible for identification of projects as per the recommendations of the 'Gram Sabha' and for executing and supervising such works. GP shall prepare the 'Annual Action Plan', decide the priority of works and recommend it to the PO at the block level for scrutiny and approval prior to the commencement of the year. The GPs have been assigned the responsibility to register the list of employment seekers, maintain details of registered household, receive applications for job, allocate employment opportunities among the applicants (as per the direction of PO), and intimate them through personal letter and public notice, maintain registers, vouchers, other documents pertaining to work and employment etc. They will also be responsible for execution, supervision and conducting regular social audit of the programme.

At the block level a Programme Officer is appointed by the State Government for implementing the scheme. The PO is under the overall direction, control and supervision of District Project Coordinator and will assist the Panchayata Samiti in discharge of its functions. He shall be responsible for matching the demand for employment and employment opportunities arising from projects, consolidating various project proposals submitted by GPs, monitoring, scrutinizing, sanctioning of works, prompt and fair payment of wages, payment of unemployment allowance, ensuring regular social audit, provision of work within 15 days of application from the job card holder and grievance redressal. The PO shall allot at least 50 per cent works in terms of its cost under NREGP to GPs.

District Project Coordinator (Chief Executive Officer, Zila Parishad, or Collector or any other district officer as designated by the Government) will be responsible for implementation of the scheme at the district level and will assist the District Panchayat to discharge its functions. District Panchayat has been entrusted with the task of consolidation of block plans for inclusion in the 'shelf of project' to be approved by Zila Parishad, accord necessary sanctions and administrative clearance, reviewing, monitoring and coordinating the POs, periodical inspection of the works in progress, preparing budget for the coming year and redressal of grievances.

At the State level, a State Employment Guarantee Council (SEGC) shall be constituted. The SEGC shall advise the State Government on matters relating the implementation of the scheme, monitoring, supervision, dissemination of information etc. In addition the SEGC shall prepare and place the Annual Report before the State Legislature.

At the central level, a Central Employment Guarantee Council (CEGC) will be constituted to deal with matters concerning dissemination of information, implementation, supervision, monitoring of the scheme and for grievance redressal.

The Central Government reserves the right to amend the scheme through the Parliament. There is a penal provision of fine to the tune of Rs. 1000/- in case of breach of conditions laid down in the Act. If the Central Government is satisfied with the complaint of misutilisation of fund, it can stop further release of fund and initiate steps for its proper implementation.

The Non Governmental Organisations have been given a prominent role in disseminating information about people's rights under NREGP.

The list of responsibilities is quite long. However, the main duties of various actors are listed in Box 2.

BOX–2

Main Responsibilities of Various Actors/Administrators Under NREGA

Responsibilities of Gram Sabha (GS)

1. Recommend 'projects' required in their area to GP.
2. Monitor the execution of works within the GP.
3. Conduct regular Social Audit of all projects taken up in the GP.

Responsibilities of Gram Panchayat (GP)

1. Register households, verify and issue job cards.
2. Receive applications for work and issue dated receipt.
3. Forward applications to the PO.
4. Inform applicants (through notice board) when work is available.
5. Prepare an Annual Development Plan as per the recommendations of GS and execute these.
6. Make available all relevant documents including muster rolls to the GS for Social Audit.
7. Prepare an Annual Report on the implementation of the scheme.

Responsibilities of Intermediate Panchayat (IP)

1. Send 'proposals' of works to be taken up to the PO and implement projects that have been sanctioned by him.
2. Supervise and monitor the projects taken up at the GP and block level.
3. Approve the block plan and forward it to the District Panchayat for final approval.

Contd...

Responsibilities of the Programme Officer (PO)

1. Receive applications for employment (with the issue of dated receipt of the same) as well as work proposals from GP/other implementing agencies. The PO is supposed to match the two.
2. Ensure that every applicant is provided work within 15 days.
3. Notify applicants to report for work.
4. Ensure prompt and fair payment of wages to all labourers.
5. Sanction and disburse the unemployment allowance.
6. Sanction projects to be taken up by the GP and monitor the projects taken up by the GP/other implementing agencies.
7. Ensure that regular social audit of all works are carried out by GS.
8. Deal promptly (within 7 days as grievance redressal officer at the block level) with any complaint that may arise in connection with the implementation of the scheme.
9. Assist the Intermediate Panchayat in discharging its functions under the Act.
10. Prepare an Annual Report on the implementation of EGS in the block.

Responsibilities of District Programme Coordinator

1. Prepare an annual district plan based on the annual block plan of all IPs and work proposals from other implementing agencies.
2. Prepare a 'Labour Budget' (about details of the anticipated demand for unskilled manual work in the district and plan for engagement of people in different works) every year during the month of December for the next financial year.
3. Assist the 'District Panchayat' in discharging its function under the Act.
4. Sanction works that are not within the jurisdiction of PO and regular inspection of the works in the district.
5. Prepare an Annual Report on the implementation of the scheme in the district.

Responsibilities of State Employment Guarantee Council

1. It is essentially an advisory body for the State Government for proper implementation of the EGS.
2. It is expected to advise the State Government on the 'Schedule of Rates', level of unemployment allowance and monitoring arrangement.
3. Other responsibilities of SEGC includes preparation of list of 'preferred works' to be taken up on a priority basis, conducting evaluations of EGS and preparing an Annual Report to be laid before state legislature.

Responsibilities of Central Employment Guarantee Council

1. Monitors the implementation of the Act countrywide.
2. Advises the Central Government.
3. Prepare an Annual Report to be laid before Parliament.

The following chart depicts the implementation and monitoring chain of the NREG Act, 2005.

Chart–1
Implementation and Monitoring Chain

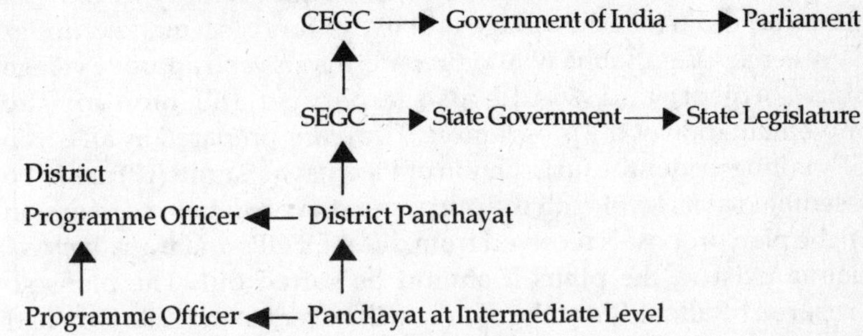

SECTION–IV

Role of PRI

Different poverty alleviation programmes were conceptualized with a view to achieve certain specific objectives but the results obtained and benefits accrued under each of these programmes were not as expected. The potent reason advanced for this is the utter sluggishness on the part of the local people for whom these programmes were evolved. All these programmes were planned and implemented by government officials and bureaucrats rather than by involving the local people. The involvement and participation of local people and grassroots institutions such as PRIs are highly essential for the success of poverty alleviation programmes.

Participation is an active process by which beneficiaries acquire knowledge about its potential benefits, understand its role and responsibilities, functions of involving institution including its own one. Hence, it is very much essential that not only the likely beneficiaries under the NREGS but also all the rural households of these villages must participate to secure all the details of the scheme, its short and long-term advantages/disadvantages, the precise role and responsibilities of all concerned individuals, GSs and GPs and Government officials in planning, execution, implementing, monitoring and evaluating different schemes. This enables the GS in particular and GP in general to put all their efforts to make the scheme a success one in achieving its desired objectives.

For the first time in the history of free India, the NREG Act assigned the PRIs a pivotal role for the implementation of the Employment Guarantee Scheme in such a way that they would implement the scheme as an integral part of rural development plan

Gram Panchayat and Gram Sabhas would decide types of work to be undertaken in the village and use of funds earmarked under the scheme. Gram Sabha would prepare, discuss and approve village plan (project) and would also supervise and monitor the implementation of the programme. The plans prepared by all GSs / GPs falling under the jurisdiction of Panchayat Samiti (IP) are to be assembled at its level with the purpose to have a detailed discussion on the plan proposals received from different GPs and if any lapses/ lacuna exist in the plans it should be sorted out. The plans so prepared by all the IPs of the district will be sent to the Zilla Parishad with the purpose of discussion at its level and finally forwarded to the DPC for onward transmission to the State Government. This is the only way through which the participation of all players of the PRIs can be operationalised for effective implementation of the EGS.

With the passage of 73rd Amendment Act, 1992, peoples' participation in the process of planning, decision-making, implementation and delivery system in rural India has been recognized. In India Rural Government comprises 232278 Village Panchayat, 5905 Intermediate Panchayats, 499 District Panchayats making a total of 238682 at all the three levels. Total number of elected representatives of panchayats at various levels are 2.92 millions of which about 1 million are women, more than 6 lakh are SC/ST. This is unparallel across the world. Therefore, the government is very keen to involve local people and PRIs for implementing the NREG Act and make them responsible to achieve the underlying objectives.

However, the study shows that people participate in the political process but show low level of interest in PRIs as an instrument of democracy and development. Around half of the village members (women) are virtually outside the Gram Sabha meetings because they are not allowed to participate by their male counterparts. Likewise another group of people mainly SC/ST and other marginalized sections do not attend the Gram Sabha meeting due to some compulsions. Political decentralization requires pursuit of collective decision-making process, responsiveness and transparent governance, adhere to the system of accountability. But all these are more or less absent. Even elected PRI representatives feel marginalized at every level.

At this juncture PRIs knowledge, skills and capabilities need to be strengthened in order to settle the problems that may arise in the way of fiscal and administrative decentralization. For this purpose, suitable capacity building measures need to be adopted so that desired functions, finance and functionaries (triple Fs) are transferred smoothly to the panchayats to enable them to function as institutions of Self Government and prepare plans for economic development with social justice at its level. Capacity building may be defined as support or intervention that empowers Gram Sabha/Gram Panchayat as organization to achieve the objectives underlying the scheme. Effective capacity building requires the interaction of learning-by-doing, access to resources, facilitation, meditation and training. Capacity building measures for GS consists of formulation of project proposals, prioritizing realistic objectives, encouraging the monitoring activities, strengthening of managerial capabilities, evaluation of progress, developing social audit skill, human resource development, creation of an enabling environment for decision making and overall development of the village infrastructure.

Gram Sabha the lowest layer of PRI plays a strategic role in the NREG Act. It acts as a planner, decision-maker and auditor simultaneously. Hence in order to ensure the effective and efficient participative role of PRIs in general and Gram Sabha in particular, following measures needs special attention:

1. Impart comprehensive training and orientation to GS/GP functionaries for transferring various skills viz., planning, implementing, monitoring, accounting, audit, ex-post evaluation etc.
2. Information technology service should be extended to create database for ready reference to maintain transparency of the scheme.
3. Emphasis should be laid on proper coordination between different segments of implementing agencies.
4. Independent professional institutions / management experts should be entrusted with the task of monitoring-cum-concurrent evaluation of the scheme, and for getting feed-back for future policy formulation.

5. Implementation progress of the ongoing scheme should be recorded continuously at a regular interval.

SECTION–V

Conclusion

The implementation of NREGS is in a very nascent stage. The fate of NREGP hinges on the level of awareness, acceptability and the mindset of the rural people. Hence an all-out effort is essential to aware the rural mass about the objectives and provisions of the scheme and their rights and responsibilities for the success of the same. The coordination between government machinery and PRIs is another prerequisite. Steps should be taken towards this end. Various officials/authorities at the Gram Panchayat level should be well-equipped with the knowledge of manpower planning. The network and institutional arrangement of Panchayati Raj system, i.e., from Village Panchayat to District Planning Committee through intermediate and apex tiers of Panchayati Raj system should be used optimally to accomplish the goal of NREG Act. Political will and administrative support to PRIs is the main ingredient of successful implementation of the Act.

REFERENCES

1. Patel Amrit (2006), Role of PRIs in Implementing Rural Employment Guarantee Scheme, Kurukshetra, Vol 54, No 10, pp. 24-29.
2. Patra Aditya Kumar (2006), NREGP: A Holistic Approach for Rural Development, Proceedings of State Level Conference on EGA held at Nayagarh Autonomus College, Orissa, pp. 87-94.
3. Economic Survey, 2005-06, Government of India.
4. Employment Guarantee Act: A Primer, October 2005, Right to Food Campaign.
5. Himanshu (2007), Recent Trends in Poverty and Inequality: Some Preliminary Results, Economic and Political Weekly, Feb. 10, pp. 497-508.
6. IGNOU Study Materials for the Course MARD, MRDE-101 (4), pp. 17-20.
7. NSSO Estimates 60th Round, 2004.

ANNEXURE-1

Chronology of Different Wage Employment Programmes

1. RWP (Rural Workers Programme, 1961-66)
   To provide 100 days of employment in rural area.
2. RMP (Rural Manpower Programme, 1966-69)
   About 2.5 million persons for 5 years by creating community assets.
3. CSRE (Crash Scheme for Rural Employment, 1971-74)
   To generate 2.5 lakh mandays of employment in each of selected districts (350 districts mostly SFDA, MFPA and DPAP) by creating productive assets and prospective irrigation.
4. PIREP (Pilot Intensive Rural Employment Programme, 1972-76)
   Provide employment to 1000 persons in a year in a district and to one person in a family in which nobody was employed by creating economic and social assets in 15 selected blocks.
5. FFW (Food for Work, 1977-80) *
   Providing gainful employment to the poor by creating rural infrastructure and payment of part wages in foodgrains.
6. NREP (National Rural Employment Programme, 1980-89) *
   Providing gainful employment to the poor by creating rural infrastructure and payment of part wages in foodgrains.
7. RLEGP (Rural Landless Employment Guarantee Programme, 1983-89) *
   Provide 100 days of employment to every rural landless by creating durable assets.
8. JRY (Jawahar Rozgar Yojana, 1989-99)
   Generate meaningful employment opportunities for the unemployed and the underemployed in rural areas though the creation of economic infrastructure and community and social assets by merging NREP and RLEGP. (Initially JRY includes IAY and MWS. Both these were made two independent scheme in 1996.)
9. EAS (Employment Assurance Scheme, 1993-2001)
   To provide employment in the form of manual work in the lean agricultural season by creating economically productive assets. Initially in drought prone areas and basically tribal and hill area blocks later extended to all blocks in 97-98.
10. FFW was started in 2000-01 as a component of EAS in 845 drought affected areas with the objective of augmenting food security through wage employment.
11. JGSY (Jawahar Gram Samridhi Yojana, 1999-2001) *
    By restructuring JRY with a view to create demand-driven

community assets/infrastructure with employment generation as a secondary objective.

12. SGRY (Sampoorna Grameen Rozgar Yojana, 2001-till date) *
    JGSY, EAS and FFW programmes were revamped and merged. Providing additional wage employment in rural areas with the creation of durable economic infrastructure and thereby food security and improvement of nutritional level.
13. NFFWP (National Food for Work Programme, 14.11.2004-2.2.2006)
    Augmenting food security through wage employment in 150 most backward districts.
14. NREGP (National Rural Employment Guarantee Programme, 2.2.2006-till date)
    By subsuming SGRY and NFFWP it guarantees at least 100 days of guaranteed employment in every financial year to every household whose adult members volunteer to do unskilled manual work. Initially in 200 most backward districts and to all districts within a period of 5 years.
    ('' indicates working of the scheme in all States and UTs)*

8

Rural Empowerment, Social Action and Gender Equity: The Case of *Kudumbashree* Projects in Kerala

Dr. V.P. Raghavan

Introduction

Poverty is a crucial problem in all developing countries in the present day world. It is felt that the problem of poverty can be solved through a concerted effort by the State. Sustainable livelihood opportunities can be provided to the deprived and the destitute by means of lending asset creating facilities.

Women households are the cruelest victims of deprivation and destitution. Therefore, any programme for poverty alleviation must aim at improving the living environment of the women folks. It is through creating livelihood opportunities for the women that they can be empowered, and the micro credit and self help groupings are a better means through which their living conditions can be improved.

Poverty alleviation schemes based on micro credit system have been implemented in many of the developing countries in recent years.[1] In all developing countries state actions are being reinforced in streamlining poverty alleviation programmes. (Buckley,1996; Hulme and Mosley, 1996; Hussain, 1998). The Institutional formations of various means are also invigorated for initiating schemes of poverty alleviation successfully. (Hulme, *et al.*,1996; Yaron, 1992; Yunus, 1999).

The Government of Kerala State in India has introduced a novel scheme of poverty alleviation based on micro credit and self-help grouping . Paraphrased as *Kudumbashree* (Prosperity of the Family), the scheme aims at improving the living levels of the poor women in rural and urban areas. It seeks to bring the poor women folks together to form the grassroots organizations to help enhance their economic security. The projects aim at removing poverty among rural women households through setting up of micro credit and productive enterprises. The activities such as micro credit and micro enterprises under the scheme were undertaken by the locally formed Community Development Societies consisting of rural households.

This chapter aims at examining the socio-economic impact of the *Kudumbashree* projects on the rural and urban poor in salvaging from deprivation and creating gender equity. The organization of the chapter is as follows. Section II overviews the projects under implementation , Section III analyses the paricipatory mechanism of community involvement in the anti-poverty programmes by highlighting the cases of the Alappuzha and Malappuram Models being the geneses of the multifaceted *Kudumbashree* mission. In Section IV we present the extended Kudumbashree programmes under operations along with some new programmes being launched most recently, and Section V contains the conclusions.

Anti-Poverty Programmes Under Kudumbashree–An Overview

It is the State Poverty Eradication Mission, that has been paraphrased as *Kudumbashree* in local language, meaning 'prosperity of the family', which helps enjoy the economic opportunities by a good number of the poor women folks in rural and urban Kerala. The anti-poverty programme under *Kudumbashree* has been launched by the State Government of Kerala with the active support of the Central Government of India and the National Bank for Agriculture and Rural Development (NABARD) aiming at removing absolute poverty within ten years with the full co-operation of the local self-governments. Poverty is a multi-faceted state of deprivation. Hence a multi-pronged strategy alone can help eradicate poverty. The Mission of the *Kudumbashree*, therefore, states: "To eradicate absolute poverty in ten years through concerted community action under the leadership of local governments, by facilitating organization of the poor for combining self-help with demand led convergence of available services and resources to tackle the multiple dimensions and manifestations of poverty, holistically."(http://.www.kudumbashree.org)

Identifying the Poor

Identification of the poor is one of the prime requisites for the implementation of the projects. The following risk factors are considered for identifying the poor:

- No land/Less than 5 cents of land.
- No House/Dilapidated house.
- No sanitary latrine.
- No access to safe drinking water within 150 metres.
- Women headed household/Presence of a widow, divorce/abandoned lady/unwed mother.
- No regularly employed person in the family.
- Socially disadvantaged groups (SC/ST).
- Presence of mentally or physically challenged person/chronically ill member in the family.
- Families without colour TV.

The Modes Operandi: The Community Based Organisation

The formation of the grassroots level Community Based Organisation (CBO) is the fulcrum of the *Kudumbashree* mission. The grassroots level poor women are organized through Neighbourhood Groups (NHGs) consisting of 20-40 women with 5 functional volunteers, viz.,

- Community Health Volunteer,
- Income Generation Volunteer,
- Infrastructure Volunteer,
- Secretary, and
- President,

The Neighbourhood Groups (NHGs) are coordinated at ward level through Area Development Society (ADS) by federating 8 to 10 NHGs. To coordinate the activities at the Panchayat level there is the apex body called Community Development Society (CDS), which is heading the Area Development Societies (ADSs).

The CBOs are the lifeblood of *Kudumbashree*. The NHG members used to meet once in a week in one of the member's house. The members, who meet together, discuss their problems and make joint effort to find solutions to their grievances with the support of the functional volunteers. This would bring up an interpersonal feelings among the members and would generate supportive attitude to build confidence among them. Apart from this, they practice small savings through thrift which should be used to create productive assets. The 'micro-plans' are prepared at the NHG meetings and the formulated plans would be sent to ADS for scrutiny and finalization to form the 'mini-plan'. After consolidating the 'mini-plans' by judicious prioritization at the CDS meeting a 'sub-plan' is formed to become the anti-poverty programme of the Local Self Government. The formulation of micro, mini and sub-plans help facilitate the poor women households to participate in planning process as a major stake holder. The local self governing body monitors the implementation of the 'plans' and thereby proper linkage, coupled with automony is ensured in the participatory system of planning for poverty alleviation.

The Participatory Modelling: The Cases of *Alappuzha* and *Malappuram*

Alappuzha Model: The Prelude

The first spark of a women based participatory approach for poverty eradication came out in Alappuzha Municipality in Alappuzha District in Kerala in 1993 when the Community Development Society of the poor women came into being as part of the implementation of the Community Based Nutrition Programme (CBNP) and the Urban Basic Service Programme (UBSP) with the assistance of UNICEF. The seven wards were selected for the implementation of the programme.

The programme began with the organization of the poor women folks to form the Neighbourhood Groups . The poor high risk families were identified to form the Neighbourhood groups on the basis of nine non-economic indicators such as: occupation in temporary houses, no access to safe drinking water, no access to sanitary latrines, illiterate adult member in the family, not more than one earning member in the family, family getting barely 2 meals a day or less, children below 5 years in the family, SC/ST family, and alcoholic or drug addict in the family. 88 neighbourhood groups were formed of women from such high risk families and 7 ward level Area Development Societies (ADS) were formed from the grassroots level NHGs. The ADSs were federated to the town level Community Development Society (CDS).

(i) Neighbourhood Groups (NHGs)

Neighbourhood group is the association of 20 to 40 women members, belonging to high risk families. They elect a woman from among themselves as Resident Community Volunteer, another one is selected as President of the NHG and the three others are selected as Community Volunteers, each of whom has specific responsibilities viz., Health, Infrastructure and Income Generation. They are, therefore, designated as Community Health Volunteer, Community

Infrastructure Volunteer and Community Income Generating Volunteer.

The Community Health Volunteer is responsible for all the health related activities of the NHG like immunization, maternal care, child care, nutrition and propogation of ideas like cleanliness, hygiene, etc.

The Community Infrastructure Volunteer is in charge of the basic infrastructure needs of the NHG such as housing, sanitation, drinking water, drainage, etc.

The Community Income Generation Activity Volunteer looks after the income generating activities of the NHG. She has to identify all potential agencies, departments and organizations to be engaged in promotion of self-employment activities. She also liaises with the National Bank for Agriculture and Rural Development and commercial banks on behalf of the NHG.

Proper training and orientation are given to the above volunteers in their respective areas. Each NHG prepares an action plan on the basis of the needs of the member households of the NHG and such plans are called Micro Plan of the NHG.

(ii) Area Development Societies (ADSs)

Area Development Societies at the ward level are formed of 10 -15 NHGs and the five-member committee of the all the NHGs constitutes the governing body of the ADS. The ADS has a Chairperson, a Vice-Chairperson and 7 other members. The Community Organisor of the Municipality acts as the Member Secretary of the ADS.

The ADS integrates the micro plans of the NHGs and after discussion and scrutiny a consolidated action plan is prepared and is known as Mini Plan.

(iii) Community Development Society (CDS)

Community Development Society is the apex body at the town level and is the co-coordinating agency for programme implementation. Chairpersons, Vice-Chairpersons and Members of all the ADSs form the General Body of the Community Development Society. A Project Officer of the Municipality acts as the Member Secretary of the Community Development Society. The Community Development Society has a President, Vice-President and seven other members elected from the General Body of the CDS to form the committee of the CDS. The Committee and the Member Secretary constitutes the Govrning Body of the CDS.

The Community Development Society monitors the programmes undertaken by the ADSs on monthly basis and takes steps to improve the implementation of the programmes.

Various developmental programmes initiated under Community Development Society and the Area Development Societies include training programme for women to start income generating units, water supply, conduct of health education camps , construction of dual pit latrines undertaking micro enterprises, raising of pathways and cultural programmes, etc.

The participatory modelling under Community Development System brought the poor women in Alappuzha to the mainstream of the social life. They began to participate in the development process with greater enthusiasm. The NHGs were encouraged to meet as many times as possible. It provided them an opportunity to sit together and discuss their common problems to find out solutions. The poor women belonging to the high risk families become empowered and seldom accept poverty as their destiny. They proved beyond any doubt that they could identify their own problems. They learned the meanings of ' self-help' and 'self-respect'. The united and empowered women fought against poverty quite valiantly and effectively. Poverty alleviation programmes began to deliver the goods through participation for the first time in history .

The Malappuram Model – The Continuum

The amazing success of the participatory system of poverty alleviation in Alappuzha Municipality prompted the Government of Kerala in 1994 to extend the scheme to the entire district of Malappuram, one of the most backward districts in India. The district of Malappuram has the highest fertility and infant mortality rates in Kerala.

The Government of Kerala, with the assistance of the UNICEF, chose the district of Malappuram to experiment with poverty alleviation programme called Community Based Nutrition Project and Poverty Alleviation Programme (CBNP & PAP) aiming at helping to reach out the unreached through community action. The strategy formed the Convergent Community Action and Self Help to enhance the capacity of the family to help meet their basic needs such as drinking water, primary health care, basic education, safe environment and food security.

Like in Alappuzha Model, CBNP was implemented through Community Development Societies of women, who belonged to high risk families. The risk index adopted in Alappuzha model was slightly modified to suit the regional peculiarities of Malappuram district.

The non-economic risk indicators adopted for Malappuram model are:

- Families with substandard houses and huts
- Family with no sanitary latrines
- Families having no safe drinking water supply within atleast 300 mteres
- Families having more than 6 members
- Families with only one earning member
- Families belonging to SC/ST
- Families having illiterate members
- Families having only 2 meals or less a day
- Families having alcoholic, widows and divorces.

The Schemata

At the bottom level of the community structure of Malappuram, there are 4763 Neighbourhood Groups, each of which consists of 15 to 40 women members belonging to the risk families of a neighbourhood. NHG prepares Micro plan based on the needs and requirements of the constituting families.

In each Village Panchayat, there are Area Development Societies at the ward level. Each Area Development Society is formed by the representatives of the NHGs in each ward. Functionaries are elected as we have seen in the Alappuzha Model. Area Development Societies prepare Mini Plans, integrating all NHG plans. There are 853 ADSs are working in Malappuram district.

Panchayat/Municipal Community Development Society functions as an apex body of all ADSs at Panchayat/Municipality level. The Society has an elected President, Vice President and seven Governing Body members. There are 91 Panchayat CDSs and 5 Municipal CDSs in Malappuram district.

At Block level there is the Block CDS, which acts as a co-ordinating body of all CDSs in a Block. Block CDS prepares Block level plans, integrating all Panchayat CDSs' plans. There are 14 Block CDSs in the district.

The District CDS is the apex body. All the Block CDS Presidents and Town CDS presidents are members of the District CDS. The District CBNP Co-ordinator acts as the member Secretary of the CDS. The District CDS prepares the Plans at the district level integrating all micro and mini plans.

The activities of the Malappuram CDS include Training and Orientation Programme for Women, Imparting Education for Children, Regular Meetings to share experiences and holding cultural programmes, Community Health Care, Environmental Sanitation and Inormal Banking through Thrift and Credit Societies and Self -Help Groupings.

The Philosophy

The philosophy of CBNP is 'convergent community action'. With this end in view, attempts have been made from the very beginning to establish linkages with other government departments and agencies such as Education, Health, Social Welfare, Local Administration and Rural Development. UNICEF and NABARD also rendered their wholehearted support for training and in financing.

The Achievements

A. Training

- More than 1,00,000 CBNP/CDS functionaries were given training on various aspects with the assistance of UNICEF.
- More than 2000 CDS/CBNP functionaries were trained by NABARD in community financial management.
- More than 4300 community volunteers were given training in community health care.
- More than 12000 CBNP functionaries were trained and deployed for the conduct of the baseline survey.
- 40 CBNP functionaries were trained and deployed as Tribal Volunteers.
- About 13,000 CBNP/Literary workers trained and deployed for the conduct of the Poverty Index Survey.

B. Awareness Programme

- 1700 Community immunization camps were organized.
- 99 Awareness Programmes against alcohol were conducted.

- 3418 Awareness programmes were organized for popularization for iodized salt.

C. Water and Sanitation

- 5600 sanitary latrines were provided to the poor families.
- 20 borewells were provided.
- 10 open wells were provided.

D. Thrift and Credit Operations

- Mobilised Rs.150 lakh through thrift savings.
- Provided Rs. 135 lakh to CDS members as loan for income generation as well as for consumption purposes.
- Created 12322 self employment were created through loans/ revolving funds.

E. Employment

- Established one Coir Training Centre to train 150 SC women in coir making.
- Set up one Coir Defibreing Production unit with an investment of Rs. 35 lakh.

The Epilogue

The coordinated effort and the convergence of resources of various agencies for the uplift of the poor women are the resultant of the CBNP in Alappuzha Municipality and Malappuram District in Kerala. An integrated approach with the coordination and convergence of inputs and services of the various ongoing programmes of the government and other sectors helped improve the health and nutrition status of the poor women and their children. A new limelight in the participatory approach has been emerging to open up the social and economic opportunities for the poor and the downtrodden and a new horizon has been visible to realize their dreams of betterment into realities.

***Kudumbashree:* Towards a New Paradigm of Participatory Development**

The Mission for Poverty Eradication: A New Beginning

Enthused by the phenomenal success of the Alappuzha and Malappuram models of participatory development with the active involvement of the stake holders, the State Government of Kerala resolved to extend the participatory women based programme to the entire State of Kerala in 1998. The Project has been envisaged as a mission for eradication of poverty, which has been christened as "*Kudumbashree.*"

("Prosperity of the Family") and becomes the *Magna Carta* of the poor.

Kudumbashree, the State Poverty Eradication Mission of Kerala, proved a revolutionary initiative that has changed the lives of thousands of poor people in the state through its various programmes since its inception in 1998. The unique experimentation is being implemented through the Community Based Organisations (CBOs) of the poor aiming at a multi-pronged attack on poverty.[2]

It is the Community Development Societies that work for the removal of risk factors, which are the basic causes as well as effect of poverty. With this end in view, the NHGs are identifying the most critical needs of the members. The micro plans or the NHG plans thus become the basis of delivery of services and resources through the CDS system. Each group is involved in the process of identifying their needs and problems, and accordingly preparing plans and implementing the programmes.

The Focus

Kudumbashree Mission focuses on:

1. Training for Change,
2. Education,
3. Share and Care,
4. Community Health Care,
5. Environmental Sanitation,
6. The Poor Women's Bank, and
7. Community Financial Management.

Let us Have a Brief Overview

1. Training for Change

It is stated that empowerment of women is the prime motto of *Kudumbashree*. Therefore, the decision-making power must rest solely in the hands of the poor women. In order to exercise this power, they need proper orientation and training. To achieve this objective a number of specially designed training programmes are being conducted with focus on community structures, leadership, roles and responsibilities, thrift and credit operation, community financial management and accounting.

These training programmes are organized with the support of UNICEF, NABARD and other institutions. More than one lakh women have been trained so far.

2. Education

The massive training programmes have helped further strengthen the already existing awareness among women on the need for educating their children and acquiring literary skills for themselves. Resultantly, the apathy in sending the children to schools has disappeared to a greater extent. The poor women are getting realized that their children do need education and that education alone can enhance their status and provide them gainful employment.

3. Share and Care

The NHGs are encouraged to meet as frequently as possible and most of them do meet once in a week. They are able to discuss every problem in the meeting and suitable solutions are come up. The NHGs provide the poor women to share their grieves and joys.

4. Community Health Care

The trained women Community Health Volunteers are now able to provide basic medical care to the poor rural and urban women folks. With the emergence of the Community Health Volunteers the health scenario in the less cared groups are undergoing revolutionary changes. The incidence of cholera, malaria, typhoid and diarrhea has come down considerably.

5. Environmental Sanitation

Environmental sanitation becomes the matter of greater concern of women today. Lack of sanitary latrines and safe drinking water are the twin basic problems faced by the poor people. Concerted efforts are made to address these problems. 5600 latrines have already been constructed in Vettom Panchayat in Malappuram district with the help of various Government Departments.

6. The Poor Women's Bank

The Thrift and Credit Societies are formed with the objective of encouraging the poor women to save their meagre means to widen the resource base of the NHGs. Women bring their little bit of savings when they come to attend the group meetings. This money is entrusted to the Community Volunteer, who in turn deposits it in the nearest bank. Each member is given an individual pass book.

The Thrift and Credit Societies are considered as poor women's bank. The poor women, who were hitherto dependent on their men folk for every need and did not know the meaning of economic independence, has managed the impossible under *Kudumbashree.*

Members can avail loans to meet their urgent needs like medical treatment, purchase of school books and uniforms for children, to pay off their old debts, etc.

It is interesting to note that more than 90 per cent of the savings in the thrift societies are given away as loans. The selection of beneficiaries, the rate of interest, the quantum of loans and the period of repayment, etc. are all decided and implemented by the women themselves. Since the decisions regarding the repayment of loans with the rate of interest are taken by the NHGs, the monitoring mechanisms are inbuilt and defaulting is rare. For the same reason the NHGs are also very considerate to genuine reasons of non-repayment and extensions are given. It is observed that 100 per cent repayments are ensured which are rare in banking history. The Thrift and Credit Societies become the largest informal bank in Asia.

7. Community Financial Management

Formation of thrift societies and conduct of income generating activities have led to a large financial flow at NHG and ADS levels. This has necessitated proper maintenance of accounts and keeping records in a systematic way. So poor women activists were given proper training in "Community Financial Management".

The Strategies

Kudumbashree aims at empowerment of women to become the active leaders rather than passive recipients. The strategies thus form of:

- *(a)* Formation of women collectives,
- *(b)* Information and training,
- *(c)* Skill upgradation,
- *(d)* Thrift-Credit operations,
- *(e)* Infrastructure development,
- *(f)* Micro enterprises development,
- *(g)* Power to the people, and
- *(h)* Leadership.

The ultimate objective, therefore, sets as 'reaching out family through women, and reaching out community through family'.

The Programmes under Operations

The programmes conceived as a part of the strategy to reduce poverty are:

- Microfinance operations/Thrift and Credit Societies
- Micro Enterprises
- Micro Housing/*Bhavanashree*
- Destitute Identification, Rehabilitation and Monitoring Programme/*Ashraya*
- Lease Land Farming/*Haritashree*
- The S3 programme
- Children's Neighbourhoods/*Balasabha*
- Solid Waste Management/Clean Keral Business
- Special Employment Programme for the Educated Youth
- Special School for the Disabled Children/Buds
- Self Employment Programme under SJSRY
- GRQ Project.

Microfinance Operations

Thrift and Credit Societies are set up at Neighbourhood (NHG) level to facilitate the poor and to avail easy credits, which have now grown up to Informal Banks of the poor women at their doorsteps. Now, 10,687 Thrift and Credit Societies are in operation in the 58 urban areas enveloping the major 58 towns. In the rural segment, 1,45,674 Thrift and Credit societies are in operation covering all the 991 Village Panchayats in the State. Most of the Thrift and Credit Societies are capable of providing financial assistance to income generating activities. Through microfinance operations, Rs. 651.42 lakh of thrift are raised and internal lending to the extent of Rs. 1473.12 lakh are provided.

(www.kudumbashree.org)

The NHGs, which are able to avail loans are linked with banks under linkage banking programme of NABARD. Till date, 99,356 NHGs were upgraded and 71,702 of NHGs were linked with banks. Rs. 258.78 crore is distributed as loan to NHGs for internal banking and credit of Rs. 32281/lakh flow through linkage banking. Linkage banking programme becomes an effective tool to augment resources of NHGs. (A few examples of microfinance models are given in Table–1).

Micro Enterprises

Micro Enterprises foster the economic status of women as an effective means to eradicate poverty. The income generating activities under individual and group initiatives to meet the livelihoods of the poor women are massively promoted . Canteens/Catering units, IT units, Group farming units, Fruit Processing units, Footware units, Condiments units, Umbrella units, Building materials units, Horticulture units, Electronics units, Readymade garments units, Soap powder units, Toys units, Grocery shops, are some of the examples of Micro Enterprises that are undertaken by poor women under *Kudumbashree* Mission. Women entrepreneurs are given training in entrepreneurship development, skill development, project management, performance improvement by the Entrepreneurship Development Institute of India, Ahemmedabad. It is drawn that , as of date, there are 15,382 individual enterprises (Annexure I), and 1345 group enterprises in urban areas (Annexure II) and 14,662 individual enterprises and 20,017 group enterprises in the rural areas are on the run with the involvement of 2,42,482 women across the state.

Micro Housing/Bhavanashree

Under this programme poor families, who are in dire need of constructing new houses are able to avail loans from banks and the repayment of which is ensured by tri-party agreement between the beneficiaries, the Community Development Societies and the Financial institutions/Banks. 19,922 houses were constructed by using credit amounting to Rs. 6765.91 lakh.

The Destitute Identification, Rehabilitation and Monitoring Programme/ Ashraya

This programme , named as "*Ashraya*" in local language (meaning 'depending') aims at uplifting the poorest of the poor from their destitution. Poorest of the poor families ,which lack adequate food, drinking water, shelter, educational facilities for children , sanitation facilities, employment opportunities, land for shelter, and worst sufferers of illness and chronic diseases are identified and rehabilitated under various schemes. The programme launched in 391 Village Panchayats and 6 Municipalities.

Lease Land Farming/Haritashree

Lease Land Farming Programme, named 'Harithashree' in local language, lend helping hands to those cultivators who are having no land at all. So *Kudumbashree* pools uncultivated lands on rent and provide the willing cultivators for agricultural operations. Last year, lease land farming was done in 18,489 hectares benefiting 3,15,613 families hailing from 31,980 NHGs in the state.

The S3 Programme

Kudumbashree addresses the multifaceted deprivations of the poor families, which lack food, health care, education, basic amenities such as shelter, drinking water, safe latrines and employment. It is felt that poverty reduction would foster economic development if it sustains the secured gains. So, sustainability economic development assumes greater importance in the process of attacking poverty. So much so, *Kudumbashree* has evolved a project to build a model in select Panchayats on the concept of comprehensive development. The projects focuses on self-sufficiency, self-reliance and sustainability (S3) of the Village Panchayats. The project envisages to address the problems of Child Development, Geriatric care, Mentally and Physically Challenged, Education, Adolescent care, Women Empowerment, Enterprise development, Unemployment of the educated youth, Agriculture/Animal husbandry/Dairy development, Revamping the traditional sectors, Basic minimum Needs and Destitute Identification and Rehabilitation.

Initially the programme was piloted in three Panchayats viz., Venganoor in Trivandrum district, Kodakara in Trichur district and Munniyoor in Malappuram district. Later on, the programme extended to 14 Panchayats and the extension of the programme to another 70 Panchayats is done.

Childrens' Neighbourhoods/Balasabha

The children from poor families are organized to develop their intellectual faculties by performing cultural activities from time to time. Termed as *Balasabhas* in local language it functions as a platform of the children to help develop their overall capabilities that combines education, entertainment and empowerment. 27463 *Balasabhas* comprising 504979 children were organized in different places in Kerala.

Solid Waste Management/Clean Kerala Business

Solid waste is serious menace for all the urban and semi-urban areas of Kerala. Now *Kudumbashree* mission tries to tackle this problem by setting up 'Clean Kerala Business' units in an organized and planned manner entrusting to women entrepreneur groups to segregate, collect and transport solid waste from the households, commercial establishments, hotels, etc. 75 Clean Kerala Business units are formed in the state so far.

Special Employment Programme for Educated Youth

A special employment programme for the educated youth has been initiated and 50,000 educated youth were assigned with the task of *Kudumbashree* such as identification process, setting up of innovative micro enterprises, etc. 211 group and 170 individual enterprises have been formed under this programme, thus benefiting 1307 people.

Special School for the Disabled Children /Buds

Special schools, called 'Buds', are set up aiming at providing for the developmental, social, and emotional needs of the disabled children. These children are being provided with the necessary medical attention, physical and mental therapy, mobility equipments, hearing aids, and vocational and educational training.

Self-Employment Programmes under SJSRY

Swarna Jayanthi Sahari Rozgar Yojana (SJSRY) is an anti-poverty programme launched by the Government of India and is meant for the urban areas of the state. It covers the 53 Municipalities and 5 Corporations. Individual enterprises and Group enterprises with a minimum number of 10 persons can be set up. 1365 group and 15382 enterprises are undertaken under this programme.

GRQ (Goat-Rabbit-Quail) Project

The Goat-Rabbit-Quail Project is a unique micro enterprises project for rearing the three species together to earn a steady income to the family entrepreneurs. The predominantly non-vegetarian population of Kerala necessarily ensures the potential market for the produce.

The GRQ project aims at utilizing the inherent advantage of the homestead farming practised by number of families. Quail rearing as an activity can ensure a weekly cash flow and that combined with the quarterly and half yearly cash flow of rabbit and goat would ensure a source of steady income to the family.

Nutrimix – The Babyfood Products Production Project

The *Nutrimix* Babyfood Production Project is an ambitious project recently launched by the *Kudumbashree* mission. The Project envisaged to start 500 babyfood production units in different parts of Kerala. 21 Nutrimix production units have already been started. It is estimated that 2500 women can find gainful employment through the programme, which targets the massive baby food market dominated by big brands. The expected turnover is Rs. 200 crore per annum.

Some select *Kudumbashree* Production units and their activities in Kannur and Kasargod Districts are shown in the given Table-2.

Conclusion

Kudumbashree became the lifeline to many of the poor women in the state of Kerala. It assumed the status of helpline to many. It is a massive anti-poverty programme of the Government of Kerala aiming at eradicating poverty and salvage the destitutes from the wretches of extreme deprivation. The formation of 1,65,840 NHGs of the women from 33,45,509 risk families, covering urban, rural and tribal areas of the state helps develop 2,42,489 poor women into vibrant micro entrepreneurs. Resultantly, the poor women of the state have become active participants in the planning and implementation process of various anti-poverty programmes. By participating in various income generating-cum-developmental activities, the morale and confidence of women become very high. Capacity of the poor women of the state in several areas has gone up considerably, status of women in families and community has also improved. *Kudumbashree* has gained national and international acclaim as an ideal and workable model of participatory development for eradicating poverty.

The State Poverty Eradication Mission – *Kudumbashree* – launched by the Government of Kerala State in India is a massive poverty eradication programme in contemporary history. It has proved without any doubt that women empowerment is the best strategy for poverty eradication. Women who were regarded as voiceless and powerless started identifying their inner power, their strength, opportunities for growth, and their role in reshaping their own destiny. The process of empowerment becomes the beacon light to their children, their families and to the society at large. It opens a new vistas in development history. A new paradigm of participatory economics has been found emerging in "God's Own Country". *Kudumbashree* presents a unique model of participatory development, which can very well be emulated by other developing countries. The strategy of participation and empowerment adopted in *Kudumbashree* mission ensures sustainable livelihoods to a many number of poor women – the positive outcome, which a policy planner can always be enthused with.

NOTES

1. Grameen Bank scheme of Bangladesh, SANASA in Sri Lanka , Mudzi Fund in Malawi, ICREP Juhudi Scheme and KIE-ISP of Kenya, Bancosol of Bolivia are a few examples. (For more details see, Chavan and Ramkumar, 2002).
2. The Kudumbashree Mission is functioning under the directorate of the Government of Kerala.

REFERENCES

Anand, Jaya S. (1999), "Self-Help Groups in Empowering Women: A Study of Selected SHGs and NHGs in Kerala", KKRPLLD, Centre for Development Studies, Trivandrum, Kerala, India.

Buckley, Graeme (1996), "Financing in Jua Kali Sector in Kenya: The KREP Juhudi Scheme and Kenya Industrial Estates Informal Programme", in Hulme and Mosley (1996)

Chavan, Pallavi and R. Ram Kumar (2002), " Microcredit and Rural Poverty – An Analysis of Emperical Evidence", *Economic and Political Weekly*, March 9, No. 10.

Government of Kerala (1999-2000), Kudumbashree Project: State Poverty Eradication Mission, Annual Report 1999-2000, Local Self Government Department, Thiruvananthapuram, Kerala, India.

Hule, David, *et.al.* (1996), "Mutual Finance and the Poor: A Study of the Federation of Thrift and Credit Co operatives (SANASA)in Sri Lanaka" in Hulme and Mosley (1996).

Hussain, M. (1998), " Credit for Alleviation of Rural Poverty: The Gramin Bank in Bangladesh", Research Paper No.4, International Food Policy Research Institute, Washington.

Yaron, J. (1992), "Rural Finance in Developing Countries", World Bank, Washington.

Yunus, Muhammed (1999), "Banker to the Poor: Micro Lending and Battle Against World Poverty", *Pacific Affairs*, New York.

http://www.kudumbashree.org

Table–1
Select Models in Microfinance

1. Kuluthupuzha CDS	
2. Started Kudumbashree operations.	July 2002
No. of NHGs.	233
No. of Members covered.	4640
Thrift mobilized.	Rs. 30,98,860
Loans issued.	Rs. 30,72,330
Capital mobilized.	
Linkage Banking.	Rs. 141,30,700
No. of NHGs linked.	88
SGSRY.	Rs. 22,76,500
PMRY.	Rs. 7,50,000
Enterprises started.	
Individuals.	2200
Group.	64
2. Kinanoor–Karinthalam CDS	
Started Kudumbashree operations.	April 2000
No. of NHGs formed.	210
No. of Members covered.	4730
Thrift mobilized.	Rs. 1,54,30,360
Loans issued.	Rs. 7,45,38,680
Capital mobilised	
Linkage Banking	Rs. 12,00,000
No. of NHGs linked.	143
3. Nedumkandam CDS	
Started Kudumbashree operation.	April 2000
No. of NHGs.	331
No. of members covered.	6750
Thrift mobilized.	Rs. 88,24,000
Loan issued.	Rs. 1,28,10,000
Capital mobilized.	
Linkage Banking.	Rs. 20,00,000
No. of NHGs linked.	33

Source: Self-compiled.

Table–2

Some Select *Kudumbashree* Production Units and Their Activities in Kannur and Kasargod Districts

Sl. No.	*Name of the Unit*	*Panchayat/Ward*	*Products*	*No. of Persons*
1.	*Udaya*	Karivellur	Chapals, Leather Products	20
2.	*Pulari*	Mokeri	Curry Powder	16
3.	*Salaya sangamom*	Mangattidam	Umbrellas	30
4.	*Puthuma*	Payam	Building Materials	23
5.	*Archana*	Punnad	Agricultural Farming	20
6.	*Samata Desabandhu*	Mangattidam	Electric Chalk	
7.	*Kairali*	Karivellur	Milk supplies	23
8.	*Gramashree*	Kalliassery	Hotel	7
9.	*Ambili*	Mangattidam	Garments	17
10.	*Souhrida*	Kunian	Washing Powder	
11.	*Aiswarya*	Uliyil	Telephone Mats	
12.	*Gramashree*	Puthur	Grocery shop	21
13.	*Navodaya*	Nellikkunnu	Bakery/Chicken	26

Source: Self-organized.

Annexure–I

List of Micro Enterprises (District-wise)

As on 31-01-06

Sl. No	*Name of District*	*DWCUA*	*USEP*
1.	Thiruvananthapuram	173	1671
2.	Kollam	51	1825
3.	Pathanamthitta	28	577
4.	Alappuzha	142	1818
5.	Kottayam	57	535
6.	Idukki	7	96
7.	Ernakulam	344	1633
8.	Thrissur	131	1016
9.	Palakkad	61	1380

(Contd...)

Sl. No	Name of District	DWCUA	USEP
10.	Malappuram	65	827
11.	Kozhikkode	164	1864
12.	Wayanad	12	102
13.	Kannur	72	1442
14.	Kasargod	38	596
	Total	**1345**	**15382**

Source: www.kudumbashree.org.

Annexure–II

List of Group Micro Enterprises in Urban Area

Sl. No.	Name of Project	No. of Units
1.	Direct Marketing	87
2.	IT unit	63
3.	Clean Kerala Business	62
4.	Soap making unit	55
5.	Catering Service	55
6.	Canteen	53
7.	Ethnic Delicacies	47
8.	Dairy unit	46
9.	IT @ School	45
10.	Garments/Readymade	45
11.	Hotel	41
12.	Provision Store	32
13.	Super Market	32
14.	Tender Coconut selling unit	32
15.	Laundry unit	31
16.	Kerashree (Coconut processing/Oil extraction unit)	29
17.	Mat Weaving/Cover making unit	27
18.	Food Products	25
19.	Paper Cover and Paper Bag	25
20.	Remedial Education Centre	25
21.	Curry Powder unit	23

(Contd...)

Sl. No.	Name of Project	No. of Units
22.	Umbrella Manufacturing	21
23.	Mobile Market (Pick up van)	20
24.	Book Binding unit	20
25,	Agricultural Nursery	19
26.	Bakery/Sweet Products	19
27.	KSRTC Canteen	19
28.	Sanitation unit	17
29.	Tailoring unit	17
30.	Grinding unit	16
31.	Solid waste processing unit	16
32.	Fish vending unit	15
33.	Palm mat unit	14
34.	Bag manufacturing	13
35.	Pickles making	12
36.	Consumer Store/Traders	11
37.	Chappel making	11
38.	Coconut Products	9
39.	Coir Yarn/Products	8
40.	Vanila Nursery	8
41.	Bamboo Products	8
42.	Cloth Bag unit	7
43.	Note Book Manufacturing	7
44.	Metal Crushing unit	6
45.	Neighbours-Support Services to Friends	6
46.	Handicrafts	6
47.	Beauty Parlour	5
48.	Bricks/Hollow bricks	5
49.	Flowers and Garland	5
50.	Toy Manufacturing	5
51.	Computer Hardware unit	5
52.	Hospital Restaurant	5

(Contd...)

Sl. No.	Name of Project	No. of Units
53.	Telephone Repair	5
54.	Herbal Nursery	4
55.	Hosiery unit	4
56.	Prasoothika	4
57.	Rice/Rice Powder Business	4
58.	Chicken Stall	4
59.	Cooking mate/Gas light/Decoration (Hiring service)	3
60.	Electronic unit	3
61.	Fish/Sea shell processing	3
62.	Instant Mix Manufacturing unit (Palada)	3
63.	Paddy Cultivation	3
64.	Pappad making unit	3
65.	United Services	3
66.	Water Meter Repair unit	3
67.	Multi Purpose Job Club	3
68.	Chips unit	3
69.	Vegetable Vending	3
70.	Agarbathi/Candle unit	2
71.	Atta Packing	2
72.	Construction work of women	2
73.	Courier Service	2
74.	Day Care centre	2
75.	Documentation/File works unit	2
76.	Electronic Choke Assembling unit	2
77.	Furniture Manufacturing	2
78.	Ice Cream Parlour	2
79.	Marketing unit	2
80.	Ornaments Manufacturing unit	2
81.	Painting unit	2
82.	Pandhal unit	2
83.	Poultry Farm	2

(Contd...)

Sl. No.	Name of Project	No. of Units
84.	Printing unit	2
85.	Shawl/Pardha Making	2
86.	Tarpolin Production/Chackuviri	2
87.	Women Hostel	2
88.	Fire Wood	2
89.	Photo Album	1
90.	Bio Technology	1
91.	Cashewnut Processing	1
92.	Cement Products	1
93.	Handloom Weaving	1
94.	Home Nursing unit	1
95.	Networks	1
96.	Plastic Chair and Mat	1
97.	Pottery unit	1
98.	Soda making	1
99.	Solar Cooker	1
100.	Sound System	1
101.	Vehicle Service	1
102.	Wire Coir Carpet making unit	1
	Total	**1345**

Source: www.kudumbashree.org.

9

Interweaving of Economic Growth, Environmental Protection and Sustainable Development of India

Dr. Lingaraj Patro and Jhum Jhum Das

India can be enumerated in the list of fastest growing economies in the world today. The reforms introduced in the country since the early 1990s have accelerated India's growth at 6-Plus per cent on an average since 1992-1993. During the next 50 years the growth of Indian Economy by leaps and bounds would make it emerge as conspicuous force in the world economy. If the speed continues in less than 40 years the share of Indian economy along with some other developing economies would be larger than the G-6 in US dollar terms. India's noticeable growth will lead to high returns and increased demand for capital which will again bring about higher economic success.

The range of real GDP growth in India is 7.5-8.0 per cent during 2006-07. Significant increase in industrial production, electricity generation, exports, services sector, foreign exchange reserves, lower revenue deficit decrease in poverty, rise in employment ratio join hands to make Indian economy faster.

Accelerating Growth Potential of Indian Economy

Indian economy grew by 8-5 per cent in 2003-04, the initial growth for 2004-05 were between 6.2 to 7.4 per cent. The central statistical organization has made an advanced estimate at 9 to 10 per cent for the year 2007. The performance of services sector and manufacturing industries boost the growth pace. The performance of the Indian economy during the 10th plan was over 8 per cent. The industry sector which accounts for about 26 per cent (till 2005) of GDP, increased by 9.0 per cent. Manufacturing brings four fifths of industrial output. The fastest growing categories contain textiles, basic metal and alloys, and transport equipment. Exports of clothing and textile to the U.S.A. went up by 34 and 22 per cent respectively in value terms in the year 2005. Exports of clothing and textiles to the European Union rose by 16 per cent in value terms in this period. It indicates a significant improvement in unit values. Growth in the transport equipment sector reflects the emergence of Tamilnadu state as an international cynosure for automobile component manufacturing.

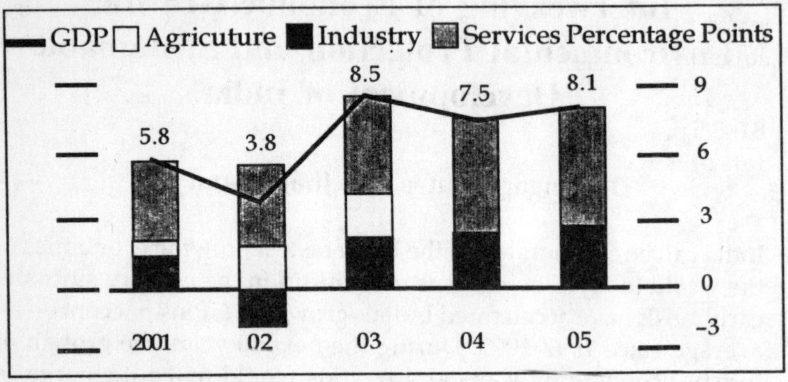

Source: Central Statistical Organization.

Contributions to Growth (Supply)

In the recent years India's services sector has risen fast. Literate young masses have brought laurels to the country. There is availability of vast skilled labour.

In the external sector, Indian economy is going to capture 1 per cent of the global trade in near future. Growing competitiveness of our manufacturing sector is indicated by merchandise exports growth of 24 per cent per annum, on average, in the past four years. Improvements in infrastructure accounts for its competitiveness encourages investment in the export production. Due to growing population demand for consumer goods is expected to grow immensely in near future.

The growth patterns over the past 50 years show that the Indian economy is riding on a trend of accelerating growth rising from 3.5 per cent upto the 1970s to 5.4 per cent in the 1980s and further to 5.9 per cent in the 1990s. Growth pace, especially in 1990s, was because of growth of services. Services growth of 7.8 per cent during 1990s, 6.1 per cent during 1980-91 and 2.7 per cent during 1950-70 was higher than growth in agriculture and industry. Industrial growth has also increased. The share of services in GDP went up from 27.9 per cent to 50.8 per cent between 1950-51 and 2002-03. In 2005 Indian economy grew by 8.1 per cent. On the supply side growth was accelerated by the opening up of space for private investment. India is consolidating its fiscal position. It is doing so while ensuring both adequate infrastructure improvements to support industrial and high skill services development and public investment to advance rural productivity. It is also improving the investment area by lowering the cost of doing business development.

The annual average growth rate over 2006-2010 is likely to exceed 8.0-8.5 per cent. The following data reflect an upward trend in growth rate of Indian economy during Five-Year Plan period.

Growth Rate of Indian Economy During Five Year Plans (GDP, % Per annum)

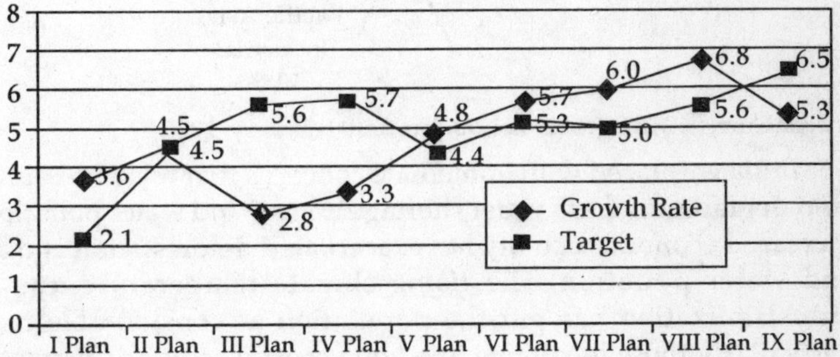

Source: National Accounts Statistics, 200 CSO.

Environmental Threat

According to the latest scientific assessment, the earth's climate system has demonstrably changed on both global and regional scales since the preindustrial era. Further evidence shows that most of the warming (of 0.10C per decade) observed over the last 50 years, is attributable to human activities. The Intergovernmental Panel on Climate Change (IPCC) projects that the global mean temperature may increase between 1.4 and 5.8 degrees Celsius © by 2100V. This is happening so due to rampant exploitation of natural resources for economic growth. It is expected to have severe impacts on the global hydrological system, ecosystems, sea level, crop production, and related processes. The impact is particularly severe in the tropical areas, which mainly consist of developing countries, including India. Hence, this environmental concern, resulting from rapid economic growth, is one of the most important challenges confronting India today. It has implications for food production, natural ecosystems, freshwater supply, health, etc.

Per cent Cumulative Global CO_2 Emissions from Industrial Sources and Land use Change During 1900-1999

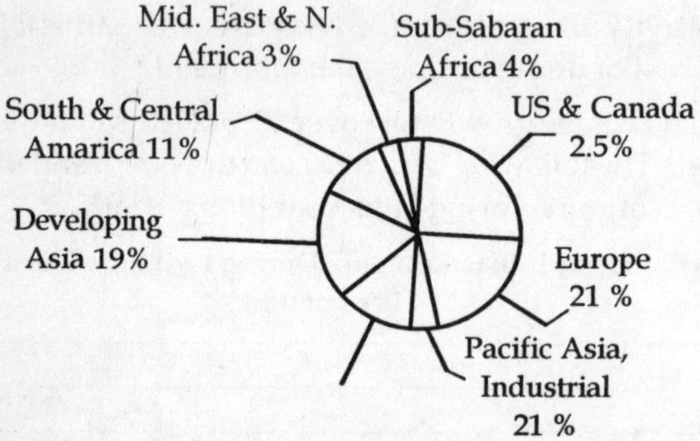

Source: Current 316 Science, Vol. 90, No. 3, 10 February, 2006.

India was faced with immediate concerns that relate to health, land degradation fresh water shortage and air and water pollution. Increased economic activity has exacerbated deforestation and air and water pollution. The rising climate temperature due to industrialization has put the population at considerable risk. Particularly those inhabiting low lying coastal areas are at greater risk of social and economic disruptions.

India's Economic Development activities have, carried with itself the seeds of environmental destruction. Activities such as manufacturing, processing, transportation, and consumption have not only depleted the stock of natural resources but also are adding stress to the environmental system by accumulating the stock of wastes. The pollution of water, air, atmosphere, and noise has emerged as the by-products of rapid economic development, particularly industrialization and urbanization. Frequent droughts, floods, rising temperature etc. as witnessed recently are some instances.

Pollution is an "external cost sometimes called as a "neighbourhood cost." Untreated or improperly treated waste incurs not only private but also social costs. The environmental degradation occurring due to rapid economic growth is causing irreversible damage in terms of human lives and loss of productivity. The move towards urbanization and industrialization has placed significant pressure on its natural resources and ecology. Air, water and land pollution has continued to worsen. The repid industrialization in India's booming metropolises have caused serious health problems.

Despite a greater commitment by the Indian Government to protect public health, forests and wildlife—The Environment Protection Act, 1986, creating the Ministry of Environment and Forests (MoEF) etc., still the importance of integrating environmental strategies into the development plan for the country is lacking. Policies geared to develop the country's economy have taken precedence over environment in the last 20 years. While industrial development has contributed significantly to economic growth in India, it has done so at a price to the environment. Industrial effluents and emission of carbon monoxide have endangered the environment. Not only industrial pollution in increasing public health risks, but the abatement efforts are also not upto the mark. Hence, the rapid pace of economic development without adequate environmental considerations is causing serious environmental damage, therefore, affecting the quality of life of the present and future generation.

Carbon Emission

India's energy consumption is increasing rapidly, from 4.16 quadrillion Btu (quads) in 1980 to 12.8 quads in 2001. This 208 per cent increase is largely the result of India's increasing population and the rapid urbanization of the country. Higher energy consumption in the industrial, transportation, and residential sectors continues to drive India's energy usage upwards at a faster rate even than China, which experienced a 130 per cent increase in energy consumption from 1980 to 2001.

Coal accounts for just over 50 per cent (6.5 quads) of India's energy consumption. The power generation sector uses the majority of this coal. Petroleum (4.4 quads) makes up 34.4 per cent of India's energy consumption, while natural gas (6.5%) and hydroelectricity (6.3%) account for much of the remainder. Natural gas is growing in importance, as its share of India's energy consumption has risen from just 1.4 per cent in 1980, while hydroelectricity—which made up 11.5 per cent of the country's energy usage in 1980—has declined in relative importance. Nuclear (1.7%) and geothermal, wind solar, and biomass (0.2%) made up a very small share of the country's energy consumption in 2001. As a result the level of carbon in the atmosphere goes on increasing.

INDIA'S FUEL SHARE OF ENERGY CONSUMPTION 2001 (BTU)

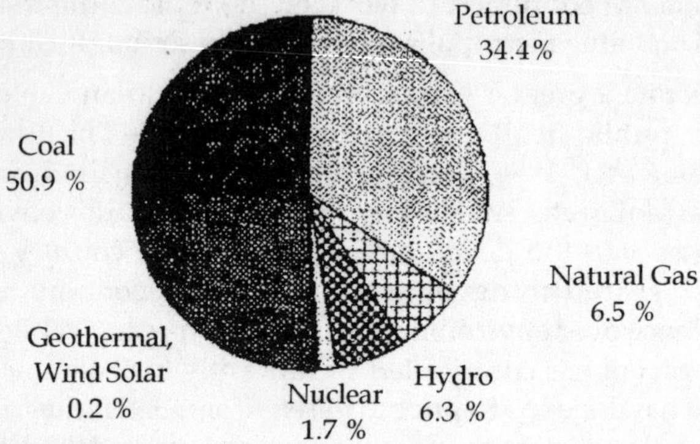

Source: EW

Industrialization and urbanization have resulted in a profound deterioration of India's air quality. India has more than 20 cities with populations of at least 1 million, and some of them – including New Delhi, Mumbai, Chennai and Kolkata are among the world's most polluted. Urban air quality ranks among the world's worst. Of the 3 million premature deaths in the world that occur each year due to outdoor and indoor air pollution the highest number are assessed to occur in India.

The main factors contributing to urban air quality deterioration are growing industrialization and increasing vehicular pollution. It has been aggravated by development that typically occur as countries Industrialize: growing cities, increasing traffic, rapid economic development, and industrial growth, all of which are closely associated with higher energy consumption. Industrial pollution is concentrated in industries like petroleum refineries, textiles, pulp and paper, industrial chemicals, iron and steel and non-metallic mineral products. Small scale industries especially foundries, chemical manufacturing and brick making are also significant polluters. In the power sector, thermal power which constitutes bulk of the installed capacity for electricity generation is an important source of air pollution.

Vehicular emission and untreated industrial smoke is a major contributor of air quality degradation. Continued urbanization has exacerbated the problem of rapid industrializations. One of the most affected cities is New Delhi, where airborne particulate matter (PM) has seen registered at levels more than 10 times India's legal limit. Vehicles are the major source of this pollution, with more than three million cars, trucks, buses, taxies, and rickshaws already on the roads.

Level of Air Pollution in the Metro Cities

Name of the Metro City	*Level of air pollution (micrograms/m²)*		
	SO_2	NO_2	*SPM*
1. Calcutta	6.0-122.0	6.0-73.1	77.3-833.3
2. Chennai	2.4-161.6	1.8-55.5	26.6-351.4
3. Coimbatore	0-8.9	0.3-19.1	2.5-133.0
4. Delhi	10.1-85.1	20.1-104.5	145.3-929.8
5. Hyderabad	5.1-70.7	7.5-124.13	59.3-458.0
6. Kochi	3.2-54.3	1.7-137.0	10.5-271.1
7. Mumbai	6.1-111.7	5.4-115.8	60.6-473.2
NAAQ/Standards	15.0-80.0	15.0-80.0	70.0-360.0

NAAQ*:* National Ambient Air Quality Standards.
Source : Central Pollution Control Board.

Vehicular traffic is the most important source of pollution in all the mega cities. The number of vehicles in these cities has increased manifold. This increase has been characterized by a boom in private transport. Other reasons for high vehicular pollution are two stroke engines, aged vehicles, congested traffic, poor roads and made structures and to country's ecology I general. It has severe health effects:

Health Effects Associated Different Types of Air Pollution

Cause	Effects due to prolonged exposure
Lead	Affects circulatory, reproductive, nervous and renal systems: suspected of lowering learning ability in children; hazardous even after exposure ends.
Particulate Matter	Fine particles may cause lung cancer; a strong correlation exists between suspended particulate and infant mortality in urban areas.
Carbon Monoxide	Affects foetal growth in pregnant women and tissue

(Contd...)

	development of young children; impairs perception and thinking. Slow reflexes and causes drowsiness, can cause unconsciousness and death.
Sulphur Dioxide	Exacerbates asthma, bronchitis and emphysema; causes coughing and impairs lung function.
Toxic Substances	Suspected of causing cancer, reproductive problems and birth defects; benzene is a known carcinogen.

Source : Asia-Pacific Environmental Outlook, UNEP, 1997.

Water Pollution

The quality of water has also suffered due to rapid economic growth. Organic pollutants from industries, discharges of domestic sewage and run off from land based industrial activities have severely affected water value. Water bodies such as lakes, rivers and underground water table is also affected. High bacteriological and heavy metal contamination has added to severe pollution.

Water quality is assessed by biochemical oxygen demand (BOD) values. A value of 6 mg/litre and above is treated to be good. Water quality, with regard to organic and bacterial pollution as observed during the year 1997 for the country as a whole, indicates that about 65 per cent of observations had quality below 3 mg/litre and only 14 per cent had more than 6 mg/litre. A number of chemical and other industries discharge their effluents into the coastal water. Furthermore, coastal areas are exposed to environmental stress like unplanned and improper developments without appropriate coastal zone management plans and shipping and sea-based activities leading to oil spills, sludge disposal and petroleum and gas exploration. The impact of climatic changes can be seen in the forms of rise in sea level (coastal flooding), erosion, storm surges, and intense wave activity.

More seriously, however, India faces a crisis of clean and potable water supply. In the country as a whole, approximately 60 per cent of the people do not get safe water for drinking and personal hygiene. Recently, a Union Minister said that over 25 per cent of the urban population in India does not have safe water and 65 per cent do not have a sewage system. It is estimated that the daily average supply of water per person in Delhi, Calcutta, Bombay and Madras is 180, 140, 130 and 80 liters, respectively. Limited supply, poor quality of water and waste are some of the major problems affecting urban areas. Considering the pace of industrial growth it is quiet certain that the water problem will further worsen.

Its water is polluted by the endless streams of effluents and poisonous gases discharged by industries, power generators, transportation systems; and other human activities. The modern agriculture has further aggravated water problem by supplying nitrogen fertilizers, insecticides, pesticides and herbicides, which are washed off by rains into rivers and the sea. Because of which many heavy metals like, mercury, lead, and cadmium are found in its water table and river bodies. Many chronic diseases such as jaundice, cholera, and gastroenteritis, related to impure consumption of water have started occurring quite frequently. Large and small water bodies in the country have become reservoirs of large quantities of effluents discharged indiscriminately. The major sources of pollution are petroleum, chemicals, paper and pulp and sugar industries.

The deteriorating ground water quality due to pollution from pesticide leaching and toxic metal leaching from the industrial effluents has had serious health effects on people all over the country. Arsenic poisoning has been detected far above the acceptable levels in drinking water in many districts of West Bengal, where thousands of people have already been diagnosed with poisoning symptoms. Arsenic in groundwater above the WHO maximum permissible limit of 0.05 mg/I has been found in six districts of West Bengal covering an area of 34,000 kms with a population of 30 million. At present 37 administrative blocks by the side of the river Ganga and adjoining areas are affected. More than 800,000 people from 37 villages/wards are drinking arsenic contaminated water and amongst them at least 175,000 people show arsenical skin lesions. Further water-borne diseases like diarrhoea and cholera claim a large no. of lives every year in the country. In 1990, there were almost 10 million cases of acute diarrhoea, 1.8 million of malaria and 3700 of cholera. It is estimated that 1.5 million pre-school children in India die every year from diarrhoea, and that dysentery and gastroenteritis are responsible for 60 per cent of the total urban deaths.

Land

One of the major impacts of rapid industrialization and urbanization has been on the land use pattern in India. Changes in the land use pattern bring associated ecological changes. Following mentioned is an overview of the land use pattern and the transformation that has taken over the period. According to the following data, Agriculture emerges as the dominant category with an increase in its share from about 42 per cent in 1950/51 to 47 per cent in 1993/94. The next major land use category for India is Forests which accounted for 22 per cent in 1993/94 and was 8 per cent higher as compared to 1950/51. The only other category to register an increase in its percentage share includes area under non-agricultural uses although the increase is quite modest from 3 to 7 per cent. In addition, barren and uncultivable land, fallow and other uncultivated land have recorded a decline in percentage terms over the period 1950/51 to 1993/94. It is understandable that, there has been an increase since then.

Changes in Land Use Pattern for India 1950/51 to 1993/94

	Units	*1950/51*	*1960/61*	*1970/71*	*1980/81*	*1990/91*	*1993/94(P)*
Total geographical areas	Mha	328.73	328.73	328.73	328.73	328.73	328.73
Reported area for land use	Mha	284.32	298.5	303.8	304.2	304.86	304.86
Forest area	(%)	14.24	18.09	21.03	22.19	22.24	22.44
Barren and unculturable land	(%)	3.29	4.97	5.42	6.46	6.92	7.23
Other uncultivated land	(%)	17.39	12.61	11.54	10.62	9.91	9.61
Fallow land	(%)	9.89	7.64	6.54	7.88	7.66	7.88
Net area sown	(%)	41.76	44.62	46.17	46.02	46.91	46.61

Source : Agricultural Statistics at a Glance, Ministry of Agriculture, March 1997.

The economic growth of India has increased the intensity of land use pattern, which has led to land degradation and loss of vegetation cover. The following data shows the extent of soil degradation that has occurred over the years.

In 1997, more than 57 per cent of the total area is degraded which was 53 per cent in 1994. Soil erosion due to water and wind actions emerge as the dominant type of soil degradation. The percentage share of land affected by soil erosion was as high as 86 per cent in 1994 as against 81 per cent in 1985 indicating worsening of the situation over time. It can be said that much of the soil in India is already degraded, is being degraded, or is at the risk of degradation.

Status of Soil Fertility in India (M.H.A.)

Sources Degradation Type	*National Commission on Agriculture* (NCA)	*Bali and Kanwar*	*Ministry of Agriculture Cooperation*		*Sehgal and Abrol (NBSS and LUP)*	
	1976	1977	1980	1985	1994	1997
Water erosion		90.0			148.9	
Wind erosion		50.0				
Total Erosion		50.0				148.9
Total Erosion	**150.00**	**140.0**	**150.0**	**141.2**	**162.4**	**167**
Saline and Alkali Soils	7.0	7.0	8.0	9.4	10.1	11
Water Logging	6.0		6.0	8.5	11.6	13
Shifting Cultivation		3.0	4.4	4.9		9
Total	**163.0**	**150.0**	**168.4**	**175.06**	**174.97**	**187.8**

- Estimate based on rates of different areas of degradation.
- Estimates by regressing with irrigated one largely due to faulty irrigation practices.

Increased economic pressures and greater aspiration are one of the major causes of land degradation in India. In order to obtain sufficient food and income and to meet immediate need farmers and other end users resort to improper crop rotations and unbalanced fertilizer use.

Most of the land area in the country shows evidence of degradation, thus affecting the productive resource base of the economy. Out of the total geographical areas of 329 million hectares, 175 million hectares are considered degraded. While soil erosion by rain and river in hill areas causes landslides and floods, deforestation, overgrazing, agricultural practices, mining and non-environmental friendly development projects have resulted in soil erosion and the presence of heavy metal in land. For instance, the current annual withdrawal of fuel wood is estimated at 235 million cubic meters against a sustainable capacity of about 48 million cubic meters. The annual demand for industrial wood is about 28 million cubic meters against the production capacity of 12 million cubic meters.

Soil Erosion and Land Degradation (Million Hectares)

1.	Total Geographical Area	328.7
2.	Area Subject to Water and Wind Erosion	141.3
Area Degraded through Special Problems		
3.	Water Logged Area	8.5
4.	Alkali Soil	3.6
5.	Acid Soil	4.5
6.	Saline Soil including Coastal Sandy Areas	5.5
7.	Ravines and Gullies	4.0
8.	Area Subject to Shifting Cultivation	4.9
9.	Riverine and Torrents	2.7
	Total 3 to 9	**33.7**

Over exploitation, and loss due to rapid industrial growth is leading to the extinction of various plants and species. According to certain estimates, over 1500 plant species are endangered and about 79 mammals, 44 birds, 15 reptiles, 3 amphibians and several insects are listed as endangered. In fact it is contributing slowly to biological impoverishment of the country.

Sustainable Development

India's ongoing rapid economic growth has placed tremendous pressure on the country's environment. The rapidly growing population, along with urbanization and industrialization, has placed significant pressure on its ecology. Deforestation, soil erosion, water pollution, and land degradation continue to worsen. As the Indian economy develops, one of the greatest challenge that it will face is to sustain that development in an environment friendly manner. Because growth do not have any meaning if it comes with at the cost of good health, dirty water/river bodies, polluted air and land. The productivity of its economy depends on the supply and quality of environmental resources. While, water, soil and air are productive assets, their pollution somewhere contravenes the pace and quality of economic development. India faces significant challenges in balancing its increased quest for economic growth with the need to protect its environment from further damage. Rapid industrialization and urbanization makes the tasks even more difficult, as increased vehicular emission contribute to existing air pollution problems, urbanization raises serious health risks from that pollution. Hence, the need for sustainable development is high for India.

The immediate and long-term impact of fast industrialization and environmental damage cannot be overlooked. Environmental consciousness has to be considered a part of the development process; any future economic strategy must consider this factor.

Integrating sustainability into the domestic supply chains can generate new trade opportunities. Producers can win access to new market, secure and even expand market share in existing areas. Thus, when India's largest textile producer obtained the Ecotext standard for its products in 1995, it gained an 8 to 10 per cent price advantage and its market grew by a tenth in the first year. Furthermore, companies can earn powerful internal productivity benefits from investing in improved labor practices and resources use. Hence, environment and development can be reconciled either through the market, state or through a combination of both. Scope for it certainly exists, but needs to be nurtured.

National Sustainable Development Strategy

National strategy for sustainable development competes with many deeply entrenched values. It forces a reconciliation of the short-term gains with long-term planning, goal of economic growth with environmental and social sustainability, advantages of policy coherence through greater coordination with the move toward decentralization. These are all difficult challenges to which there are no easy answer.

For over a decade now, the United Nations has been asking all countries to pursue strategic and coordinated action for sustainable development through the creation of national sustainable development strategies. This call was first made at the 1992 UN Conference on Environment and Development (UNCED) and through its programme of action for sustainable development—Agenda 21—the conference asked countries to adopt a national strategy for sustainable development to "build upon and harmonize the various sectoral economic, social and environmental policies and plans that are operating in the country." Way for sustainable development cannot be charted in advance. Rather, it must be navigated through a process of learning, adaptation and innovation.

Poverty Eradication and Sustainable Development

Poverty and a degraded environment are closely inter-related, especially where people depend for their livelihoods primarily on the natural resource base of their immediate environment. Restoring natural systems and improving natural resource management practices at the grassroots level are central to strategy to eliminate poverty. The survival needs of the poor force them to continue to degrade an already degraded environment. Removal of poverty is therefore a prerequisite for the protection of the environment.

Development has to be conscious of its long-term as well as immediate impacts. The problems are complex and the choices difficult.

Avoiding Unsustainable Patterns of Consumption and Production

Increasing consumerism linked with market driven purchasing power and wasteful consumption is putting tremendous stress on the environment. It is important to put a check on this through education and public awareness. In several areas, desirable limits and standards for consumption and production need to be established and applied and applied through appropriate mechanisms including education, incentives, and legislation. In India, several traditional practices that are sustainable and environment friendly continue to be practised by the people. This need to be encouraged. Technologies exist through which substantial reduction in consumption of resources is possible. Efforts to identify, evaluate, introduce, and use these technologies must be made.

Protecting and Managing the Natural Resource Base

The integration of agriculture with land and water management, and with ecosystem conservation is essential for both environment sustainability and agricultural production. An environment perspective must guide the evaluation of all development projects, recognizing the role of natural resource in local livelihoods. A comprehensive understanding of the perceptions and opinions of local people about their stakes in the resources base must inform this recognition. To ensure the sustainability of the natural resources base, the recognition of all stakeholders in it and their roles in its protection and management is essential.

Integrated Approach

There is a need to develop an integrated institutional approach that can allow an analysis of inherent tradeoffs and interlinkage among the economic, social and environmental dimensions of development. Presently MOEF is working as a nodal agency, but it lacks functional coherency. Integrated sets of sustainability indicators should be identified and systemically monitored and, through an application of formal and informal approaches and tools, they are adapted accordingly. Steps towards evolving a national sustainable development indicators and reporting, sustainable development audit committees and spending reviews, sustainable development research networks should evolve.

Strategic Management

Sustainable development process calls for rethinking the current policy initiatives as well as developing new ones to address key issues. It shall include a rethinking of expenditure and revenue generation process. Most national sustainable development approach remains at the periphery of government decision making until finance ministries or departments play a central role in it. Fiscal priority by setting national expenditure and revenue generation should be encouraged.

Institutional Access

Elected officials and the courts are quiet accessible to the public and the pro-environment concerns they might bring. The corpus of laws passed in national parliament and state legislative assemblies must acknowledge voters who are concerned about environment issues. Any citizen may send a letter of complaint or a writ petition to the Supreme Court, and this letter may begin a judicial process. It is a well-known fact that writ petitions have been applied to environmental issues since 1986 and they have generated impressive results, but more needed to be done in this direction. More stringent and broader environmental orders should be passed and it should be ensured that they are enforced.

India's rapid economic development to be locally appropriate and sustainable must be guided by local consideration that lie in its diverse culture and traditions. Hence, this recognition of India's cultural diversity at the policy level must include, as an important precondition, its approach towards sustainable development.

The challenge of India's sustainable development is a complex one. It calls for more than simply managing the environment or the economy, it seeks prosperity for the poor, their involvement in the management process, assisting in finding way to live in synergy with the environment. For this to happen, we must make globalization to work by initiating the Second Generation of Economic Reform and linking the ideas and institutions with different parts of the world. Ending extreme poverty is an imperative for sustainable development; hence, there is a need to accelerate India's economic progress. India must learn to invest in the well-being of its poor. India's Science and Technology is increasing at a rapid pace. It must take this opportunity to explore avenues for technologies that can assist in sustainable development. Incentive based approach to environmental protection must be promoted. The use of market to limit pollution can be of great help. Firms must regularly report their emissions to air, water and land.

There is an urgent need for investment in environmental infrastructure like improved quality of air and water, capping greenhouse gas emissions, protection of biospheres etc. With a significant part of India's population, yet to achieve a reasonable standard of living, social issues must be an important consideration for policy makers in India. While the Indian economy has been notching up impressive gains, it is important for stakeholders operating in the Indian economy to be aware of the significant place environmental and social issues occupy in the mainstream debate in India. The Indian Government has repeatedly stressed the mantra of "inclusive growth" that is yet to be taken up by market and companies.

Endnotes

Environmental pollution is the unfavourable alteration of our surroundings, wholly or largely as a by-product of man's actions, through direct or indirect effects of changes in energy patterns, radiation levels, chemical and physical constitutions and abundances of organisms. These changes may affect man directly or through his supplies of water and of agricultural and other biological products, his physical objects or possession or his opportunities for recreation and appreciation of nature—U.S. President's Science Advisory Committee, Environmental Pollution Panel, Restoring the Quality of our Environment, Washington, D.C., U.S. Government Printing Office 1965.

REFERENCES

Adil Najam and Nick Robins, "Seizing the Future: The South Sustainable Development and International Trade", International Affairs, January, 2001, Vol. 77, No. 1, pp. 57-58.

Darren Swanson and Laszlo Pinter (2004), "National Strategies for Sustainable Development: Challenges, Approaches and Innovation in Strategic and Coordinated Action", International Institute for Sustainable Development, Manitoba, Canada, p. 1.

EIA, India: Environmental Issues, February 2004, p. 2.

Goldman Sachs, Global Economics Paper No. 99, GS Financial Workbench, p. 2.

India Economic Bulletin, December 2003, Vol. 1, No. 4, Asian Development Bank, India Resident Mission, New Delhi, p. 10.

Indian Economic Survey 2005-06.

Jayant Sathaye, P.R. Shukla and N.H. Ravindranath, "Climate Change, Sustainable Development and India: Global and National Concerns" Current Science, Vol. 90, No. 3, 10 February 2006, p. 314.

Patro, L.R. (2002), Toxicological effects of cadmium chloride on fresh water fish, Tilapia Mossambica, Peters, and its ecological implicating Ph.D. thesis submitted to Berhampur, University, Orissa.

Patro, L.R., M. Mishra and A.K. Panigrahi (2004), Eco-toxicological effects of cadmium on the Haemotology of a fresh water fish, Oreochromi's Mossambicus, Peters, National Journal of Life Science I (i), pp. 47-55.

Patro, L.R., M. Mishra, A.K. Panigrahi (2005), Impact of cadmium chloride on the ATPase activity of different organs of a fresh water fish , Oreochromis Mossambicus Peters, Journal of Industrial Pollution Control, 21(I), pp. 121-133.

Rashmi Mayur, "Environmental Problems of Developing Countries", Annals of the American Academy of Political and Social Science, Vol. 444, The Environmental and the Quality of Life – A World View", Jul. 1979, p. 93.

TERI Report No. 97/ED/52, 1998, pp. 45-46.

10

Rainwater Harvesting: A Key for Rural Development

Professor R.K. Khitoliya

A major portion of India's population (72.2%) lives in villages. Village economies are based on agriculture and livestock which supports about 70 per cent of Indian population. Thus by neglecting agriculture comprehensive development cannot be achieved. Agriculture sector largely depends upon the availability of water and rainfall pattern. With an average annual rainfall of 1,170 mm, India is one of the wettest countries in the world. Though the average rainfall is adequate, ironically three-quarters of the rain pours down in less than 120 days, from June to September making the rainfall erratic.

Out of total area under cultivation approximately 61 per cent is rainfed, thus making rainwater harvesting of paramount importance. The present chapter emphasizes means by which harvested rainwater can be used at a large scale in agriculture thereby eradicating poverty and transforming the living standards in rural areas. It observes the ways in which rainwater harvesting can prevent precious groundwater from depletion thus preventing desertification and provide affordable potable water by replacing other sources which suffers from quality and quantity problems.

The present chapter analyses the effects of rainwater harvesting on socio-economic and ecological status in rural India as whole with reference to case study of a small village in lower Shivalik hills where by active community participation rainwater harvesting has restored the ecology as well as improved the economic status of its residents. It examines the ways in which rainwater harvesting has contributed to the flora and fauna of the region.

Water has been a very important commodity in rural India since centuries. Shortage or excess of water has forced many settlements to migrate in the past. Its impact on rural life is so great that it has become part of its culture. Rural life in India is largely dependent on agriculture and livestock which are the primary sources of income. They support more than 70 per cent of Indian population either directly or indirectly.

Output from these resources depends largely on the availability of water. Unfortunately situation is not in favour on water front. With an average annual rainfall of 1,170 mm, India is one of the wettest countries in the world. Though the average rainfall is adequate, ironically three-quarters of the rain pours down in less than 120 days. In such a situation watershed management gains tremendous importance. The idea behind watershed management is to trap the water where it falls. This helps in reducing runoff losses, soil erosion and impurities in water. Water is made available in proximity to its users thus considerably reducing transmission losses. For this purpose water is conveyed utilizing gravity flow therefore eliminating the role of electricity which is hardly available in such areas.

Citing these reasons watershed management was initiated in the Shivalik hills by the Central Soil and Water Conservation Research and Training Institute (CSWCRTI). The project which later became famous as Sukhomajri Watershed Management programme, was initially conceived for reducing silt deposition in Lake Such. Such was an integral part of the master plan of city of Chandigarh as a place of relaxation, seclusion and sports. Incidently this project became a model project of watershed management for rural development. In the years to come similar projects were undertaken in other catchments. They included Bunga and Railmajra. Experience gained from previous projects helped various agencies to make future projects more economical and efficient. The progress of watershed management in Shivalik hills can be best reviewed in a chronological order.

Technical Meaning of Rainwater Harvesting

Rainwater harvesting means capturing the rain where it falls.

Various suggested ways of harvesting water are:

(a) Capturing run-off from rooftops
(b) Capturing run-off from local catchments

(c) Capturing seasonal flood water from local streams
(d) Conserving water through watershed management.

Need for Recharging Groundwater

Requirements given below, justify the need for recharging the groundwater through rainwater harvesting:

(a) To meet the ever increasing demand for water.
(b) To reduce the runoff which chokes storm drains.
(c) To avoid flooding of roads.
(d) To augment the groundwater storage and control decline of water levels.
(e) To reduce groundwater pollution.
(f) To improve the quality of ground water.
(g) To reduce the soil erosion.

Advantage of Recharging Groundwater

Following advantages are associated with groundwater recharge through rainwater harvesting:

(a) Reduces the cost for pumping of groundwater by raising to groundwater table.
(b) Provides high quality water, soft and low in minerals thus improves the quality of groundwater through dilution.
(c) Reduces soil erosion in urban areas as runoff is reduced.
(d) Rainwater harvesting is less expensive.
(e) Rainwater harvesting systems are simple which can be adopted by individuals.
(f) Rainwater harvesting systems are easy to construct, operate and maintain.
(g) In saline or coastal areas, rainwater provide good quality water and reduce salinity and also help in maintaining balance between the fresh saline water interfaces.

Components of Rainwater Harvesting System

The functional components of a rainwater harvesting system are as under:

(a) *Catchments area* : The catchments area is the surface through which rainwater runoff is harvested.
(b) *Rainfall efficiency:* Generally a loss of upto 20 per cent may take place due to evaporation and inefficiencies in collection processes. Thus collection efficiency of 80 per cent is often used.

(c) *Rainfall reliability*: Average monsoon rainfall over a period of 10 years is safely considered as reliable for arriving at the availability of water.

(d) *Availability of rainwater:* To determine how much water would be generated from a given roof area, following formula is used: Total quantity of water to be collected (cum)

= 0.8 × {Roof Area (Sqm) } × { Average Monsoon Rainfall (m) }

(e) *Inflow structures*

(i) *Gutter:* Gutters are of great significance especially in hilly terrains. Gutters collect rainwater from the root and transport it to the inflow pipe.

(ii) *Inflow pipes:* Inflow pipe or drainpipe is the pipe which connects the gutter to the filter and then to reservoir.

(iii) *Bye-pass arrangement:* A bye-pass arrangement should be made at the point where the inflow pipe is connected to the filter. The objective is not to collect first shower water. This can be done by using a stopper and a by-pass pipe just above the filter.

(iv) *Silting pit:* For recharge to groundwater reservoirs, the filter in the inflow structure is not required. The water, however, should pass through a desilting pit before entering the aquifer. A desilting pit is essential to let the suspended material settle down before the water is introduced into the aquifer.

(f) *Storage (Groundwater Reservoir)*: Rooftop rainwater collected may be recharged to groundwater reservoir through:

(i) Abandoned dug well;
(ii) Abandoned/Running hand pump;
(iii) Recharge pit;
(iv) Recharge trench;
(v) Gravity head recharge well;
(vi) Recharge shaft;
(vii) Defunct borewell;
(viii) Trench with injection wells; and
(ix) Inundation/spreading of water.

Abandoned Dug Well

Water to be recharged is guided through a pipe to the bottom of the dry/unused dug well or below the water level to avoid scouring of bottom and entrapment of air bubbles in the aquifer. Precautions to be taken are:

(a) Bottom of the dug well should be cleaned and all fine deposits should be removed before its use for recharge. Recharge water should be silt free.
(b) The well should be cleaned regularly.
(c) Periodic chlorination is required in order to control bacteriological contamination.
(d) This method is suitable for large buildings having the roof area of more than 1000 sq.m.

Abandoned/Running Hand Pump

Water is diverted from the rooftop to the hand pump through pipe of 50 to 100 mm diameter. For running hand pump, a closing valve is fitted in conveyance system near the hand pump to avoid entry of air in suction pipe. This method is suitable for small buildings having the roof area upto 150 sq.m. Care should be taken that:

(a) Recharge water should be silt free.
(b) During the period the water is being recharged, water extracted from the hand pump should be used after proper chlorination.

Recharge Pit

1 to 2 m wide and 2 to 3 m deep recharge pit is constructed to recharge the shallow aquifer. The method is suitable for small buildings having the rooftop area upto 1000 sq.m.

(a) After excavation, the pit is refilled with boulders and pebbles at the bottom followed by gravel and then sand at the top.
(b) The collected water from the rooftop is diverted to the pit through a drain pipe.
(c) Recharge water is filtered through the pit.
(d) The sand layer; in the pit should be removed and replaced every year after rainy season.
(e) Recharge pit can be of any shape i.e. circular, square or rectangular. If the pit is trapezoidal in shape, the sides' slopes should be steep enough to avoid silt deposition.

Recharge Trench

0.5 to 1.0 m wide and 1 to 1.5 m deep recharge trench is constructed to recharge the shallow aquifer. The method is suitable for alluvial soil and buildings having the of top area upto 1000 sq.m.

(*a*) After excavation, the trench is refilled with boulders and pebbles at the bottom followed by gravel and then sand at the top.

(*b*) The collected water from the rooftop is diverted to the trench through a number of drain pipes.

(*c*) Recharge water is filtered through the trench.

(*d*) The sand layer in the trench should be removed and replaced every year after rainy season.

(*e*) Recharge trench can be of any shape i.e. circular, square or rectangular. If the pit is trapezoidal in shape, the sides' slopes should be steep enough to avoid silt deposition.

Gravity Head Recharge Well

Bore wells/tube wells can be used as recharge structures. The rooftop rainwater is channelised to the well and recharged under gravity flow condition.

(*a*) The technique is most suitable in areas where groundwater levels are very deep.

(*b*) Recharge water should be silt free.

(*c*) The well can also be used for pumping.

(*d*) The number of recharge structures can be determined in limited area around the buildings depending upon the rooftop area and aquifer characteristics.

(*e*) This method is applied where land availability is limited and when aquifer is deep and overlain by impermeable strata.

Recharge Shaft

Recharge shaft is constructed where shallow aquifer occurs below clay layer. A recharge shaft is dug manually or drilled by the reverse/direct rotary drilling method.

(*a*) Diameter of recharge shaft varies from 0.5 to 3 m depending upon the availability of water to be recharged.

(*b*) Recharge shaft is backfilled with boulders, gravel and coarse sand.

(c) The bottom of the shaft should end in permeable strata i.e. sand.
(d) Recharge shaft should be constructed 10 to 15 meters away from the buildings for their safety.
(e) It should be cleaned regularly by scrapping the top sand layer and refilling it periodically.

Quantity of Water which can be Harvested

Urban Scenario

The total amount of water that is received in the form of rainfall over an area is called the *rainwater endowment* of the area. Out of this, the amount that can be effectively harvested is called the *water harvesting potential.*

Water harvesting potential = Rainfall (mm) × Collection efficiency.

Consider your own building with a flat terrace area of 100 sq. m. Assume the average annual rainfall in your area is approximately 600 mm (24 inches). In simple terms, this means that if the terrace floor is assumed to be impermeable, and all the rain that falls on it is retained without evaporation, then, in one year, there will be rainwater on the terrace floor to a height of 600 mm.

Area of plot = 100 sq. m. (120 square yards)
Height of the rainfall = 0.6 m (600 mm or 24 inches)
Volume of rainfall over the plot = Area of plot × height of rainfall
Assuming that only 60 per cent of the total rainfall is effectively harvested. Volume of water harvested = 36,000 litres (60,000 litres × 0.6).

This volume is about twice the annual drinking water requirement of a 5-member family. The average daily portable water requirement per person is 10 litres.

Rural Scenario

Community based rainwater harvesting in rural areas of India – the paradigm of the past – has in it as much strength today as it ever did before. It is, in fact, only with this rudimentary technology that people are able to survive in water scarce areas. Recognising this fact, our ancestors had learnt to harvest water in number of ways:

They harvested the rain drop directly. From rooftops, they collected water and stored it in tanks built in their courtyards. From open community lands, they collected the rain and stored it in artificial wells.

They harvested monsoon runoff by capturing water from swollen streams during the monsoon season and stored it in various forms of water bodies.

They harvested water from flooded rivers.

Let us assume that India's 587,000 villages can harvest the runoff from 200 million hectares of land, excluding inaccessible forest areas, high mountains and other uninhabited terrains, that still gives every village an average access to 340 hectares or a rainfall endowment of 3.75 billion litres of water. These calculations show the potential of rainwater harvesting is enormous and undeniable.

SUKHOMAJRI—The Model Project

Sukhomajri is a small hamlet located in Shivalik foothills 30 km north-east of Chandigarh on Pinjore-Nalagarh road at 30"53' latitude and 76"53' longitude in Panchkula district of Haryana. In 1975, village had no source of irrigation. The entire agricultural land (52 ha) was under rainfed single cropping. Small land holdings (less than one hectare per family) and frequent crop failures due to skewed pattern of rainfall made agriculture undependable. Each family was keeping large number of goats to eke out a living. Goats were allowed to graze freely in the nearby hills. Years of overgrazing had made even toughest of shrubs and grasses scrawny. Villagers resorted to illicit cutting of trees from hilly areas for fuel wood. Denudation in the surrounding hills was so fast that the hill slopes once clothed with green cover were rendered totally naked. Not even a blade of grass was to be seen. Sheer needs of sustenance forced the poor villagers to decimate the very base of their survival.

The Operational Research Project (ORP) was started in May 1975 by the Chandigarh centre of the CSWCTRI. The large scale denudation of hills near Sukhomajri was the cause of silting of Such Lake in Chandigarh. The cycle of poverty and denudation operating in the entire region of Chivalric foothills was clearly visible which typically represented soil, climate and socio-economic conditions of the region. The land use was such that the rainfed agriculture occupied the valleys and degraded forest the adjoining hill slopes. Uneven and undulating topography further added to the problems of soil erosion and impoverishment of soils.

Under a Ford Foundation financed ORP three earthen dams which were constructed to store rainwater from the barren hills which was not only going waste but also posing environmental hazards near Sukhomajri. Subsequently seven more dams were constructed in the hills around the region providing the facility of supplemental irrigation to farm lands. In a period of ten years (1976-1985), 95.6 ha forest catchments area was treated with soil and water conservation measures and 425400 cub. metres of water storage capacity was created at a cost of Rs 1.612 million to provide life saving irrigation to 181.9 ha of farm lands located in the valley area.

Table–1
Details of Dams in Sukhomajri

Name of project	*Yr of construction*	*Catchments area (ha)*	*Storage capacity (m3)*	*Command area (ha)*	*Cost (Rs.)*
Sukhomajri I	1976	4.3	8000	6.0	72000
Sukhomajri II	1978	9.2	55600	20.9	109000
Sukhomajri III	1980	1.5	9500	2.0	23000
Sukhomajri IV	1985	2.6	19300	5.0	150000

Agricultural and Economical Impacts

Local people were involved in planning and implementation of entire programme since its inception. They were engaged as daily wage workers for most of the physical works thus providing them employment.

After the implementation of the watershed the crop production was increased by nearly three times. Between 1977 and 1986, because of the availability of irrigation water, wheat production increased from 40.6 tonnes in 1977 (with a productivity of 0.68 tonnes per hectare) to 63.6 tonnes in 1986 (with a productivity of 1.43 tonnes per hectare) and maize production increased from 40.9 tonnes in 1977 (with a productivity of 0.61 tonnes per hectare) To 54.3 tonnes in 1986 (with a productivity of 1.22 tonnes per hectare) (Table–2).

Simultaneously the protection of the forest area, greatly increased grass and tree fodder availability. Protection of the watershed led to increased grass production which steadily went up from 40 kg per hectare in 1976 to 3 tonnes per hectare in 1992. Increased availability of fodder led to a transformation in the livestock composition. The number of goats went down from 246 in

1975 to 10 in 1986 while the number of buffaloes went up from 79 in 1975 to 291 in 1986. This led to increased milk production which increased from 334 liters per day in 1977 to 579 liters per day in 1986 (Table–2). This in turn lead to increased milk production. With growing prosperity, Sukhomajri's economy underwent a change. The villagers replaced their thatch-arid-mud dwellings with brick-and-cement houses and most of the houses now boast of radio sets, electric fans, sewing machines and television sets. Annual household income also increased (Table–3). A combination of public, private and community investments and the participatory efforts of the villagers produced, according to one cost benefit analysis, a rate of return of the order of 19 per cent. The Sukhomajri project proved that it is possible to get sustained development with limited financial investments from the outside. One of the most impressive savings resulting from the project was the cost of desilting the Such Lake which supplies water to the downstream city of Chandigarh. The inflow of sediment came down from 141 to 19 tonnes per hectare per year (by over 90 per cent). This saved the government Rs. 7.65 million ($0.2 million) each year in dredging and other costs.

Table–2
Impacts on Agriculture and Livestock

Particulars	*1975*	*1977*	*1981*	*1986*	*1988*
Total foodgrain production (t/yr)	45.0	65.0	154.4	182.4	185.0
Total fodder from agriculture (t/yr)	73.1	104.6	246.4	292.0	317.0
Air dry grass in hills (t/yr)	0.10	0.50	1.84	2.05	2.51
No. of goats	246	144	36	10	6
No. of buffaloes	79	129	148	291	313
Milk production (l/day)	248	334	658	995	1200

Watershed protection also resulted in increased production of a highly fibrous grass that is commonly found in the region called bhabhar (Eulialopsis binata). This grass provides good fodder when it is young but is also very good pulping material for paper mills when it is mature. This grass was very widely used traditionally to make ropes that were commonly used to make beds across north India. Villagers of Sukhomajri used bhabhar both as fodder and for sale to paper mills.

The economic benefits have been substantial. By the mid-1980s, Sukhomajri had turned from a food-importing village to a food-exporting village. In just five years, from 1979 to 1984, its household income went up from about Rs. 10,000 to Rs. 15,000. It today earns about Rs. 3, 50,000 from sale of milk and another Rs. 1, 00,000 or so is earned collectively from sale of bhabhar. The village has yet to earn anything from the wood in the forest because the forest department has not yet decided how it will share the proceeds with the villagers. But, as indicated above, it will run into several crores (10 million) of rupees. Increase in the income of villagers can be ascertained from the income of the village hill resources management society (Table–3).

Table–3
Net Income (Rs.) of HRMS Sukhomajri

Source of income	*1984*	*1985*	*1986*	*1987*	*1988*	*1989*	*1990*	*1991*	*1992*	*Mean*
Irrigation	-	152	261	1960	1153	406	1400	300	1500	805
Forage grasses	2600	1255	3550	7610	6288	5945	5462	5608	7683	5103
Bhabhar grass	-	-	-	6534	-	7709	2520	4575	8000	3048
Fish	-	-	455	1800	-	-	-	-	2500	321
Others	-	3750	-	1470	-	-	-	-	-	745
Total	2600	5157	4265	19374	7441	14060	9382	10475	19683	10022

Ecological Impacts

Ecological recovery in the area started beginning in 1980's. This was a result of massive soil conservation measures taken, which now included construction of silt retention dams. Thousands of cubic metres of silt was retained in the catchments itself which would have otherwise gone to the Such Lake. The area was treated with soil conservation measures in the form of live hedge plantations, bhabhar grass plantations and brushwood structures etc. Further, hundreds of small loose stone structures, cratewire structures, retaining walls, masonry spurs and reventments etc. were constructed along the bed of the streams so as to properly train the course of the streams and minimize soil erosion. Side by side massive afforestation schemes were taken (Table–4).

As a result of various soil conservation measures and afforestation, a sizeable part of the catchment was stabilized and

Table-4

Tree Stocking and Water Runoff from Forest Catchments

Year	*Sukhomajri reservoir no.*			*Rainfall (mm)*
	I	*II*	*III*	
1980 (trees/ha)	103	64	27	
1988 (trees/ha)	288	161	112	
	Runoff %			
1978-80	41.3	42.3	45.5	810
1986-89	14.1	24.4	40.5	

covered under thick vegetation. Some of the steep slopes also emerged as well wooded pockets as a result of the angle of repose after requisite treatment. A number of water bodies were made available to the wildlife. In many of these water remains impounded throughout the year. Micro-climatic conditions of each dam were improved. The seepage line extended down along the relief. In fact some of the streams tended to become perennial. Due to regeneration of forest vegetation several perennial and palatable grasses came up in the area. Edible fruits and drinking water became available to birds and other wildlife. There was an appreciable increase in the population of peacocks, red jungle-fowl, partridge, parrots, spotted deer, sambhar, porcupines etc. Thus soil water conservation led to emergence of pockets as models of micro-ecological recovery.

Bunga Watershed Management Project

Bunga is a small hamlet in Ambala District of Haryana State situated at 77°10′ longitude and 30°42′ latitude and 300 m above mean sea level in the foothills of Shivalik range in North India. Ecological conditions in Bunga were not very different from Sukhomajri before implementation of watershed management. People have been depending heavily on the hills for their fuel and fodder requirements. The demands went on increasing and so also the problems of hill denudation and soil erosion. Consequently the productive slopes have been rendered barren and the villagers lost their grazing grounds.

The project work at Bunga was started in 1984. It was seen as another potential success after Sukhomajri by Central Soil and Water Conservation Research and Training Institute (CSWCRTI). The planning and designing of the project was done by (CSWCRTI). The primary objective of the project was environmental improvement through rainwater harvesting for supplemental irrigation. For this purpose an earthen dam was constructed in addition, 1400 small earthen check dams (gully plugs) were also constructed.

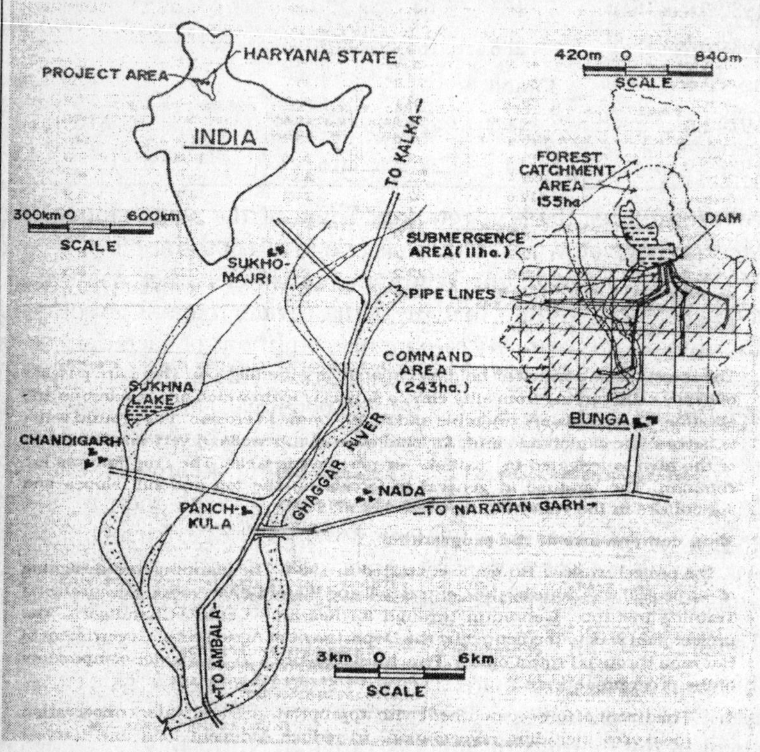

Fig. 1: Location Map of the Project Area

Details of the Water Storage Reservoir (Bunga)

Year of construction	*1984*
Forest catchment area (ha)	55
Dam height (m)	16
Storage capacity (ha-m)	59.6
Command area (ha)	243
Total cost (lakhs)	35.46
Cost per ha (Rs)	10900

Socio-Economic Impacts

The social and economic impacts have been inferred on the basis of the data collected before, during and after the project completion during a span of seven years. The data clearly shows the tremendous progress the project village has made. There has been a manifold increase in the pucca houses from mud and thatched dwellings. Economically there has been an 84 per cent growth in the income of the villagers. Apart from this the literacy rate has also improved with total literacy increasing from mere 14 to 35 per cent. It has also been observed that there has been a change in status of women with increased literacy rate. Another important fact has been brought to light that although the time of women engaged in unproductive activities like cattle grazing and fire wood collection has reduced and they are now involved in more labour intensive and fruitful work in agricultural fields.

Table–5

Improvement in Housing Patterns After the Project (area/sq.m)

Particulars	*Before the project*	*After the project*	*% increase/ decrease*
1. Covered area			
(a) Mud roof, wall and floor	8244	1688	- 388
(b) Mud roof and floor with pucca wall	575	3198	456
(c) Brick roof and wall with mud floor	239	2348	897
(d) Brick roof wall and cemented floor	108	4362	3938
2. Boundary			
(a) With mud wall and floor	3004	1478	- 103
(b) Brick wall and mud floor	880	1478	817
(c) Open boundary	749	10661	1323
3. Cattle shed			
(a) Thatched with mud wall	2130	4270	100
(b) Thatched with brick wall	563	1737	208
(c) Brick wall with mud floor	411	1271	209

REL MAJRA – Another Success Story

The project area is located just above the village of Rel Majra in tehsil Balachaur, District Nawanshahar (Latitude 31° N, Long 76° E) and 280 m above sea level. The village is situated just above the Kattardhar range of Shivalik about 9 km from Ropar on Ropar-Hoshiarpur highway in Punjab. The watershed is spread over 627

Table-6
Improvement in Educational Status in the Project Village

	Before the Project (1983-84)			After the Project (1991-92)		
	Male	Female	Total	Male	Female	Total
Read and write	5	0	5	15	0	15
Upto primary level	49	23	72	112	58	170
Middle	23	2	25	77	26	103
Matric	18	0	18	56	4	60
Intermediate	1	0	1	2	0	2
Graduate	2	0	2	7	0	7
Total	98	25	123	269	88	357
% of literacy	19	7	14	46	20	35

Table-7
Increase in Gross Income in Lakhs

Particulars	Before the project	After the project	% Increase
Agriculture	21.20	47.50	124
Animal husbandary	43.10	69.56	61
Others	4.24	10.18	140
Total	68.54	127.24	86

ha, drains into river Satluj through six seasonal streams locally known as choes. These streams used to bring heavy load of detritus and sand, which used to be deposited on agricultural fields, drains and highways thus disrupting the communication systems. The mean annual rainfall of the region was about 1149 mm, varying between a low of 613 mm to a high of about 1800 mm. It was bimodal in nature. About 80 per cent of the annual rainfall was received during the monsoon period (June end to September). Such yearly rainfall was not too low to manage two good crops, but its skewed pattern of distribution was the major concern.

A number of project interventions were carried out which involved plantation of vegetative cover in 59 ha sub catchment area of Badhole choe, tree enumeration and bio mass production among various other implementations. Amongst these the single most important was the construction of earthen dam for rainwater harvesting from 59 ha hilly catchment for supplemental irrigation to about 22 ha land. A network of about 2.9 km long underground pipeline system was laid down to convey water through gravity.

Socio-Economic Impacts

Rel Majra set an excellent example of community based participation in rural development. A village-based institution called the 'Water Users Society (WUS)' was set up to carry out all the functions related with the project and also to maintain the accounts and settle disputes among the villagers.WUS generated social funds by mobilizing various resources like collection of one time membership fee, sale of napier grass and fruit plants on community lands and leasing out the reservoir water to a contractor for fish culture. WUS now generates income out of interest from its bank deposits. WUS has been using these funds for financing various social activities. Rail Majra is one of the few villages with its own Community Centre which was funded by the village WUS.

Table–8

Social Fund Generated by Water Users Society, Rel Majra (INR)

Particulars	*1993-94*	*1994-95*	*1995-96*	*1996-97*	*1997-98*	*1998-99*	*1999-2000*	*2000-01*	*2001-02(Sept.)*	*Total*
Membership fee	400	400	550	250	–	–	–	–	–	1650
Sale of irrigation water	1040	5190	11535	12782	2202	4541	520	4675	5128	47613
Sale of napier grass	2060	4405	3825	5250	1300	1450	–	500	–	18790
Sale of saccharum munja	–	–	3700	5000	7900	6800	10000	7800	6500	47700
Sale of bhabhar grass	–	1430	1950	100	3500	2500	–	4300	–	13780
Sale of fruit plants	–	–	–	1250	–	–	500	–	–	1750
Lease of reservoir on fish	1000	5800	3000	–	–	–	–	7000	7700	24500

(Contd...)

Particulars	*1993-94*	*1994-95*	*1995-96*	*1996-97*	*1997-98*	*1998-99*	*1999-2000*	*2000-01*	*2001-02(Sept.)*	*Total*
Contribution by society members	–	–	–	–	2710	–	–	–	–	2710
Hiring of community center	–	–	–	–	–	–	–	10700	4000	14700
Interest on bank deposits	–	–	1038	454	507	–	–	–	–	1999
Grant received by Deputy Commissioner	–	–	–	–	89705	–	–	–	–	89705
Miscellaneous	–	–	–	300	–	100	500	–	–	900
Total	4500	17225	25598	25386	107824	15381	11520	34975	23328	265747

Table–9

Expenditure Incurred by WUS Rel Majra (INR)

Particulars	*1993-94*	*1994-95*	*1995-96*	*1996-97*	*1997-98*	*1998-99*	*1999-2000*	*2000-01*	*2001-02(Sept)*	*Total*
Construction of community center	–	–	–	–	100822	66029	–	4810	27371	199033
Furniture and utensils	–	–	1987	–	–	–	5925	2600	–	10512
Repair of dam/pipeline	–	150	9475	5425	2400	2400	3590	3590	1960	28990
Purchase of poplar plants	–	–	–	–	1000	–	–	–	–	1000
Electricity charges for community center	–	–	–	1737	633	235	92	771	918	4386
Hand pump for community center	–	–	–	–	–	–	–	13427	–	13427
Miscellaneous	79	–	692	–	–	–	–	–	–	771
Total	79	150	12154	7162	104855	68664	9607	25198	30250	258119

Table–10
Benefit and Cost Stream for Working Overall Economics

Year	*Benefits stream (Rs.)*	*Cost stream (Rs)*
0	754471	3363520
1	1313840	809160
2	1024281	790614
3	1877105	973085
4	1579172	1299972
5	2469849	2928151
6	2342932	1820810
7	32792341	2216311

Overall benefit = Rs. 2,30,90,820
Overall cost = Rs. 1,45,69,057
C/B ratio = 1.58

Ecological Impact

The environmental impacts of this project have also been tremendous. There has been a marked improvement in the groundwater level and also the fluctuations in the groundwater level have reduced to a considerable extent.

Apart from improvement in groundwater the vegetative cover has also changed. Now more percentage of the land is under environmentally desirable groups.

Before

After

It is clearly observed that how the vegetative pattern has changed in the area. With area under non-productive plants reducing from 29.97 ha in 91-92 to 14.23 ha in 98-99. Area under desirable plants

Table–11
Vegetation Cover Rel Majra

Groups	*1991 -92*	*1992-93*	*1993-94*	*1994-95*	*1995-96*	*1996-97*	*1997-98*	*1998-99*
Environmentally desirable like bhabhar, napier, irrigated crops, fodder crops	–	5.15	6.09	8.14	9.24	10.36	10.41	11.57
Environmentally undesirable like rainfed crops, fallow land	29.97	28.57	16.07	13.07	15.18	13.73	14.44	14.23

increased from null to 11.57 ha. This cover has two-fold beneficial as this has grown on the area, which was earlier occupied by undesirable plants and shrubs.

Conclusions

Over-exploitation of groundwater reservoir has sent water table drastically down. The various methods discussed above of recharging groundwater through rainwater will not only arrest the depleting water table but also bring out the widespread benefits.

It can be inferred from the above observations that watershed management has played a crucial role in the social, economical and ecological development of the project areas. Thus watershed management in conjunction with soil conservation is capable of catalysing change at grass roots level wherever social status is directly or indirectly linked to the availability of water. Such conditions are generally prevalent in developing countries. Watershed management practices are being implemented in other parts of India (Karnataka, Maharashtra, Tamil Nadu, North East India and Rajasthan) as well.

These projects are micro level Hydrologic schemes which can be easily installed and managed locally. Hence it is required to identify such locations around the globe with an objective of sustainable development.

REFERENCES

1. Swarn Lata Arya and J.S.Samra 1995, Socio-Economic Implications and Participatory Appraisal of Integrated Watershed Management Project at Bunga, Bulletin No. T-27/C-6, CSWCRTI, Chandigarh.

2. Grewal S.S. *et al.*, Sukhomajri Concept of Integrated Watershed Management, Bulletin No. T-26/C-5, CSWCRTI, Chandigarh.
3. S.P. Mittal *et al.*, Environmental Impact Assessment of Participatory Watershed Management in Shivaliks -Rel Majra CSWRTI, Chandigarh
4. Aggarwal R.K. *et al.*, Development of Sukhomajri Model of Integrated Watershed Management in Shiwalik foothills.
5. Mittal, S.P., Participatory Water Resource Development and Management for Sustainability in Shiwalik Foothill Watersheds.
6. Background Paper, 2003. National Conference on Water Management: Public-Private-Partnership, Ministry of Water Resources, May 27th, New Delhi.
7. V.Suresh, 1998, Financing and Private Sector Participation in Urban Water Supply Projects: Indian Experience. Worshop on Financing and Private Sector Participation in Water Resources Projects, 6th November, New Delhi.
8. S.K.Katara (2006),"Groundwater Recharge through Rainwater Harvesting". All India Seminar on Potable Water for All—Challenges and Solutions, October 13-14, New Delhi.

11

Promoting Rural Labour Banks: A Corporate Social Responsibility Perspective

Dr. P.N. Sankaran

Introduction

It is a truism that 'India lives in the villages'. An overwhelming portion of land area is rural and so are the majority of the people. But the definition of '*rural*' is residuary; what is not 'urban' is known as rural. The term '*rural settlement*' in India essentially means an area, which is characterized as non-urban in style of life, occupational structure and settlement pattern. With industrialization, better communication, facilities for education and employment, the rural settlements are getting more closely integrated with the mainstream economy and the urban centers. The rural-urban interface develops in terms of increasing incidence of the flow of people, goods, services and knowledge towards urban settlements. However, the natural tendency towards urbanization may not always bring good results to the rural settlements on the urban fringe. Thus rural India lags behind urban India in terms of its accessibility to livelihood options and basic amenities of life. The saga of those who migrate to the city for better employment, education, amenities of life, etc. gives a mixed picture of the majority forced to join the already swelling slum dwellers. Neither the fortunate minority nor the unfortunate majority gets back to their original rural settlement. While the plight of migrants from rural to urban settings is well-documented, institutional options for employment security of those who are forced to continue in the rural settlements, despite the proximity of their settlements to the mega cities, have not been examined in detail. The present chapter has been conceived in the above backdrop.

Objectives and Methodology

As already indicated at the outset, there exists large number of backward rural settlements in the urban frontier as islands unto themselves, with little prospect of accessing the socio-economic avenues available in the urban periphery. The proximate causes for the seemingly paradoxical predicament may be lack of productive assets, infrastructure, skill, education, awareness/information, access to local governments, and promotional institutions in the third sector [like cooperatives, voluntary agencies, NGOs etc]. The present study was carried out to test the above proposition in terms of empirical information. In view of the above perspective of the study, a census survey of three rural settlements was carried out in August 2004 in Anekal Taluk, Bangalore Urban District,[1] Karnataka. Centre for Rural Welfare (Jnana Jyothi), an NGO managed by the Karnataka Jesuit Educational Society at Anekal [having micro credit, educational and SHG linkage programmes in the area] collaborated effectively with the study team. The selection of the settlements was made on a random basis out of the total settlements/villages served by the NGO partner for the study. Detailed information on a household basis was collected through personal interview, using a semi-structured questionnaire under active association of community informants/SHG leaders and key animators of the supporting NGO. Simple statistical tools have been used for data analysis and interpretation.

The Study Area: Socio-Economic Profile

Anekal, one of the smallest taluks of Bangalore Urban District, lies on the border of Tamil Nadu. Nature has blessed the taluk with forests, valleys and lakes making it a viable spot for eco-tourism. Majority of the people are economically backward [mostly belonging to SC and ST category like Nayakas, Nakkipikki, semi nomads etc.] with agriculture and weaving forming their main occupation, apart from sericulture, dairy farming, poultry, looms and cottage industries. The population of Anekal according to the *Makkala Samikshe* [Census of Children 2004] is 342395 with sex ratio 871:1000 [See Table–1].

The Settlements

Madhappanadoddi, the first settlement covered by the study, is a tribal hamlet located about 22 kms from Anekal. It is on the periphery of the Kalluballu Panchayat under the Jigani Hobli. The hamlet is

Table–1
Socio-Economic Profile, Anekal Taluk, Bangalore Urban District

Area of Taluk [sq km]	*535*
No. of Panchayats	32
No. of villages inhabited	346
No. of towns	1
Total No. of families	80944
No. of town wards	23
Density of population [town]	640
Density of population [general]	309
SC/ST Population %	30
Total No. of revenue blocks	04 [Sarjapura, Athibele, Jigani, Kasaba]
Total No. of Educational Blocks	05 [Sarjapura, Chandapura, Athibele, Jigani, Anekal Kasaba]
Literacy rate	40.74% (State average 67.04%)
Total No. of Anganvadis	219
Major economic activity	Agriculture, weaving, dairy farming, poultry and cottage industries

Source: Block Education Office, Anekal, Bangalore.

home for the Kadu Pujari tribes, who first settled in the region in 1962-63, when the government allotted 80 acres of land for the entire community. At present they are left with less area of land, as part of the original assignment of land was sold or alienated in order to repay the mounting debts. They engage themselves primarily in agricultural operations for three months in an year for the cultivation of ragi. They also go to Jigani to work in the quarry, where they get a paltry sum of Rs. 30-50 per day for another two months. The remote location of the hamlet denies it most of the facilities for income earning and regular employment. The group does not participate fully in the Grama Sabha meeting, primarily because they are not aware of their rights and they lack information on Grama Sabha. Unsanitary conditions of life and malnutrition make women and children vulnerable to communicable diseases. Cases of child death, for want of medical attention, are also reported in the settlement. The government provides water and electricity, as common facility services. The leader of a local SHG narrated to the study team his personal experience of mounting debts. *Jnana Jyothi* has set up a Balawadi for children in this area. The NGO, which arranges occasional visit of health workers, proposes to set up a small community health center for the tribes, whose health would be regularly monitored by Doctors and Interns from St. John's Medical College Hospital, Bangalore.

Muthurayapanadoddi, the second settlement is an SC colony located about 30 kms away from Anekal town and comes under Kallubalu Gram Panchayat. Since the inhabitants do not have any agricultural land assigned to them by the government, most of them make a living as farm wage employees, construction workers and wage earners in brick kiln. Apart from a single teacher, newly started primary school, temporarily housed in a portion of a building, basic facilities are absent for educating the children; the state of health facility is deplorably poor, which again tells the unfortunate story of neglect by the local panchayat.

Siddayanadoddi, the third settlement, located close to Madappanadoddi on the opposite side of the village road separating the two, is an exact replica of the latter, but for the limited number of households inhabiting the tribal settlement. The settlement is situated in Inglawady Panchayat and shares all the characteristics of Madappanadoddi tribal settlement.

Socio-Economic Issues: A Discussion

Karnataka's villages have experienced diverse social and political changes in the last three decades. Most of these have occurred gradually, but over time, many have had considerable cumulative effects (Manor, 2007). In the years since 1972, agriculture in Karnataka has gradually declined in importance both economically [as people turn increasingly to non-farm incomes], and socially [as the interdependence and hierarchical bonds anchored in old patterns of agricultural production have been eroded]. According to Aurora (2004):

- The potency of hierarchy and interdependence with villages has declined.
- Links to and dependence upon external forces have increased.
- Individuals now count for more than collectivities within villages—which increases both the liberty and the vulnerability of individuals.

- The result is a society that is more open and democratic, but in which people face greater risks – since the old hierarchical order entailed not only injustices but also certain collective protections against uncertainties.

The broad lesson that may be drawn from the above observations is that the livelihood support system of the village communities, anchored in agriculture, has collapsed over the years and that they are more vulnerable to poverty, exploitation and marginalization. In other words, despite the glitter enveloping the urban economy, the villages in the periphery [sometimes characterized as peri-urban] continues to wear the pal of gloom. The above predicament has triggered our interest towards development of a viable option, given the burgeoning opportunities associated with urban growth.

The information collected from the survey is summarized in Tables 2 and 3. The insights from the survey of the above settlements on the urban fringe of Bangalore are an eye-opener in many respects. The settlements are typical examples of shocking backwardness and deprivation, where the spin off/linkages from urban growth fail to percolate to the rural surroundings of the city. Majority of the rural folk in the study area is engaged in agriculture and cultivates ragi, paddy and jowar. Ragi and green gram constitute their staple food. In areas where water is available for cultivation, paddy is grown; however, most regions are arid, with the result that many parts of the taluk face severe water scarcity. Secondary occupations comprise casual work at construction sites, brick kilns and quarries where men and women toil from dawn to dusk. Villages in the interior parts do not have proper transport facilities and the poor commute by foot. They need to cover long distances to reach their place of work or education. The most vulnerable strata is the Scheduled Caste and tribal people, who comprise nearly 30 per cent of the population. Most of the landless labour comprise the Dalit community, who often fall into debt trap for non-repayment of borrowings and lose at times their only asset, namely land, to the moneylenders. The survey has indicated two types of resources worth considering for local level development, namely:

- Tribal skill in bamboo crafts, and
- Unskilled labour with seasonal engagement in agriculture.

Employment Generation: Rationale of a Labour Bank

Bamboo, being a forest plant, is short in local supply and the people don't have direct access to it; the market for bamboo products is also unsteady because of competition from alternative packing and other materials. A better alternative would be planned/centralized utilization of unemployed [though unskilled] labour in terms of

Table–2
Socio-Economic Status of Rural Settlements

Socio-economic characteristics	*Settlements*			
	Madhappana-doddi	*Muthuyapana-doddi*	*Siddayanadoddi*	*Total/ Average*
Households	33	24	9	66
Population	178	116	64	358
Sex: Male	105	58	29	192
Female	73	58	35	166
Children	58	27	10	95
Size of family:				
Joint	9	14	5	28
Nuclear	24	10	4	38
Educational Status				
Illiterate	122	84	26	232
Primary	40	19	16	75
Secondary	1	6	3	10
Higher Secondary	0	2	0	2
Borrowings (*HHs)	29	18	3	50
Average borrowing [Rs]	7725	11438	4333	7832
Purpose of borrowing:				
Agriculture	5	2	0	7
Social (marriage, birth, funeral)	5	4	0	9

(Contd..)

Socio-economic characteristics	Settlements			
	Madhappana-doddi	*Muthuyapana-doddi*	*Siddayanadoddi*	*Total/ Average*
Consumption, health	16	5	0	21
House repair	3	7	3	13
Sources of borrowing				
Institutional	1	2	0	3
Non institutional	28	16	3	47

Source: Field Survey 2004.

Table–3

Status of Employment and Wage in Rural Settlements

Nature of Employment	Settlements			
	Madhapana-doddi	*Muthuraya-panadoddi*	*Siddayana-doddi*	*Total/ Average*
Agriculture	13	5	6	24
Farm labour	4	2	1	7
Non farm labour	20	14	4	38
Bonded labour	2	3	0	5
Village crafts (bamboo)	2	0	1	3
Domestic help	0	3	0	3
Child labour	3	4	2	9
Beneficiaries of Employment guarantee	1	2	0	3
Annual days of Employment	124	132	108	121
Average daily wage (Rs.)	60	55	50	55

Source: Field Survey 2004.

suitable institutional arrangements for accessing employment opportunities. One option in this regard would be to organize unskilled workers into people-centered participatory institutions like Labour Contract Cooperative Societies (LCCSs), affiliated to the state level cooperative structure in Karnataka. Funds of the local panchayat can be utilized to register an LCCS, under capacity building schemes for the promotion of SHGs, cooperatives etc. However, given the fact that cooperatives are, by and large, losing their autonomy and lacking professionalism in operations, a better option would be the formation of a '***Labour Bank***'[2] [under the Societies Registration Act] that would combine the core functions of LCCSs and the active support of Information Technology [IT] service and other companies in the Electronic City of Bangalore, under Corporate Social Responsibility [CSR] initiative. The proposed labour bank can receive/register deposits of labour [willingness to offer labour services] and can make investments of pooled labour through appropriate [labour] contracts with individuals/agencies in construction, house-keeping, production of goods and provision of services. To begin with, promoters of the labour bank and others in the corporate sector would be able to offer in-house contracts to the labour bank and train the labour for better employment.

Promotion of Labour Bank: CSR Perspective

According to the World Bank, CSR consists of "the commitment of business to contribute to sustainable economic development, working with employees and their families, the local community, and society at large to improve their quality of life, in ways that are both good for business and good for development". The term Corporate Social Responsibility [CSR] may be relatively new in the Indian context; but the concept is certainly not so. Our traditions of "trusteeship", "giving" and "welfare" have existed and grew. Historically too, the concept of social good has been part of the Indian psyche. Corporate India has contributed significantly to the development of the country since independence and continues to do so. The global framework and standards of CSR need some adaptation to make them applicable to the Indian context. The reason is that each stakeholder group in India is so heterogeneous, that they cannot equally access the benefits that a company's CSR activities provide. For example, unionized and organized workmen have access to the collective bargaining process whereas casual and contract labour do not. Similarly, amongst communities, some sections are more disadvantaged than others like women, tribes, girl children etc. [BCCI, 2005]. In the domain of social and community initiatives, the CSR checklist, according to TERI Corporate Social Responsibility Awards 2003-04, consists, *inter alia*, of:

- Establishment of trust/foundation/NGO by the company to implement social activities.
- Positive impacts provided by the company, which benefit the community, like employment for the disabled/poor, social infrastructure, environmental protection etc.
- Strategies adopted by the company to undertake developmental activities for the marginalized/under-privileged/poor communities.

Thus, companies look at Communities, NGOs and the Government—Union, State and Local—to pursue their social responsibility programmes.[3] It is in the above specific context of company-community partnership for employment generation that the concept of labour bank is mooted.

Aims of Labour Bank

The objectives of the proposed bank are:

- To undertake registration of labour.
- To arrange basic and skill-related training to labour.
- To find suitable employment for labour by securing small/medium contracts for execution of construction work, maintenance, house-keeping, supplies, catering, laundry, manpower supply etc.
- To acquire tools, equipments, accessories and related machinery for own use/leasing.
- To advance loans to clients in the form of labour [man days] against future repayment [wages].
- To build up/mobilize funds for financing the housing, educational, and other needs of members , through pooling the wage incomes of members and facilitation of loans for the purpose, through institutional guarantee.
- To provide essential goods and services to the registrants.
- To promote and sustain the socio-economic interests of registrants.

Conclusion

In the model outlined above, the transfer of agricultural labour to the production and service sectors of the urban industrial economy is conceived not only as a strategy to make effective use of surplus labour (without a fall in agricultural output), but also as a means of linking the workforce with the industrial sector through social responsibility initiatives of industry, the framework being corporate-community partnership for capacity-building (the labour bank). Notwithstanding the debate in the corporate circles over the key drivers in CSR (where industry initiatives are sometimes stated to be not properly built into core business pursuits/processes), the present model is fully justified as mutually beneficial to the partners in progress. The workers benefit from regular employment, training and development in education, health care, housing etc. Industry partners, on the other hand, are assured of workforce and services under social responsibility schemes in community-networking. Since avenues for contracts in construction, maintenance, leasing, house-keeping, supplies, catering, laundry, manpower supply etc. exist in Anekal [mainly because of its close proximity to the Bangalore IT hub, *Electronic City*], there is scope for a labour bank in Anekal. Construction work of Local Self Governments (LSGs) can also be undertaken in terms of preferential arrangements like *Beneficiary Contracting*. Jnana Jyothi, a reputed NGO in Anekal, would be an ideal choice for networking with corporate agencies for the promotion of a labour bank. Since the labour bank model has been visualized in a range of urban activities beyond construction works as well, it could be stretched successfully to the upcoming activities in Smart City-Cochin and the Special Economic Zones envisaged across the country.

Notes

[The chapter is a substantially modified version of the article 'Rural Labour Banks: Promoting Employment Generation' published in Kurukshetra, Vol. 54, No.11, 2006. I am thankful to the Director and the Coordinators of Jnana Jyoti, Anekal, Bangalore for facilitating the survey. Valuable services rendered by IPGDM students (2004-2005) of St. Joseph's College of Business Administration, Bangalore in connection with collection of primary data are gratefully acknowledged.]

1. Though the study areas come under Bangalore Urban District, they exhibit typical characteristics of rural settlements.
2. An interesting example of the concept of labour bank is the

Kunnathukal Grama Panchayat experiment in Thiruvanathapuram district, Kerala, conceived in the formative phase as *Labour Army*. Labour Army refers to a body of different categories of labourers with adequate training in the use of agricultural machinery such as tractor, power tiller, winnowing and spraying machines etc. to be pressed into service on request from farmers. These labourers were registered under the *Karshaka Sahaya Samithi* of the Gram Panchayat, a society registered under the Charitable Societies Act. The basic objective of the formation of the institution of labour bank was to provide land and labour saving measures to the farmers to revive the agricultural production sector while guaranteeing not less than 20 days of employment in a month of the agricultural labourers covered under the network. The name *Labour Army* has subsequently been changed to *Labour Bank* from the second stage of the institutional setup. The institutional network was later developed in the third phase into a full-fledged body encompassing labourers and farmers with diversified interventions like advancing loans to farmers in terms of labour hours which can be repaid in cash after harvesting and also by leasing in agricultural lands from part-time farmers for the cultivation of annual crops. See Mohanakumar and Girishkumar 2000.

3. For a detailed analysis of the why, what and how of CSR in India, see Shrivastava and Venkateswaran [2000].

REFERENCES

1. Aurora, G.S (2004): 'Core Issues in the Agrarian Economy and Society of Karnataka', in Baumgartner, R and Hogger, R (eds). *In Search of Sustainable Livelihood Systems: Managing Resources and Change*, Sage Publications, New Delhi, Thousand Oaks and London, pp. 247-64.
2. Bombay Chamber of Commerce and Industry (2005): *Corporate Social Responsibility Handbook*, Mumbai: BCCI.
3. Manor, James (2007): 'Change in Karnataka over the Last Generation: Villages and the Wider Context', *Economic and Political Weekly*, Vol. XLII No. 8, pp. 653-60.
4. Mohanakumar, S and Girishkumar, K.G (2000): 'Labour and Development under People's Plan: The Experience of Kunnathukal Gram Panchayat', paper presented in the International Conference on Democratic Decentralisation, pp. 23-27.

5. May 2000, Thiruvananthapuram, Kerala, organized by the Kerala State Planning Board.
6. Shrivastava, Harsh and Venkateswaran, Shankar (2000): *The Business of Social Responsibility: The why, what and how of corporate social responsibility in India.*

12

Income and Assets Generation of Beneficiaries of the Governments Sponsored Programmes: A Study with Reference to Virudhunagar District in Tamil Nadu

Dr. A. Subbiah and A. Muthumani

Introduction

The central and state governments have introduced several subsidy programmes for the welfare of the weaker sections of the community. These government subsidy programmes are implemented through various types of financial such as public and private sector commercial banks, regional banks and co-operative banks.

This chapter deals the assets generation and income generation of beneficiaries of two government-sponsored programmes SGSY and THATCO by commercial banks (PSBS and PVTBS). For the purpose of this study 300 sample beneficiaries were proportionately from four blocks namely Sivakasi, Sattur, Viruthunagar and Vembakkotai.

By means of interview schedule the income and assets of the beneficiaries before availing loans under SGSY and THATCO were collected. As like the assets and income of the beneficiaries after availing loan by giving a clear gap of not less than three years were also collected. *t test* has been used to know whether there is any significant difference in the income generation of beneficiaries after availing of loan under SGSY and THATCO. The following formula is used:

$$t = \frac{\overline{X}_1 - \overline{X}_2}{\overline{S}E\ X_1 - X_2}$$

Where,

$\overline{X}_1$ = Average per capita income of pre-loan period

$\overline{X}_2$ = Average per capita income of post-loan period

$SE_{\overline{X1}-\overline{X2}}$ = Standard error.

The following hypotheses were framed for analysis:

1. There is no significant change in per capita income of the respondents during pre and post loan periods.
2. There is no significant change in per capita income of the respondents activity wise, during pre and post loan periods.
3. There is no significant change in assets generation of the respondents during pre and post loan periods.
4. There is no significant change in assets generation of the respondents activity wise, during pre and post loan periods.

   For testing the above hypotheses, t-value was calculated. The calculated t-value was computed, with the table value of t-located from t-table for the desired level of confidence on the given degrees of freedom.

If the calculated t-value is less than the table value of 't' it indicates that the hypothesis can be accepted but if the t-value is higher than table value of 't' it indicates that the hypotheses is rejected.

Income and Asset Generation

Income Generation

The assets that are financed by commercial banks under SGSY and THATCO are expected to produce returns within a period of one year from the commencement of the project and commercialization of produce or services. The success of the loan lies in its ability to generate additional income to the beneficiaries, which results in a chain of reinvestment returns from the additional assets created. The impact of the loan on the beneficiaries has been identified in terms of its additional income-generating capacity to the families of the borrowers and it is discussed in this section.

Per Capita Annual Income

The impact of commercial bank loans under SGSY and THATCO on per capita income of the borrowers is shown in Table–1.

This distribution of average per capita income of the beneficiaries before and after receiving the loan assistance under commercial bank loan under SGSY and THATCO has been furnished in Table–1. It is observed that the percentage increase in per capita income varied between 9.36 per cent and 41.63 per cent. The highest increase in per capita income is found in the income group of below Rs. 3000, at

41.63 per cent, followed by the income group of Rs.3000-4000 where the increase was 39.31 per cent. The percentage increase in per capita income is found to decline with higher income groups.

Table–1
Impact of Commercial Bank Loan on Per Capita Income of Borrowers Per Annum

(in Rs.)

			Pre-loan Period	*Post-loan Period*		
Sl. No.	*Income Group*	*No.of Beneficiaries*	*Average per capita Income*	*Average per capita Income*	*Percentage Increase*	*t-value*
1.	Below 3,000	72	2,754.29	3,876.11	41.63	5.25*
2.	3,000-4,000	124	3,676.33	5,111.56	39.31	4.26*
3.	4,000-5,000	66	4,451.48	6,085.26	37.61	5.65*
4.	5,000-6,000	28	5,424.73	6,626.46	22.15	6.14*
5.	6,000-7,000	10	6,391.41	6,989.49	9.36	4.75*
	Overall	300	3,879.26	5,233.25	34.90	5.28*

*Significant at 5 per cent level.

The activity-wise impact on the changes in per capita income of the borrowers commercial bank loan under SGSY and THATCO has revealed that the absolute change in per capita income has been found high in agricultural and allied activities than in non-agriculture activities. Percentage-wise it is revealed as 54.28 per cent increase in per capita income in agricultural activities and 51.69 per cent increase in per capita income in non-agricultural activities. As per t-test, the null hypothesis is accepted.

On the whole, there has been a positive increase in per capita income of the beneficiaries even though the percentage increase has been observed to vary for different types of ventures. The details of activity-wise changes in per capita income has been presented in Table–2.

Data was collected regarding the family assets of the beneficiaries before and after getting financial assistance under the commercial bank loan under SGSY and THATCO in order to assess the additional income accruing to families of the beneficiaries for setting up the projects at concessional rates of interest. As per t-test, a higher income is observed during post-loan period than in pre-loan period.

Table–2
Changes in Per Capita Income of Commercial Bank Loan Under SGSY and THATCO Beneficiaries Families Sector-wise

(in Rs.)

Sl. No.	*Activity*	*No.of Beneficiaries*	*Pre-loan Period Average per capita Income*	*Post-loan Period Average per capita Income*	*Percentage Increase*	*t-value*
1.	Non-agricultural	182	2,974.65	4,466.67	51.69	3.31*
2.	Agriculture and Allied Activities	118	2,718.19	4,164.18	54.28	5.19*
	Overall	300	2,997.42	3,765.97	26.74	3.31*

*Significant at 5 per cent level.

Family Asset Positions Before and After Joining the Commercial Bank Loan under SGSY and THATCO

The distribution of assets among the four different asset classes shows the average family assets of the respondents before and after getting financial assistance as commercial banks loan under SGSY and THATCO. This has been presented in Table–3.

Table–5.3
Classifications of Family Assets Before and After Joining the Commercial Bank Loan under SGSY and THATCO

(in Rs.)

Sl. No.	*Asset Classes (in Rs.)*	*No.of Beneficiaries*	*Pre-loan Period Average per capita Income*	*Post-loan Period Average per capita Income*	*Percentage Increase*	*t-value*
1.	Below 20,000	96	16,897.48	26,117.19	55.57	5.32*
2.	20,000-30,000	128	22,467.37	37,767.19	64.85	5.19*
3.	30,000-40,000	47	39,761.89	59,417.19	50.59	4.17*
4.	More than 40,000	29	46,618.37	67,876.11	47.59	5.19*
	Overall	300	27,347.12	39,998.19	47.26	5.81*

*Significant at 5 per cent level.

As far as the assets of the family are concerned there has been an increase in the assets position of the beneficiaries after getting financial assistance under commercial bank loan under SGSY and THATCO. The percentage of increase in assets is found to be the highest, that is 64.85 per cent for those in the asset group of Rs. 20,000-30,000. It is followed by 55.57 per cent for the asset class below Rs.20,000. An increase of 50.59 per cent and 47.59 per cent in asset position is found in the asset classes of Rs. 30,000-40,000 and more than 40000/-respectively. It has been found that the commercial bank loan is successful in improving the standard of living of the borrowers families through improvement in their assets position. As per t-test, asset is found to be higher during post-loan than pre-loan periods.

Changes in family assets during pre-loan and post-loan periods for the different types of ventures are shown in Table–4.

Table–4
Changes in Family Assets During Pre-Loan and Post-Loan Periods Sector-wise

Sl. No.	*Activity*	*No.of Beneficiaries*	*Pre-loan Period*	*Post-loan Period*	*Percentage Increase*	*t-value*
			Average per capita Income	*Average per capita Income*		
1.	Non-agricultural activities	182	31,319.19	49,818.69	58.06	3.21*
2.	Agricultural and allied activities	118	21,965.66	36,466.30	62.49	4.21
	Overall	300	25,367.19	36,976.99	51.72	4.19

*Significant at 5 per cent level.

In absolute terms an increase in the assets has been found to be more in agricultural and allied activities than in non-agricultural activities. There has been 62.49 per cent increase in asset position for those engaged in agricultural and allied activities followed by 58.06 per cent increase in non-agricultural activities of the families of beneficiaries. According to the t-test, in both non-agricultural and agricultural and allied activities, the assets are more higher during post-loan than pre-loan period.

Conclusion

From the analysis, it is observed that an effort has been made to assess the impact of commercial bank credit on weaker sections in terms of income, and assets generations. It has been found that due to income generation after getting the loan there has been a very high increase in per capita income by 41.63 per cent in the income group "below Rs. 2,000", followed by 39.21 per cent the income group of "Rs. 2,000-3,000" by 39.31 per cent. The increase in per capita income is 51.69 per cent, 54.28 per cent and 26.74 per cent in non-agricultural, agricultural and allied activities and overall respectively.

As per t-test, established null hypothesis has been accepted and it may be concluded that per capita income of the beneficiaries is found to be higher during post-loan period than pre-loan period.

With regard to the asset position, it has been found that after getting the loan, the position of the beneficiaries under the asset group of "Rs. 30,000-40,000" has improved and it has been followed by the asset class "below Rs. 20,000" and "Rs. 20,000-30,000". The results of t-test have showed that there is a significant difference in per capita assets between pre and post-loan periods.

The venture-wise increase in the asset position has been found to be the highest in the case of agricultural and allied activities followed by non-agricultural activities.

The commercial banks play a vital role in the implementation of several subsidy schemes of central and state governments in Virudhunagar district (Tamil Nadu). This helps for the upliftment of weaker sections not only in Virudhunagar District but also other districts of our country.

13

NABARD Refinance Assistance for Rural Entrepreneurship Development Programme (REDP): Use Efficiency in Tamil Nadu During 1999-2000 to 2004-05

Dr. K. Prabakkar Rajkumar

Introduction

National Bank for Agriculture and Rural Development (NABARD) is established as a Development Bank for providing and regulating credit and other facilities for the promotion and development of agriculture, small scale industries, cottage and village industries, handicrafts and other rural crafts and allied economic activities in rural areas with a view to promoting integrated rural development and securing prosperity of rural areas and for matters connected therewith or incidental thereto. The main objectives of NABARD are facilitating credit flow for agriculture and rural development, promoting and supporting policies, practices and innovations conducive to rural development and strengthening and regulating rural credit delivery system through institutional development measures and effective supervision. NABARD has always keen on promoting projects, which can provide employment and accelerate capital formation in the rural areas in farm and non-farm sectors.

Importance of REDP

The Indian economy needs to generate a large number of jobs in the rural areas in the decentralised Rural Entrepreneurship Development Programme comprising small, tiny, cottage, village industries and rural artisans in order to arrest the rising unemployment and urban migration in the country. Apart from inadequate credit support, another major impediment in development of REDP is the lack of motivation, proper guidance and training for development of necessary skills for rural youth. Entrepreneurship Development is the quick and tested route for establishment of small enterprises both in the manufacturing and service sector. REDP approach becomes highly relevant where the motivation and familiarisation process coupled with access to bank credit and the support by way of escort services could enthuse rural youth with certain basic skills of hand or technology, to start income-generating enterprises.

Objective of REDP

Developing entrepreneurial and activity-oriented among the educated and unemployed rural youth by assisting Voluntary Agencies (VAs)/Non-Governmental Organisations (NGOs)/ Development Agencies (DAs) with good track record to conduct REDP for those willing to set up small/ micro-enterprises for creation of sustainable employment and income-opportunities in 'rural areas' in a cost-effective manner. The agency conducting the REDP is expected to monitor the progress of trainees in setting up their units for, at least, 2 years and also required to provide the requisite information/ feedback to NABARD.

Under REDP, NABARD has particularly provided financial assistance through State Co-operative Agriculture and Rural Development Banks, State Cooperative Banks, Commercial Banks, Regional Rural Banks, and Primary Urban Co-Operative Banks for farmhouse involving pig, sheep and goat rearing for commercial purpose. The importance of the scheme, guidelines to get financial assistance and terms and condition of NABARD for refinancing assistance under the scheme are analyzed below.

Objectives of the Study

The main objectives of the study are:

1. To study the importance of REDP and refinancing condition of NABARD under the programme.
2. To examine the trend in refinance assistance rendered by NABARD and its impact on REDP in Tamil Nadu during 1999–2000 to 2004-2005.

Methodology

The study covers the refinancing performance of NABARD for REDP in Tamil Nadu. The Study is based on the secondary data that has been collected from the Annual Reports of NABARD and its publications. The refinancing performance of NABARD has been studied by number of projects achieved the amount of refinance assistance by NABARD and assistance by financial institutions under this scheme during the study period from1999-2000 to 2004-2005.

Hypothesis

The hypothesis relating to the role of NABARD in providing refinance is formulated and tested at 5% significant level. It is as under:

Significance of the difference between top 5 and top 10 districts in respects of the mean value of projects, mean amount of refinance provided by NABARD and mean amount of financial assistance provided by financial institutions for REDP during 1999-2000 to 2004-05, to test whether or not the top 5 and top 10 districts differed significantly.

General Criteria and Conditions for Promotional Support

NABARD has identified financing, promotion and development of REDP as one of its thrust areas and has introduced several measures to enlarge and diversify the credit and developmental activities in the field of rural development. NABARD has been providing refinance to banks against loans for manufacturing, processing and service activities in small, tiny, cottage and village industries sector including the Industries, Services and Business component of Rural Entrepreneurship Development Programme (REDP). The credit package covers financial needs of different segments of rural non-farm sector, like traditional industries (handloom, handicrafts, coir, sericulture, etc.), agro-industries, modern industries (mother units, common service centers), services and goods transport sector, etc. The NABARD's refinance, mainly focuses on rural artisans, handicrafts, tiny, cottage and village industries.

Promotion of Rural Entrepreneurs

NABARD recognizes promotion as an important function for expanding the choices available to rural entrepreneurs. The promotional strategy is recognized as a useful and essential adjunct to the core refinancing function of NABARD. Besides, it also provides opportunities to test different hypothesis, to learn what works and what does not, and also provides a forum for interacting with agencies having a shared commitment.

A large number of NGOs have realized the importance of income-generating activities for the rural poor and have diversified into enterprise promotion through training and savings and credit programmes through groups. Many NGOs have been able to develop a close and enduring relationship with the rural people. These NGOs articulate the local people's needs and aspirations and translate them into effective action plans and implement them with people's active participation. As a strategy for development of rural micro enterprises, NABARD has, therefore, been involving NGO's/VAs and other development-oriented organizations in its efforts to improve the access of rural micro-enterprises to credit and non-credit facilities and linkages.

The objective of NABARD's promotional programmes is to generate or enhance opportunities for livelihood both in terms of income and employment in rural areas in a sustainable, demonstrative and cost-effective manner. The major promotional concepts evolved by NABARD and implemented in partnership with Voluntary Agencies (VAs)/Developmental Agencies (DAs) over the last few years are:

Training-cum-Production Centres (TPCs)
Rural Entrepreneurship Development Programmes (REDPs)
Training for/by Master Craftsmen (TMC)
Market-oriented Training (MOT)
Artisan Guilds (AGs)
Mother Units and Common Service Centres (MUs and CSCs)
Assistance for Rural Women in Non-Farm Development (ARWIND)

The above programmes are purely experimental in nature and sanctioned selectively to NGOs/VAs/DAs with good track record and capacity to implement the same with a view to drawing lessons for the suitability/replicability. In view of the experimental nature, close monitoring and documentation of the experiences are essential. The agencies, which could satisfy NABARD about their capability to closely monitor and document the project impact, are likely to be preferred. The salient features of the programmes, the eligibility norms for seeking assistance, etc., are given below.

The promotional programmes are experimental in nature and intended for learning lessons on the suitability and replicability of different concepts. NABARD will, therefore, be very selective in sanctioning such programmes. The promotional support would be provided by NABARD strictly on merits, on a case-by-case basis, taking into account the feasibility of the project as well as the track record, commitment and capability of the NGO/VA/DA concerned.

Eligible Institutions

The NGOs/VAs / DAs satisfying the following requirements would normally be considered eligible for promotional support:

The organization should be a legal entity;
It should have been working in the rural area, at least, for three years;
Its accounts should have been audited regularly;
It should not discriminate on the basis of religion, caste, sex or race;
Its officers should not be office-bearers of any political party; and
It should have the professional competence to plan, manage, monitor and document the experiences in the implementation of the project.

Location

Generally, the REDP should be implemented in 'rural areas' as defined in the NABARD Act, 1981 (i.e. area comprised in any village irrespective of population and also in any town, the population of which does not exceed 50,000).

Credit Linkage

All the promotional programmes are credit-linked, i.e., the financial support provided by NABARD will have to supplemented by bank loan. The NGOs/VAs/ DAs should, therefore, involve the banks in the projects proposed to be implemented by them and indicate in the project proposal, the details of the credit tie-up being arranged (e.g. name of the bank, assistance proposed, whether consent, in principle, to support the proposal has been received from the bank, etc.).

Monitoring

NABARD lays emphasis on close and effective monitoring of the promotional projects. The implementing agency should ensure regular follow-up and monitoring with the necessary extension services to the beneficiaries to achieve the ultimate objective of the concerned promotional programme. The programmes will be monitored by a committee set up in consultation with the NABARD Regional Office concerned and through the submission of periodic monitoring reports by the implementing agency to NABARD in the prescribed formats.

Number of Projects Assisted in Tamil Nadu

Table-1 gives the district-wise number of projects under REDP assisted by NABARD in Tamil Nadu during the period 1999-2000 through 2004-05.

During 1999-2000, the number of projects assisted under REDP in Tamil Nadu was 578. Kanyakumari district got the first place with 126 projects, followed by Cuddalore district with 85 projects, Toothukkudi district 59 projects and Tirunelveli and Coimbatore districts got 56 projects each. The remaining districts got below 40 projects each.

During 2000-2001, the number of projects assisted was 144. Composite Madurai district got the highest number 100 projects, followed by Cuddalore district 23 projects, composite Salem district 9 projects and Tiruvannamalai district 5 projects. These four districts accounted for 95 per cent of projects assisted. During 2001-02, no project was assisted in whole Tamil Nadu.

During 2002-2003, the number of projects assisted increased to 3848. The highest number of 500 projects went to Thiruvallur district followed by Salem district (466 projects), Coimbatore district (454 projects), Villupuram district (396 projects), Cuddalore district (362 projects), Kanyakumari district (357 projects), Tirunelveli district (241 projects), Madurai district (176 projects), Dharmapuri district (133 projects), and Vellore district (99 projects). The above ten districts accounted for 83 per cent of projects assisted.

During 2003-2004 the number of projects assisted decreased to 3006. The highest number of 323 projects went to Virudhunagar district. The next places went to Villupuram district, Cuddalore district, Kanyakumari district, Tirunelveli district, Coimbatore district, Tiruvannamalai district, Dharmapuri district, Salem district and Erode district respectively 266, 241, 211, 210, 178, 143, 122, 111 and 110 projects. These ten districts accounted for 64 per cent of projects assisted.

During 2004-2005, the number of projects assisted increased to 181,084 projects. Vellore district got the first place with 60,649 projects, followed by Tiruchirapalli district with 24,918 projects, Dindigul district with 24,397 projects, Sivaganga district with 15,649 projects, Kancheepuram district with 14,760 projects, Tirunelveli district with 12,164 projects, Virudhunagar district with 9550 projects, Kanyakumari district with 3939 projects, Ramanathapuram district with 3421 projects and Nilgiris district with 3066 projects. These ten districts accounted for 95 per cent of projects assisted.

Mean and Standard Deviation

The annual mean number of projects by district assisted was 26, 20, 167, 104, and 6244 for the 5 years (1999-2000 through 2004-05 except 2001-02) and the Std. deviation was 32, 33, 163, 78 and 12468 for the 5 years. For the top 10 districts the annual mean number of projects assisted was 51, 20, 318, 191 and 17251 and the Std. deviation figures were 33, 33, 138, 68 and 16300.

Test of Hypothesis

The null hypothesis is that there is no significant difference between the top 5 and top 10 districts mean values of number of projects assisted under REDP. Out of 6 years under study, in 4 years (1999-2000, 2002-2003, 2003-04 and 2004-05), the null hypothesis is rejected. Hence, there was a significant difference between top 5 and top 10 districts in this regard.

Total District-wise Amount of Assistance by Financial Institutions and NABARD Refinance

Table 2 gives the amount of assistance provided by financial institutions under REDP and refinance to these institutions by NABARD.

During 1999-2000, Toothukkudi district got the maximum amount of Rs.11.04 lakh of financial assistance and Rs. 5.96 lakh of refinance. The second highest amount of financial assistance and refinance went to composite Salem district, respectively Rs. 5.75 lakh and Rs. 3.37 lakh. Third and fourth places went to Villupuram and Kanyakumari districts respectively Rs. 5.23 lakh and Rs. 5.03 lakh of financial assistance and Rs. 2.94 lakh and Rs. 2.51 lakh of refinance. The top ten districts accounted for 85 per cent of financial assistance and refinance.

During 2000-2001, seven districts only got the financial assistance and refinance. The highest amount of financial assistance and refinance went to Cuddalore district respectively Rs. 2.45 lakh and Rs.1.90 lakh. The second and third places went to composite Salem district (Rs. 88000 and Rs. 62000) and Coimbatore district

(Rs. 33,000 and Rs. 17,000). During 2001-2002, no financial assistance and refinance was given to whole Tamil Nadu.

During 2002 -2003, the following districts were got the maximum amount of financial assistance and refinance. Thiruvallur district (Rs.83.38 lakh and Rs.58.76 lakh), Coimbatore district (Rs.67.86 lakh and Rs.61.01 lakh), Salem district (Rs.62.15 lakh and Rs.55.94 lakh), Sivaganga district (Rs.60.27 lakh and Rs.42.65 lakh) and Cuddalore district (Rs.49.49 lakh and Rs.44.39 lakh). The top ten districts accounted for 77 per cent of financial assistance of refinance.

During 2003-2004, again, Thiruvallur district got the first place with Rs. 230.55 lakh of financial assistance and Rs. 229.87 lakh of refinance. The next places went to Kanyakumari district (Rs.174.69 lakhs and Rs.171.91 lakh), Tirunelveli district (Rs. 117.11 lakh and Rs. 117.05 lakh), Kancheepuram district (Rs. 115.12 lakh and Rs. 114.41 lakh) and Dharmapuri district (Rs.106.99 lakh and Rs. 105.74 lakh). The top ten districts accounted for 57 per cent of financial assistance and refinance.

During 2004-05, Erode district got the highest amount of financial assistance and refinance (Rs.1752.33 lakh and Rs.1579.88 lakhs). The next places went to Vellore district (Rs.1258.37 lakh and Rs.1142.71 lakh), Truchirapalli district (Rs.1229.98 lakh and Rs. 1166.81 lakh), Tirunelveli district (Rs.1152.99 lakh and Rs.1049.68 lakh) and Kanyakumari district (Rs.1119.73 lakh and Rs.950.73 lakh). The top ten districts accounted for 73 per cent of financial assistance and refinance.

Mean and Standard Deviation-Finance

The annual mean financial institutional loan by district assisted was Rs.2 lakh, Rs.0.64 lakh, Rs.53 lakh, Rs.72 lakh and Rs. 501 lakh for the 5 years (1999-2000 through 2004-05 except 2001-02) and the standard deviation was Rs.3 lakh, Rs.0.77 lakh Rs.124 lakh, Rs.46 lakh and Rs.452 lakh for the 5 years. For the top 10 districts the annual mean financial institutional loan assisted was Rs.5 lakh, Rs.0.64 lakh, Rs.50 lakh, Rs.12 lakh and Rs.1057 lakh and the standard deviation figures were Rs. 2 lakh Rs.0.77 lakh, Rs. 18 lakh, Rs. 44 lakh and Rs. 309 for the 5 years.

Test of Hypothesis

The null hypothesis is that there is no significant difference between the top 5 and top 10 districts mean values of financial institutional loan for REDP. Out of 6 years under study, in 3 years (2002-03 to 2004-05), the null hypothesis is rejected. Hence, the differences between the two groups were significant for three years only.

Mean and Standard Deviation-Refinance

In the case of NABARD refinance, the annual mean NABARD refinance by district assisted was Rs.1 lakh, Rs.0.47 lakh, Rs.45 lakh, Rs.71 lakh and Rs.461 lakh for the 5 years and the standard deviation was Rs.1 lakh, Rs.60 lakh, Rs.106 lakh, Rs.46 lakh and Rs.411 lakh for the 5 years.

For the top 10 districts the annual mean NABARD refinance assisted was Rs.3 lakh, Rs.0.47 lakh, Rs.42 lakh, Rs.119lakh and Rs.970 lakh and the standard deviation figures were Rs.1 lakh, Rs.0.60 lakh, Rs.13 lakh, Rs.45 lakh and Rs.275 lakh for the 5 years.

Test of Hypothesis

The null hypothesis is that there is no significant difference between the top 5 and top 10 districts mean values of NABARD refinance for REDP. Out of 6 years under study, in 4 years (1999-2000, 2002-03, 2003-04 and 2004-05), the null hypothesis is rejected. Hence, there was a significant difference between top 5 and top 10 districts in this regard.

Overall Assistance

Table–3 gives the six-year period aggregates and average. During the study period 1999-2000 through 2004-05, 1,88,660 projects under REDP were taken-up. Vellore district (61.021 projects), Kancheepuram district (14825 projects) and Tirunelveli district (12671 projects) were the major benefited districts. In terms of financial assistance and refinance, the following were the top three districts, namely Erode district (Rs.1826.89 lakh and Rs.1649.97 lakh), Vellore district (Rs.1362.64 lakh and Rs.1239.89 lakh) and Kanyakumari district (Rs.1336.54 lakh and Rs.1158.53 lakh).

Conclusion

The financial assistance provided by different financial institutions in Tamil Nadu during the 6-year period of study (1999-2000 to 2004-05) under REDP, stood at Rs.17,327.05 lakh. Against this, these institutions got a refinance totalling Rs.16,015.79 lakh from NABARD accounting for 92 per cent of total assistance extended to various beneficiary borrowers by these institutions. Besides, during the same period, NABARD had sanctioned 1,88,660 projects under this scheme to Tamil Nadu. The top 5 districts by total amount of refinance for the 6-year period for NFS Composite Scheme were: Erode, Tirunelveli, Vellore, Tiruchirapalli, Kanyakumari and the amounts of total assistance were Rs.1,649.97 lakh, Rs.1,255.46 lakh Rs.1,239.89 lakh and Rs.1,235.33 lakh and Rs.1,158.53 lakh, respectively. Besides, during the same period, NABARD had sanctioned 1,88,660 projects under this scheme to Tamil Nadu.

The difference between top 5 and top 10 districts was significant with respect to *(i)* mean number of projects assisted in 4 out of 5 years, *(ii)* mean amount of financial assistance in 3 out of 5 years, and *(iii)* mean amount of refinance assistance in 4 out of 5 years.

REDP is a successful scheme of NABARD. NABARD has to consider the following suggestions for further increasing refinance disbursements:

- Recommend to the Government to establish direct-level market center to provide marketing infrastructure for rural non-farm products.
- Technology transfer centers may be established in each district for providing guidance, technical know-how, etc., to the entrepreneurs.
- In select blocks/district, rural artisan complexes/common work sheds may be established.
- Provision of adequate water facilities and uninterrupted power supply to be ensured.

The study shows that the NABARD refinance disbursement for this scheme is successful.

Table–1
Number of Projects Under REDP

Sl.No.	*District Name*	*1999-00*	*2000-01*	*2001-02*	*2002-03*	*2003-04*	*2004-05*
1.	Chennai	-	-	-	1	3	31
2.	Coimbatore	56	3	-	454	178	743
3.	Cuddalore	85	23	-	362	241	714
4.	Dharmapuri	8	-	-	133	122	585
5.	Dindigul	9	-	-	37	29	24397
6.	Erode	6	-	-	83	110	1222

(Contd...)

Sl.No.	*District Name*	*1999-00*	*2000-01*	*2001-02*	*2002-03*	*2003-04*	*2004-05*
7.	Kancheepuram	3	-	-	-	62	14760
8.	Thiruvallur			-	500	108	122
9.	Kanyakumari	126	-	-	357	211	3939
10.	Tiruchirapalli			-	94	89	24918
11.	Karur	6	-	-	-	87	18
12.	Perambalur			-	-	65	106
13.	Madurai	3	100	-	176	58	402
14.	Theni			-	-	24	78
15.	Nagapattinam	-	-	-	50	59	444
16.	Salem	36	9	-	466	111	606
17.	Namakkal			-	-	61	290
18.	Nilgiris	15	-	-	14	77	3066
19.	Pudukottai	-	-	-	4	50	443
20.	Ramanathapuram	8	-	-	33	33	3421
21.	Sivaganga	4	-	-	81	67	15649
22.	Thanjavur	6	-	-	92	38	383
23.	Thiruvarur			-	-	57	208
24.	Tirunelveli	56	-	-	241	210	12164
25.	Tiruvannamalai	7	5	-	38	143	459
26.	Toothukkudi	59	-	-	94	37	489
27.	Vellore	6	1	-	99	266	60649
28.	Villupuram	44	-	-	396	323	1228
29.	Virudhunagar	24	-	-	43	87	9550
30.	Unspecified	3	3	-	-	-	-
31.	Multi District	8	-	-	-	-	-
	TOTAL	**578**	**144**	**-**	**3,848**	**3,006**	**1,81,084**
	Top 5 Mean	76	28	-	436	250	28075
	Top 5 Standard Deviation	27	37	-	50	42	16830
	Top 10 Mean	51	20	-	318	191	17251

(Contd...)

Sl.No.	*District Name*	*1999-00*	*2000-01*	*2001-02*	*2002-03*	*2003-04*	*2004-05*
	Top 10 Standard Deviation	33	33	-	138	68	16300
	Z-Value	2.075	0.664	-	2.343	2.377	1.819
	H_o	Rejected	Accepted	-	Rejected	Rejected	Rejected

Source: NABARD Unpublished Data.

– Composite Tiruchirapalli Dt. includes Karur and Perambalur Dts.
– Composite Kancheepuram Dt. includes Thiruvallur Dt.
– Composite Madurai Dt. includes Theni Dt.
– Composite Salem Dt. includes Namakkal Dt.
– Composite Thanjavur includes Thiruvarur Dt

Table–2
Financial Institutional Loan and NABARD Refinance for REDP

(Rs. in lakhs)

Sl. No.	District Name	1999–2000		2000-2001		2001-2002		2002-2003		2003-2004		2004-2005	
		F.I. Loan	NABARD Refinance	F.I. Loan	NABARD Refinance	F.I. Loan	NABARD Refinance	F.I. Loan	NABARD Refinance	F.I. Loan	NABARD Refinance	F.I. Loan	NABARD Refinance
1	2	3	4	5	6	7	8	9	10	11	12	13	14
1.	Chennai	-	-	-	-	-	-	2.02	1.82	10.03	9.03	93.76	84.39
2.	Coimbatore	4.60	2.27	0.33	0.17	-	-	67.86	61.01	104.18	102.16	823.23	773.60
3.	Cuddalore	3.10	1.89	2.45	1.90	-	-	49.49	44.39	69.92	65.95	263.16	240.36
4.	Dharmapuri	1.74	1.20	-	-	-	-	10.25	9.22	106.99	105.74	137.28	125.85
5.	Dindigul	1.17	0.57	-	-	-	-	4.44	3.88	28.12	27.66	1037.34	937.47
6.	Erode	0.69	0.35	-	-	-	-	14.07	12.48	59.80	57.26	1752.33	1579.88
7.	Kancheepuram	0.56	0.21	-	-	-	-	-	-	115.12	114.41	646.43	602.00
8.	Thiruvallur					-	-	83.38	58.76	230.55	229.87	158.54	156.41
9.	Kanyakumari	5.03	2.51	-	-	-	-	37.09	33.38	174.69	171.91	1119.73	950.73
10.	Tiruchirapalli					-	-	12.45	11.21	58.39	57.04	1229.98	1166.81

(Contd...)

1	2	3	4	5	6	7	8	9	10	11	12	13	14
11.	Karur	0.53	0.27	-	-	-	-	-	-	56.67	55.02	19.21	19.15
12.	Perambalur					-	-	-	-	66.45	65.72	90.22	88.57
13.	Madurai	0.68	0.34	0.18	0.12	-	-	26.11	23.49	58.00	57.38	291.75	279.55
14.	Theni					-	-	-	-	16.83	16.65	67.03	63.46
15.	Nagapattinam	-	-	-	-	-	-	5.44	4.90	61.28	60.38	206.21	184.59
16.	Salem	5.75	3.37	0.88	0.62	-	-	62.15	55.94	94.30	93.17	317.54	293.13
17.	Namakkal					-	-	-	-	35.43	34.34	132.46	122.96
18.	Nilgiris	0.59	0.22	-	-	-	-	8.78	7.90	25.96	24.86	113.58	105.66
19.	Pudukottai	-	-	-	-	-	-	3.45	3.10	64.35	63.93	267.37	256.42
20.	Ramanathapuram	0.71	0.43	-	-	-	-	21.72	19.53	18.55	18.12	362.78	321.49
21.	Sivaganga	1.24	0.88	-	-	-		60.27	42.65	65.12	63.42	849.58	787.91
22.	Thanjavur	0.47	0.24	-	-	-	-	12.63	11.37	36.46	36.39	318.26	300.85
23.	Thiruvarur					-	-	-	-	50.52	50.17	153.08	141.44
24.	Tirunelveli	4.51	3.18	-	-	-	-	40.77	40.55	117.11	117.05	1152.99	1094.68
25.	Tiruvannamalai	0.54	0.27	0.21	0.15	-	-	14.63	13.17	67.41	66.08	193.75	179.39
26.	Toothukkudi	11.04	5.96	-	-	-	-	23.03	20.73	45.89	45.72	330.23	310.65
27.	Vellore	1.61	0.88	0.25	0.20	-	-	9.00	8.10	93.41	88.00	1258.37	1142.71

(Contd...)

1	2	3	4	5	6	7	8	9	10	11	12	13	14
28.	Villupuram	5.23	2.94	-	-	-	-	43.82	39.47	105.20	101.15	434.85	397.42
29.	Virudhunagar	4.04	3.17	-	-	-	-	25.82	18.78	66.73	65.70	704.11	662.99
30.	Unspecified	0.65	0.32	0.21	0.14	-	-	-	-	-	-	-	-
31.	Multi District	0.78	0.39	-	-	-	-	-	-	-	-	-	-
	TOTAL	**55.26**	**31.86**	**4.51**	**3.30**	-	-	**638.67**	**545.83**	**2103.46**	**2064.28**	**14525.15**	**13370.52**
Top 5 Mean		6	4	0.82	0.61	-	-	65	52	149	148	1303	1187
Top 5 Std. Deviation		2	1	0.85	0.67	-	-	11	7	47	47	230	210
Top 10 Mean		5	3	0.64	0.47	-	-	50	42	121	119	1057	970
Top 10 Std. Deviation		2	1	0.77	0.60	-	-	18	13	44	45	309	275
Z-Value		1.370	2.740	0.640	0.639	-	-	2.283	2.107	1.743	1.766	2.181	2.162
H_o		Accepted	Rejected	Accepted	Accepted	-	-	Rejected	Rejected	Rejected	Rejected	Rejected	Rejected

Source: NABARD unpublished Data.

Table–3
Overall Assistance (1999-2000 to 2004-05) for REDP

Sl No.	District Name	Total Assistance F.I. Loan (Rs. in lakhs)	Total Assistance NABARD Refinance (Rs. in lakhs)	Total Number of Projects	Per Project F.I. Loan (Rs. in lakhs)	Per Project LABARD Refinance (Rs. in lakhs)
1.	Chennai	105.81	95.24	35	3.02	2.72
2.	Coimbatore	1000.20	939.21	1434	0.69	0.65
3.	Cuddalore	388.12	354.49	1425	0.27	0.25
4.	Dharmapuri	256.26	242.01	848	0.30	0.28
5.	Dindigul	1071.07	969.58	24472	0.04	0.03
6.	Erode	1826.89	1649.97	1421	1.28	1.16
7.	Kancheepuram	762.11	716.62	14825	0.05	0.04
8.	Thiruvallur	472.47	445.04	730	0.65	0.61
9.	Kanyakumari	1336.54	1158.53	4633	0.29	0.25
10.	Tiruchirapalli	1301.35	1235.33	25107	0.05	0.04
11.	Karur	75.88	74.17	105	0.72	0.70
12.	Perambalur	156.67	154.29	171	0.92	0.90
13.	Madurai	376.72	360.88	739	0.15	0.49
14.	Theni	83.86	80.11	102	0.82	0.78
15.	Nagapattinam	272.93	249.87	553	0.49	0.45
16.	Salem	480.62	446.23	1228	0.39	0.36
17.	Namakkal	167.89	157.30	351	0.48	0.45
18.	Nilgiris	148.91	138.64	3172	0.05	0.04
19.	Pudukottai	335.17	323.45	497	0.67	0.65
20.	Ramanathapuram	403.76	359.57	3495	0.11	0.10
21.	Sivaganga	976.21	894.86	15801	0.06	0.05
22.	Thanjavur	367.82	348.85	519	0.71	0.67
23.	Thiruvarur	203.60	191.61	265	0.77	0.72
24.	Tirunelveli	1315.38	1255.46	12671	0.10	0.09
25.	Tiruvannamalai	276.54	259.06	652	0.42	0.40
26.	Toothukkudi	410.19	383.06	679	0.60	0.56

(Contd...)

Sl No.	District Name	Total Assistance: F.I. Loan (Rs. in lakhs)	Total Assistance: NABARD Refinance (Rs. in lakhs)	Total Number of Projects	Per Project: F.I. Loan (Rs. in lakhs)	Per Project: LABARD Refinance (Rs. in lakhs)
27.	Vellore	1362.64	1239.89	61021	0.02	0.02
28.	Villupuram	589.10	540.98	1991	0.29	0.27
29.	Virudhunagar	800.70	750.64	9704	0.08	0.07
30.	Unspecified	0.86	0.46	6	0.14	0.07
31.	Multi District	0.78	0.39	8	0.09	0.05
	TOTAL	**17,327.05**	**16,015.79**	**1,88,660**	**0.09**	**0.08**

REFERENCES

NABARD's Annual Reports (1996-97 to 2004-05).

NABARD's State Level Credit Seminar—State Focus Paper (1996-97 to 2004-05).

NABARD's Statistical Reports (1996-97 to 2004-05).

NABARD's News Letters.

The Hindu Survey of Indian Agriculture-1996-97 to 2000,01,02,03, and 2004

The Economic Times-2005.

NABARD unpublished data.

RBI Bulletins (1999-2000 and 2003-04) .

Model Project for REDP–NABARD publication (several).

www.nabard.org

14

Trusting Attitude in Rural Talent: The Better Way to Survive

Dr. C. Karthikeyan

The HR Scenario in India

Even attitude has taken a sea change due to an "infectious factor" called the competitiveness, due to relationships and trust has an important role for the smooth functioning of organizations these days. The essential ingredient of collaborative effort is trust. High performance teams are characterized by high mutual trust among members. Leaders succeed in bringing about change because constituents to reflect their values and aspirations trust them. An organization climate of trust enables employees to surface their ideas and feelings, use each other as resources and learn together. Without trust people assume self-protective, defensive postures that inhibit learning.

Trust is the quality seen as an essential ingredient now and a guiding star to effective teamwork. It has been proved by research that team-based organizations are more efficient and give better results than the traditional ones.

The concept of trust seems to be quite simple superficially, but an in-depth study of the same reveals that some complex concepts relating to trust, a concrete definition is not possible. To put it simply why is this trust required is that today the HR Market is in turbulence, one side there is plenty of opportunities, the otherside is scarcity of talent, and on one angle lot of education, on the one angle demands for dynamic skills, when you try to merge all these, there is another overriding factor called the attrition, so trusting from all levels that is, from the employer and employee level alone can change the existing turbulence. A look at the following paragraphs will reveal why.

So before going deep into the statistical diagnosis of the turbulence I would like to tell the characteristics of trust so that the factor gets relevant to the concept.

Multi level trust –	to attain effective coordination between all the members of the business concern.
Culturally rooted –	linked with the culture the person concerned comes from.
Communication based –	inclusive of both verbal and non-verbal communication largely affecting the development or downfall of trust in a relationship.
Dynamic –	varies with the change in the variables it is dependent upon.
Multidimensional –	cognitive, emotional and behavioural levels.
Dependency and vulnerability –	involves a level of being on the/to the actions of the other party.
The Types of trust	
Vertical trust –	between organization and customer.
Horizontal –	involves two people of the same hierarchy
Diagonal Trust –	two people having a diagonal relationship in the organizational hierarchy.
Dyadic Trust –	it is cognitive-based trust and affect based trust
Cognitive based –	where trust on the other party is based on a rational decision.
Affect based –	exists where the relationship involves a deep emotional investment.
Institutional trust –	that an employee or a member of particular organization has in the same.
Deterrence based –	between individuals who does not have any sound foundation.
Knowledge based trust –	knowledge that one party has about the other.
Identification based trust –	relationships where there is an emotional connection between the parties.

While all the above are said and done, why still the turbulence in HR market is the misconception that only the urban level talent has been spotted and not in entirety.

Tap the Rural Settings

India has a huge potential of everything required in the world in the rural economy, but quite often oversee things due to "cascading effect of urban thinking". HR must now pervade into the rural sectors and tap the existing potential to arrest this turbulence. The educational institutions (private) also must touch upon the rural talents in management and professional education, to arrest the huge losses occurring at organizational level.

A look at the statistical picture given below would justify this statement.

In any HR market when demand outstrips supply attrition is the natural outcome. An attrition rate is 14 per cent (2005) (find last year) means that out of every 100 employees a company will employ–14 will leave each year.

ITES sector has the worst attrition rate of over 30 per cent and Other sectors like manufacturing, banking, healthcare, pharmaceuticals, construction and engineering, telecom, aviation and aviation feels the attrition. This has a greater impact on the wage bills and indirects costs on labour. The high wage bill rising at about 14 per cent per annum is affecting competitiveness of Indian companies; in terms of training and acquisition costs.

The Employment Grid

Now that employees know that demand-supply balance is clearly in favour of employees, we as corporates must need to think in terms of other behavioural and ethical matters to settle out the issue. The other positive side in them is in 1st half of 2006, 52 per cent of India Inc increased its workforce on an average 02.89 per cent.

Indian economy expects more Indian and foreign companies stepping up investment, manufacturing and service growth, and creation of new economy sectors like retail and biotech among others. IT and ITES professionals are still the most in demand, with hiring from the sector growing at an aggressive 11.9 per cent rate. Construction and manufacturing sector are also seeing an increase in hiring at 6.43 per cent and 1.9 per cent respectively. Companies from Communication, Transport and retail sectors have future career options. Increasing in hiring is by 4.75 per cent and 3.18 per cent respectively.

- 10,30,040 more jobs to be created. (The Financial Express, 14 October, 2006).

The sector expected to drive job demand going forward remains with IT and ITES, manufacturing, retail and communication and transport. Surprisingly, the Banking and Financial Services Industry is not creating as many jobs as expected, the main reason being strict government regulations and closed nature of the sectors. Rise in manufacturing will bring more cheer to the services sector as one job in manufacturing creates jobs in services as a thumb rule.

The Reality Grid

Phase–1 (Bottom line)

Despite a surplus labour pool, 1 per cent of India Inc feels that "lack of skilled workers will be the single largest determinant going forward – Mckinsey survey (vide Financial Express, 14 October, 2006).

The Fulcrum (the very basic human talent i.e. student profile) in doldrums

- 50 per cent of Indian students drop out of high school after 10th
- 75 per cent of drops out at 12th level
- Of the 3 million, only 15-20 per cent are hirable
- Only 10 per cent get into research

So the need is to train and develop people to reduce the gap and obviously the associated long-term costs. "India at present has ton rate of enrolment at 2-5 per cent levels with low quality of educational inputs and low rate of conversion to employment for the student."

"Until enrolments grow exponentially with improvement in education quality and conversion to employment increasing with most graduation, getting employed India could be leading for a high rate of unemployment."

- Social unrest
- Rapid wage inflation
- Economic non-competitiveness
- Our advantages are turning into disadvantages

Educational Scenario

25 mn	Enrolment in 9th/10th:	large base level talent production-quality as big question
12 mn	Enrolment in 11th/12th:	50 per cent drop in secondary and higher secondary enrolments
3 mn	Graduation:	not more than 15-20 per cent of the graduate pool is hirable
0.3 mn	Post Graduation:	Demographical economics at 2050.

A close look at the aging population of various countries would clarify why talent management is now vital and why rural tapping is necessary at the earliest.

	Dependency Ratio	*Support Ratio*	*Aging Index*	*Growth Rate %*
India	22.6	4.4	105.0	0.4
USA	34.9	2.9	144.9	0.5
UK	73.3	2.1	226.7	(0.3)
Japan	71.3	1.4	338.2	(0.6)
Singapore	50.0	2.0	258.8	(0.6)
Spain	73.8	1.4	386.4	(0.6)
China	37.2	2.7	183.3	(0.3)

Dependency Ratio	*Support Ratio*	*Aging Index*
Retires (>64 years) Workers (15-64 years) Number of old people dependent on every 100 workers	Workers (15-64 years) Retires (>64 years) Number of workers a available to support every one retiree	Retires (>64 years) Children (<15 years) Number of retirees per 100 children

Industrial Sector	*No. of Companies*	*MBA%*
IT and ITES	207	11.91
Construction	63	6.43
Communication and Transport	82	4.75
Retail	73	3.18
Other Services	182	2.08
Manufacturing	1309	1.90
Energy	60	1.21
BFSI	153	1.12
Mining	14	0.16

(Ma foi Employment Index)

Number of Jobs Created

Ventures	*August 2006*
BFSI	(-) 1,31,120
Communication and Transport	10,860
Construction	8,540

(Contd...)

Energy	19,620
IT and ITES	7,04,400
Manufacturing	23,000
Mining	(-)7,090
Retailing	15,620
services	3,86,210

India and Asia Pacific Attrition

ITES	30%	23%
IT/Telecom	18%	17%
FMCG/Pharmaceutical	10.5%	15%
Manufacturing	11%	11%
BFSI	21%	25%

Attrition: (other cause of concern)

14%	: India
14-16%	: Asia Pacific

Attrition

The effect of Globalisation continues to be Global, Economic and Technological developments are producing dramatic, indeed, revolutionary changes in the cross border movement of talent and capital.

- Highly fluid of turbulent period: Attrition is no longer restricted to local or regional boundaries and attraction and retention are the crucial changes.
- Coupled with high attrition, this has led to quality manpower crunch. There hasn't been any single common vehicle that organization have employed to retain talents. Some of that can be:
  - Ensuing *"pay above market"* by using approaches like salary hikes using promotional, retention and sign on bonuses and equity-based grants.
  - *"Providing opportunity to learn new skills"* by identifying key talent of providing with development opportunities.
  - Supporting "work life Balance."

"More industries are demanding talent with jobs moving to the organized sector." "The employment are now to 10.3 lakh due to in the economic activities of the country."

The Aging Talents

Today's new generation of retired people have more money on the average than the 25-35 years old: they do respond to the ad campaign and they don't stick to a particular brand or way of life.

Some Lessons from "How the Aged and Talent Manages:

For Narayana Murthy or Mittal, the yardstick for success has always been making a difference by carrying out their share of the market. In a sentence, there is a hint of Megalomania about these men and certainly Shiv Nadar or Asim Premji will now be accused of being self effacing.

What driven these men is not the scent of money life that had been so he would have sold off long ago and made his billions, the promise of leaving imprint on the sands of India's business history. For men like Nadar and the Premji, money is just an accessory, a necessary persuit of the overall goal. They move on with the same passion and energy with which they have built their reputations.

What Others Say

"The anti-dumping duties on Chinese and Vietnamese footwear have created a huge opportunity for India. Just 12 per cent of the exports is to the U.S. We need to focus on this market" – *Jairam Ramesh, Minister of State for Commerce.*

"Companies like Tesco and Wal-mart would contribute to this economy hugely and keep local companies on their – *Mukesh Ambani, Chairman of Reliance Industires.*

Talent Management Framework Addresses

"Hire a guy who knows English, and a li more"
"Keep them happy if you want to keep them"
"HR people need to speak the same language as CEO's."

- We have to meet the aspirations of people. If companies take care of their employees, everything else falls into place – VP.HR.TCS.
- While we market Maruti to candidates when we recruit, we know that it's also important to understand the candidates expectations from Maruti – Head HR Maruti Udyog.
- Our business would not be able to run without employee empowerment – ED, Oriental Bank of Commerce.
- Quality workforce is the hottest subject today, it is hotter

than technology than itself, because there would be no technology without people—Erve Director, TATA Sons.

- Quality is an industry and organization specific term. Each organization should develop quality benchmarks in its own context.
- Retention is about driving accountability to frontline leader—Head HR Heurtt Association.
- Employees need to prove others what they are capable of and just need a chance to do so—Head HR LG Electronics.

So finally the ultimatum is TAP the rural and prepare for a balance than crying and wasting money and energy on unstable talent grids, so that consistency be streamlined and economy grows horizontally also. LET US TRUST IN OUR RURAL ECONOMY.

"This subject is the hottest subject today. In fact it is hotter than technology itself, because there would be no technology without people." There has been so much debate today over the fact that people are the key differentiators between organizations. But if this is so evident then why do we have seminar to discuss them?

And what is learnt from most of interview are that we are depriving over people, of that human moment, wherein energy is transmitted between people. So the real challenge here is to find and restore those human moments, which would bring is restoring humanity in human resources. Building a quality workforce has to do with assembling wise people and using their wisdom (which is a mix of existing knowledge and institution). Those who value and recognize their people and understand their needs will direct future. "It is important that the learning derived from the event find resonance across industries and among the HR as a whole. Creating a great organization driven by excellent people is not only the prerogative of top companies.

- "When employees have become less standardized, unchallenging work environment, limited career growth, less promotional opportunities, bad leadership and compensation could attend organization immensely."
- Indian economy being a knowledge economy, it's the prerogative of organizations to focus on training and create a resource pool for the future. Companies that can attract and retain the best and brightest will succeed. Those that get the wrong talent on the Board will fail.

- Without an exciting work environment, its difficult to keep people working for a company for a long time.
- The need to have a sound succession planning policy in place for the future. While there is a constant need to innovate and empower employees at the workplace, planning for the future is the must.

REFERENCES

Stephen, P. Robbins, *Organisational Behaviour*, Prentice Hall of India Private Ltd. New Delhi, 9th edn., 2001.

D.E. Zand, *The Leadership Traid: Knowledge, Trust and Power*, Oxford Press, New York, 1997), p. 164 as cited from, Stephen P Robbins, Organizational Behaviour, Prentice Hall of India Private Ltd., New Delhi, 9th edn., 2001, p. 337.

John, W. Newstorm and Keith Davis, *Organisation Behaviour; Human Behaviour at Work*, Tata McGraw Hill Publishing Co. Ltd., New Delhi, 11th edn., 2002.

ARTICLES

Multi-dimensional study of trust in organizations, journal of managerial issues. Fall 1998; Vol. 10, No. 3, pp. 303-317 as citied from *www.spiderquery.com/orgam/trust.htmwww.spiderquery.com/orgman/trust.htm*, Last visited on April 10, 2004.

Guidelines of Measuring Trust in Organisations, The Institute of Public Relations Commission on PR Measurement and Evaluation, University of Florida, *www.instituteforpr.com/pdf/2003_measuring -trust.pdf*, Last visited on April 5, 2004.

15

Community Participation in Rural Development

C. Siva Murugan and Dr. V. Anbumani

The idea of community participation originated in India, many centuries ago, when a temple pond in a village had dried up and no artificial feeding could revive it. A young villager snatched a sickle from a passing peasant and started digging deep, another villager followed, yet another and another till the last man of village joined followed by women and village children. In no time fresh water came out sparkling. The villagers called it "Kar Sewa" (People's Participation), the sophisticated experts, the planners, the economists termed it as 'Community Participation'. The UNDP Report's call it as 'Participatory Movement'.

Reading these reports it is obvious that the people are anxious to participate in development, in governance and in raising the quality of life in the village. The last ten Five-Year Plans have shown that no community development programme can succeed without community participation and no community development programme can fail with it, even a bad programme can succeed.

According to *Shri S.K. Dey*, the father of community development programme in India and the author of many books on the subject, a Community Development Programme, should be a programme of development of the community, by the community, for the community and with the widest diversity both in approach and content. A programme in Delhi has to be different from a programme in Arunachal Pradesh. This diversity has to be respected from Kashmir to Kanyakumari.

The community development programme was started in India in 1952 as a drop in the ocean, today it is the ocean. Historically there are three great pioneers of community participation namely *Mr. F.L. Brayne, ICS, Dr. Ms. Randhawa, ICS and Mahatma Gandhi.* As Deputy Commissioner, Gurgaon of erstwhile Punjab, Brayne ordered the digging of manure pits by which he sought to combine better farming and clean village. Reviewing the Gurgaon experiment, Sir Malcolm Darling writes: "Pits were dug in thousands, Hissar buls and Gurgaon ploughs brought in hundreds, Persian wheels in plenty. Villages were cleaned and re-caimed peasants, to most docile section of village India were activated. Multitudes attended the annual Palwal fair, boys and girls went to schools together. The activity was unprecedented. The district is talking and thinking. With the transfer of Mr. Brayne the district went to slumber again."

Pioneers

'The urge for betterment should come from the people themselves', said M.S. Randhawa sixty years ago in a book entitled 'Developing Village India' published by the ICAR, then known as the Imperial Council of Agricultural Research. Published in 1946 the book is dedicated to the 'Indian peasants whom now lies the deciding vote power'. 'What is required is to dig deep and expose the well springs of village life. The work done under official control is likened to pouring water in pond. Some of it seeps down, some of it evaporates, some of it is used, all of it stagnates and ultimately the pond dries up when artificial pouring is stooped'. Randhawa did excellent work when he was Deputy Commissioner Faizabad in UP. He gave a new lease of life to the district, but all the disappeared with his transfer.

Gandhi Ashrams

These were short-lived experiments whose importance is only historical. It was only Gandhiji who understood the village India. The village problem has to be solved by the villagers alone. He said every village should have an Ashram (later known after him as Gandhi Ashrams). These Ashrams will produce everything what the village wants... from spinning of yarn to growing of vegetables, from tanning of leather to preparing shoes and chappals, paper-making moonj-mats, swollen blankets, 'khes', 'durries'. The village schools should not buy anything from outside. They will produce their paper, their own ink, their own chalk, their own tat patties. In other words the village will be self-sufficient. The result was that villagers shook off their 'dependence' on others and stood on their own legs firmly. 'Dependence' said Gandhi, 'is a sin'. The villagers thus found occupation for their leisure hours and many idle hands were put to useful and productive work. He made it a duty of the villagers to keep their village clean and free from disease. Gandhi's basic education scheme was based on community participation where the community ran the schools and the dispensaries and took complete charge of its sanitation. The Mahatma was convinced that the innocent villagers are quite capable of looking after themselves, they do not need highly paid consultants who come to the village as if they were on a picnic, they give false assurances and disrupt the smooth span of their lives. In fact all rural development advisers should be withdrawn. Let the community look after itself. In Gandhiji's ideal village even government grants are not necessary, the community can generate its own resources. The example of Barefoot College at Tiloni in Rajasthan can be a role-model of community-based village.

Oldest Development Programme

Community development programme is one of the oldest programmes of the Government. No other programme has been subjected to greater probe and scrutiny than this programme meant to bring about an all-round improvement in the living conditions of rural India. Addressing both Houses of Parliament on May 16, 1952, Dr. Rajendra Prasad, India's first President announced an 8-Point Programme to raise the quality of life in Indian villages where the heart of India still beats. The Programme included:

1. Reclamation of wasteland, providing water for agriculture, development of other agricultural facilities for farmers;
2. Development of Roads and of Animal transport;
3. Provision of free and compulsory education upto primary stage in every village of India;
4. Provision of Public Health and Community Medical measures;
5. Providing houses for all villagers;
6. Imparting training to villages in different trades, including traditional trades handed over in the family from father to son;
7. Promotion of cottage industries and small-scale industries for self-employment; and
8. Other community programmes such as sports, khel-melas, and other cultural and entertainment programmes.

Although the above programme was financially supported by the United Stated Government and the Ford Foundation, it was expected that very soon it would be fully funded by national funds.

The First Five-Yea: Plan envisaged the establishment of 500 Community Centers. In 1953 'National Extension Service' was started. But Balwant Rai Mehta Committee (1957) found that the people's participation was not there and the Village Panchayats were not even involved. The Committee, therefore, recommended a three-tire system of rural local government namely the Village Panchayats at the local level, i.e., village, the Panchayat-Samiti at Block level and Zila Parishad at the district level. This was considered as a Magna Carta of Community participation in the New Village which was to emerge in Free India. The Panchayati Raj Institutions particularly the Gram Panchayats known as tiny legislatures worked very well till the mid-sixties but they fell out of favour as a form of local government.

The Ashok Mehta Committee Report (1978) sought to strengthen the Panchayati Raj not only through community participation but also open participation of political parties, induction of women and youth to make Panchayati Raj a people's movement. He made 100 recommendations including the two-tier system of Panchayati Raj instead the earlier three, viz., the Mandal Panchayats and the Zilla Parishad.

Elected directly by and from among the villagers all adult inhabitants of the village are its members. Most of these recommendations were theoretical. The result was the dream of 'Gram Rajya' remained unfulfilled till Rajiv Gandhi came on the scene, with his ideas of 'participatory development'. He wanted rural development to be based on science and technology, where the Panchayati Raj system should play a pivotal role. He was of the view that this system alone can enhance the awareness of the villagers about the various schemes launched by the government.

Gram Rajya

On 24th April, 1993, the Constitution (73rd Amendment) Act, 1992 came into force. It was a Red-Letter Day for the Panchayati Raj. It gave constitutional status to the Panchayati Raj Institutions. The Act provides for a three-tire system of Panchayati Raj in all states having a population of 20 lakhs, regular elections of these bodies every five years, reservation of seats for scheduled castes, scheduled tribes and women, with not less than one-third of the seats reserved for them appointment of state finance commissions to recommend financial powers to the Panchayats and to have district planning committees for preparing development plans for the entire district. The state governments lost no time to enact enabling legislation. The results have been spectacular. All-Women Panchayats have come into being. People's participation in decision making is on the increase. The onus of development in the rural sector is now on the villagers themselves, the fate of the villagers is no longer in alien hands. From being the creatures of history for centuries they are fast becoming the creators of history.

Present Position

There are at present more than two lakh Panchayats in the country with about 30 lakh elected representatives, out of whom six lakhs belong to scheduled castes and scheduled tribes and 10 lakhs of women. The 11th Schedule of the Constitution lists 29 subjects to the Panchayati Raj Institutions. If this army of elected representatives in converted into a community force, the six goals of Bharat Nirman will be met within the target year 2009. In a broader perspective they are almost the same as the 8-point programme announced by Dr. Prasad in 1952. The big difference was that it was not implemented, remained only on paper.

Rural-Urban Divide and Role of Panchayats

According to census 2001, out of the total population of 1027 billion, 285 million, i.e., 27.87 per cent people live in urban areas while 72.22 per cent live in rural areas but whereas 77.70 per cent people live in pucca houses in urban areas, only 29.20 per cent have this facility in rural areas. 81.38 per cent people in urban areas have access to drinking water whereas in rural areas only 55.34 per cent have this advantage. As regards electricity the urban-rural ratio is 75 per cent versus 30 per cent. In literacy it is 80 per cent versus 59 per cent. Life expectancy in rural areas is 59.4 per cent as against 66.34 per cent in urban areas. There are 6,38,000 villages in India and only 5,161 towns. The 2,17,300 Village Panchayats have provided an opportunity to the villagers to halt, even reverse this trend. The rural community's participation in this effort can yield extraordinary results. According to Prof. P.V. Indiresan, the author of PURA (Providing Urban Amenities in Rural Areas), the tests for any scheme for rural development are: whether it will generate enough jobs for educated rural youth to curb rural-urban divide and check rural-urban migration and whether it will be self-sustaining. I think, the Gram Panchayats have the last word, they alone can ensure community participation in this challenging task.

Bharat Nirman

In fact the role of community participation through Village Panchayats is even greater, to fulfill the six objectives of the Bharat Nirman viz. rural irrigation, rural roads, rural water supply, rural housing, rural electrification and rural telephony. With the active participation of the people the Government is determined to make this flagship programme a time-bound success. Truly speaking it is people's own programme where every village will have electricity, every habitation a road, safe drinking water, a telephone and every village family hopefully a pucca house. In the field of education and health the role of community cannot be over-emphasized. 'Mahila Samakhya' (Empowerment of Women through Education) has transformed the lives of 10,000 villages through a unique women's movement where women demand education, run schools and banks in rural areas. Under the scheme of inclusive education teachers visit the homes of the children who cannot come to the school. This participatory programme will ensure that very soon no child will be out-of–school, no adult illiterate and nobody without work. The emphasis is on the skill-training and not on the paper degree. In order to promote of participation of girls and women at all levels, there is need for and integrated approach in designing and implementing the schemes that would address all the factors that inhibit their education. Mere implementation of disaggregated schemes such as opening of non-formal centers for girls, adult education centers for women by themselves are not adequate. The Sarva Shiksha Abhiyan has taken care of these limitations.

Participative Educational Order

It is now being increasingly realized that only involvement of people and the community through participation can bring about the environment for genuine rural reform. Creation of school complexes, school clusters and the Common School System as originally recommended by Kothari Education Commission (1966) and endorsed by the National Educational Policies of 1968, 1986 and 1992, co-ordination between the primary, middle and the high schools, forging education industry inter-action through Community Polytechnics, involvement of the entire village community in non-formalizing the formal system of education true to the rural character are some of the important modalities for this new educational order. India is already the second largest education system in the world. Emphasis on participatory aspect will make it the largest and the finest qualitatively. The school, the college and the university must have social responsibility.

Empowerment of Rural Women

Participation of women is vital and a critical pre-condition in the new educational order which emphasizes the process rather than more fulfillment of targets. Mahila Samakhya to which a reference has been made earlier seeks to bring a change in the perception of rural women about themselves and the perception of the society in regard to women's traditional roles. There is a tide in the affairs of women creating a new environment for them to learn at their own pace, set their own priorities and seek knowledge and information to make informed choices. This essentially involves enabling rural women especially from socially and economically disadvaged and marginalized groups to address and deal with problems of isolation and lack of self-confidence, oppressive social customs, struggle for survival all of which inhibit their learning. It is in this process that rural women become empowered. Empowerment does not mean giving more powers to them, it only means giving them their long denied due.

The result of this empowering process is that a demand for education has been generated, women activists have emerged in rural areas, participation in Panchayati Raj bodies has increased, accountability of Government's delivery system is being insisted and an awareness of the need to struggle for gender-just society for effective participation is being strengthened. Thus the accumulated distortions of the past are being neutralized and there is a well-conceived edge in government's policies in favour of women, particularly rural women, indeed as a result of participatory movements.

Participatory Movements and Bharat Nirman

There are two types of participatory movements in the context of rural development viz., People's Organization and the Non-Governmental Organization. Both are voluntary in character, they work for the people and are non-profit-no loss organizations, funded by the tax-payer's money and having democratic credentials. However the distinction is not rigid as, more often than not, they run into each other. In India, SEWA (Self-Employed Women Association) is an NGO, a trade union of poor Indian women, both rural and urban, which concentrates on their problems in towns as well as villages. Their contribution to rural development is as praiseworthy as in the small towns.

Some NGO's are not as non-governmental as they appear to be. Although technically independent, they depend on the Government for sustenance and survival. Some of the rural voluntary organizations are a carbon copy of the government, their employees are retired government servants who cannot be accused of any new ideas. Times has thus come to review the performance of such organizations. But the fact must be faced that many NGO's reach where government cannot, particularly in rural areas. Besides people distrust the Government, not the NGO or a people's own organization. In other words the rural development in India cannot succeed without the help of participative agencies, the NGO's and the voluntary organizations. There will be no Bharat Nirman without the people's participation. Mobilising such participation means responding sensitively to the felt-needs of the people and the community. Vinoba Bhave used to say that if you do not take care of the villages, the village will not take care of you sooner than later.

Participatory movements are difficult to curb because they are demo critic and are generally peaceful. Besides their objective is raising the quality of life in the rural society. There are some experts who feel that providing urban facilities to rural areas is not the solution because that will take away the rural character of our villages – the fountain head of our culture and knowledge. In ancient India all our universities such as Nalanda, Vidarmsila, Taxila were located in villages. Today we have no rural universities except Gandhi Gram. Time has come to shift the IIT's and IIM's to rural areas as in South Korea with 100 per cent literacy or in Japan. We need not follow the Chinese model of 'rural business hubs'. The Indian village must remain Indian and indeed a village. In fact there is need to ruralise our urban areas.

It will thus be seen that people's participation in development is no longer a development jargon, a vague ideology or a closed door seminar, nor even a headline of a newspaper to be forgotten the next morning. It is a pre-condition of any development programme, and now a condition of survival for the civil society. To quote from a UNDP Report (1993) on Human Development: 'If states are to survive, they will have to establish new relationship with their people. Governments that have been able to respond sensitively and flexibly have so far been able to keep their countries in tact.'

Needless to say that India is one of them. India might have lost a few battles against poverty but now with people's participation, it will win war. It will not only survive, it shall prevail.

REFERENCES

1. Developing Village India (1946) published by the Imperial Council of Agricultural Research, New Delhi.
2. Community Development Vol. I (1960) and Community Development Vol. II (1961) by S.K. Dey published by Kitab Mahal, New Delhi.
3. Community Development in India (1961) published by Orient Longman by B. Mukerji.
4. Report of the Committee on Panchayati Raj Institutions (1978) published by the Ministry of Agriculture and Irrigation (Department of Rural Development).
5. Rural Development in India: Some Facts (1981) published by the National Institute of Rural Development, Hyderabad.
6. Basic Rural Statistics (2001) published by the Ministry of Rural Development.
7. Emerging Rural Development through Panchayats (2004) edited by Bibek Debroy and P.D. Kaushik.
8. Economic Survey (2005-06) published by the Ministry of Finance.
9. UNDP-Reports on Human Development (1993 onwards till date) Community Participation, Kurukshetra, A Journal of Rural Development 2007.

16

Artisans and Rural Development in Haryana: A Study of Kurukshetra District

Dr. Rajesh Kumar

Introduction

Rural development is a strategy to a specific group of people, poor rural women and men, to gain for themselves and their children more of what they want and need. It involves helping the poorest among those who seek a livelihood in the rural areas to demand and control more of the benefits of rural development. In this sense, it is a comprehensive and multi-dimensional concept and the development of agriculture and allied activities—village and cottage industries and crafts, socio-economic infrastructure community services and facilities, and above all the human resources in rural areas.

Historical Background of Rural Artisans

In pre-industrialized India, the village community was self-sufficient in economic terms. The rural artisans such as potters, carpenters, weavers, cobblers, blacksmiths, tailors, goldsmiths, plumbers etc. helped rural economy sustain on its own. In the earlier time they most often adopted their forefathers' vocations; their role was significant in maintaining rich cultural life. Consequently, this enclosed self-sufficient life-style paved the way to rich cultural traditions and practices in self-sufficient isolated villages. After the harvesting operations were over peasants households used to give a traditionally determined share out of their output to craftsmen and artisans and others. Due to progress of market economy this age-old bond of community living was destroyed and the artisans and craftsmen started getting payments for their services in rupees, right at the time of doing the work. Due to increasing magnetization of trade in rural areas enterprising artisans started to go out of their villages in the search of customers. This process continued throughout the independence movement.

Lack of capital, inferior techniques and obsolete looks and equipment were the main weaknesses of the rural artisans and craftsmen. The artisans and craftsmen of villages suffered very much. The weavers, potters, cobblers, goldsmiths, oilmen and dyers etc. all of them could not escape and fight with the competition of industrial goods. Further rapid growth of media communication and transportation network transformed the rural culture into a new life style, among the rural masses. The new generations discontinued their family occupations and attracted towards the city in search of factory, office jobs.

Meaning of Rural Artisan

A person deriving more than 50 per cent of his income from village crafts like carpentry, black smithing, handloom, leather works etc. is called rural artisan. As an independent occupation, rural artisans represent that class of rural households whose main function is to provide services ancillary to agriculture and farming. They also include households primarily engaged in such handicrafts as are needed largely to meet the local needs. In a sense, rural artisans the peculiars features of a subsistence village economy which has since undergone a process of fast disintegration—carpentry, blacksmith, goldsmith, masoning, weaving, dyeing etc. are some of the important trades of rural artisans.

The rural artisans conduct their activities at their own residence and mostly the family labour is employed and their market does not extend beyond the locality. They also utilize local raw materials, local skills and produce articles to meet local demand.

Problems of Rural Artisans

The rural artisans like potters, carpenters, weavers, shoemakers, blacksmiths etc. are facing many difficulties and problems these days. The importance of their artwork is decreasing in their respective villages and adjoining towns. The quality of their output is decreasing and they have to face great competition with the industrial sophisticated products. Major factors which are responsible to their failure in this regard can be listed and explained as under:

1. *Illiteracy of Artisans*

Mostly rural artisans are still illiterate or uneducated, some of them are not educated upto the matric level. Their illiteracy also a crucial factor which disposed of their family occupations, because they are not aware of the various policies and strategies of marketing and various artisans programme organised by the state and center government.

2. *Non-Availability of Raw Material*

Due to industrialization these rural artisans are facing the problems of non-availability of raw materials. For this raw material they have to depend upon the middle men and dealers on a very high prices and even of the poor quality. So these rural artisans have to shift as a labour to agriculture sector.

3. *Income Level of Rural Artisans*

The income level of rural artisan is also a main constraint for them. Most of the rural artisans are still below the poverty line. They cannot purchase good quality of raw material, modern tools and equipments.

4. *Use of Old and Obsolete Machinery and Equipments*

Most of the artisans basically engaged in handicraft or handloom business are using their old and obsolete tools, machinery and equipments which caused a drastic effect upon the quality and quantity of their output.

5. *Lack of Financial Assistance*

These rural artisans have to depend on money lenders for their financial requirements, who charged a great interest to their loans. However, government have announced loans on concessional rates and finance for tool-kits and equipments, yet that is not enough. They are still waiting to be awarded which can help them to survive their business and linked to the modern industries.

6. *Seasonal Demand of Their Products*

The demand of the product of rural artisans like, potters, weavers, carpenters etc. are quite seasonal in nature. There are so many factors which effect their sales such as crops, festivals (Holi, Diwali, Dussehra, Amavashya etc.), marriage and other social and cultural factors. In addition the maximum part of their sale is on credit because their main customers are rural persons, who make their payments on the crops and in exchange of foodgrains. They get their necessity goods throughout the year from these rural artisans. Hence, these poor artisans get their payment only two or three times in a year.

7. No Means of Transportation and Communication

These poor artisans are lacking the various facilities of transportation and communication in rural area. They have to depend on the means of transportation provided by the landlords on high charges. In addition to this they have no distribution centre from where they can distribute their products. They have to get to fairs and melas organised in the cities, where they can get some fair prices of their artwork.

8. Shift of Rural Customers Towards the Industrial Products

The growth of industrialization the demand of their product decreased substantially and attracted the rural buyers towards the machine-made, good looking, attractively packed products. The rapid growth of media communication and transportation network transformed the rural cultural life into a new life style among the rural masses.

Policies and Programmes

Different policies have been launched time to time by Government of India for the development of rural artisans under the different five-year plans. Some policy initiations regarding this can be studied as under:

Under the First Five Year Plan (1951-56) it was considered desirable to start regular programmes for artisans in rural areas. Further the plan emphasized the need for technical improvement in traditional artisans and craftsmen.

Under the Second Five Year Plan (1956-61) also included the policy of providing satisfactory arrangement for marketing research, rural electrification and improvement of housing conditions of rural artisans, credit and finance etc.

Under the Third Five Year Plan (1961-66) emphasis was laid on the programme of introduction of improved tools and equipments. The programme of improvement of Ambar Charkha, Oil Ghanies, equipments used in hand pounding of paddy in KVl Sector, coir spinning equipments, cottage basin in place of 'Charkhas' for reeling in sericulture and equipments and tools used in handicrafts.

The Fourth Five Year Plan (1969-74) emphasized to be placed on a variety of positive measures of assistance including liberal credit, adequate supply of raw materials, provision for technical assistance and improved appliances, tax concessions and different excise duty etc.

The Fifth Year Plan (1974-79) stressed to facilitate the attainment of some major tasks for the removal of poverty and inequality in consumption standards of artisans' dependent on traditional industries for fuller and additional productive employment and improvement of their skills so as to improve the level of earnings.

The Sixth Five Year Plan (1978-83) stressed the development efforts in the proposed plan were directed. "To generate opportunities for fuller and full time employment, to raise the level of earnings of rural artisans, handloom weavers, craftsmen and other employed in these industry in rural areas. The role of subsidies by providing these selectively for credit and development of skills, designs and marketing. The problem of obtaining raw material and lack of marketing arrangements have derived the artisans of a good part of the earning which should have accrued to them. The National Bank of Agriculture and Rural Development (NABARD) was set-up to provide refinance facilities, loans and advances to artisans.

The Seventh Five Year Plan (1985-90) was aimed at strengthening of infrastructure facilities of various levels, improve, productivity and quality and to lessen the dependence on subsidies.

Under the Eight Five Year Plan (1992-97) Haryana Khadi and Village Industries Board was established to provide financial assistance to the traditional artisans for setting up industry in the field assigned to the Board. It also provides financial assistance in the form of 50 per cent grant and 50 per cent loan for the purchase of tools, construction of work-sheds and working capital for the rural artisans and entrepreneurs.

Under the Ninth Five Year Plan (1997-2002) Government give the priority to rural development and rural artisans with a view to generating adequate employment and eradication of poverty.

Under the Tenth Five Year Plan (2002-07) Government provide finance through regional banks to agricultural and rural development.

Present Study

In present study area approach was followed villages (Sandhola, Sandholi, Ghumti, Malikpur, Dhudla) were selected adjoining to the Kurukshetra and studied comprehensively with respect to the difficulties and problems of rural artisans working in these villages. The area is semi-urban and full of rural cultural life on the Haryana State. There are number of rural artisans who have kept alive their family occupations. Potters, carpenters, weavers, shoemakers, blacksmiths, etc. are contributing their significant role.

The study in hand being the deeper analysis of the different problems of rural artisans from their raw-material to sale of their products for different earning their livelihood in the villages adjoining to Kurukshetra. The artisans were studied as they facilitate in attainment self-sufficiency rural economy. The study will also enable to suggest some policy measures to survive the artwork of rural artisans.

Rural Artisans Programmes in Haryana (1971-72)

The Rural Artisans Programme is a part of the central schemes of 'Small Farmers Development Agency' (SFDA) and 'Marginal Farmers' and Agricultural Labours (MF AL) launched by the Ministry of Food and Agriculture in 1971-72. The scheme was introduced in some selected areas of the country for a period of five years beginning from 1971-72. The main objectives of the programmes were:

- To upgrade the skills of rural artisans by imparting training in the use of improved tools and equipments.
- To meet the changing needs and demands of rural primary.
- To provide tools and equipments and working sheds at subsidized rates.

The Ministry of Agriculture issued financial and administrative sanctions to this programme whereas the Ministry of Industrial Development and the office of Development Commission (SS 1) scrutinized the proposal in relation to training, supply of tools and equipments etc.

Rural Artisan Programme (1976-77)

The Rural Artisan Programme was also introduced in 1976-77 to provide a short-term training to the rural artisans in Haryana State and 88 artisans were trained under this programme. But artisan development programme could not be wholly successful in achieving their objectives owing to certain problems. Also to ensure that the benefits of this programme reached to the weaker sections.

Rural Industries Scheme

It was undertaken by the government in the middle of the year 1977-78. The primary objective of this scheme was to protect, help and promote industries, specifically rural industries in rural areas of the state. It was expected that scheme would provide arrangements or facilities to modernize the units of traditional artisans and discourage them from abandoning their occupations.

Under Rural Industries Scheme (RIS), the rural artisans and entrepreneurs were provided loans at concessional rates, cash subsidy, training facilities, assistance in marketing, technical guidance etc. The rural and industrial artisans and their sons or dependents, landless labourers and other entrepreneurs were also to be assisted in raising their standard of living, their skills and motivating them to set-up tiny and college industries.

The Haryana State Small Industries and Export Corporation

It has launched training-cum-common facility centers for training the rural youth in various skills and also has made available to them common facilities in the shape of expensive machinery, design assistance, quality control apparatus and further government has established "Artistic Pottery Centre" under the handicrafts. Development Scheme at Jhajjar, a leather goods complex in 'Rewari'. The trade covered under the scheme in existing training centres include artistic pottery, leather goods, ban mudha, making hosiery and punja durries etc.

It also provides financial assistance in the form of 50 per cent grant and 50 per cent loan for the purchase of tools and equipments, construction of work-sheds and working capital.

Haryana State Handloom and Handicrafts Corporation

It was established in 1976 with the aim to promote the development of handloom and handicraft in the state. Today, it runs intensive development project at Bhiwani, Export Production Project at Panipat, two collective weaving centres and seven carpet training centres etc.

Further, to help in marketing the handloom products the corporation has opened showrooms at Chandigarh, Delhi, Bangalore, Madras, Calcutta and small retail showrooms at Bhiwani, Jind, Rohtak, Hisar, Sirsa, Chandigarh, Gurgaon, Yamuna Nagar, Solan, Kamal, Shimla, Jaipur etc. industry in the field assigned to the Board. It also provides financial assistance loan for the purchase of tools and equipments, construction of work-sheds and working capital.

Analysis and Interpretation

The present chapter includes the result of analysis and interpretation of data collected by researcher.

Analysis means the categorizing, ordering, manipulating and summarizing of data to obtain answer to research questions. The purpose of analysis is to reduce data to intelligible and interpretable form so that the relation to research problems can be studied and tested.

Interpretation calls for examination of results of one's analysis in the light all the limitations of one's data. Interoperation is most important step in total procedure of research. Analysis and interpretation of data also help future researchers to attach the related problems with appropriate technique to avoid the unnecessary labour.

It is clear from the Table–1 showing sources of raw material for rural artisans that 39 artisans acquire raw material for their products from their own village out of 50 i.e. 78 per cent. 9 artisans out of 50 i.e. 18 per cent acquire raw material for their products from adjoining villages. Only 2 artisans out of i.e. 4 per cent fulfill their raw material requirements from towns. Hence, he is accepted i.e. the main source of raw material for rural artisans is their own village itself.

Table–1
Showing Various Sources of Raw Material for Rural Artisans

	Own village	*Adjoining village*	*Town*	*Total*
Kumhar	6	3	1	10
Jullaha	10	-	-	10
Khati	7	3	-	10
Mochi	7	3	-	10
Lohar	9	-	1	10
	39	9	2	50

Table–2
Showing Possible Uses of Products of Rural Artisans

	Own village	*Adjoining village*	*Town*	*Total*
Kumhar	7	2	1	10
Jullaha	5	3	2	10
Khati	8	1	1	10
Mochi	6	-	4	10
Lohar	10	-	-	10
	36	6	8	50

Table–2 express that there are 36 artisans who are making daily used products out of 50 i.e. about 72 per cent. There are 6 artisans out of fifty i.e. 12 are producing products for decoration purpose and there are only an artisan out of 50 per cent i.e. 16 per cent are producing products and articles for cultural usage. Hence we can conclude that maximum products are of daily use produced by rural artisans.

Table–3
Showing Annual Output of Rural Artisans

	More than 20,000	*More than 30,000*	*More than 35,000*	*More than 40,000*	*Total*
Kumhar	2	5	3	-	10
Jullaha	7	3	-	-	10
Khati	8	1	-	1	10
Mochi	9	-	-	1	10
Lohar	10	-	-	-	10
	36	9	3	2	50

Table–3 shows that there are 36 artisans out of 50 i.e. 72 per cent whose annual output is more than Rs. 20,000. There are 9 artisan out of 50 per cent i.e. 18 per cent whose annual output is more than Rs. 30,000. There are 3 artisans out of 50 i.e. whose annual output is more than Rs. 35,000. In the same way there are 2 artisans out of 50 i.e. 4 per cent who are producing an annual output more than Rs. 40,000.

Table–4
Showing Number of Family Members Involved

	All members	*Single member*	*Self & labour*	*Total*
Kumhar	10	-	-	10
Jullaha	9	1	-	10
Khati	9	-	1	10
Mochi	9	1	-	10
Lohar	10	-	-	10
	47	2	1	50

It is clear from Table–4 that there are 47 artisans out of 50 i.e. 94 per cent whose all the family members are involved in their business activities. There are just 2 artisans out of 50 i.e. 4 per cent where no family members is involved and there is only 1 artisan out of 50 i.e. 2 per cent where labour is also appointed to carry on the business operation.

Table–5
Showing Factors Affecting Sale of Rural Artisans

	Crops and Festivals	*Taste of New Generation*	*Media*	*Total*
Kumhar	9	-	1	10
Jullaha	7	1	2	10
Khati	9	1	-	10
Mochi	9	1	-	10
Lohar	5	3	2	10
	39	6	5	50

Table–5 shows that there are 39 artisans out of 50 i.e. 78 per cent whose sale is affected by crops and some festivals like Holi, Diwali, Dussehra etc. There are 6 artisans out of 50 i.e. 12 per cent whose sale is affected by the preferences and taste of new generations in the rural area. There are only 5 artisans out of 50 i.e. 10 per cent whose sale is affected by the media communication network. Hence, we conclude that the demand of their products upon the crops and festivals. It is seasonal in nature so we accept H6 i.e. the demand of their product is in season.

Table–6

Showing Barter System Still Prevailing in Rural Artisans

	Yes	*No*	*Total*
Kumhar	10	-	10
Jullaha	10	-	10
Khati	10	-	10
Mochi	10	-	10
Lohar	10	-	10
	50	-	50

The Table–6 shows that 50 artisans gave the answer in yes out of 50 to the question It is barter system still prevailing in the village or rural economy. Hence, we conclude that the barter system is still prevailing in the rural economy and H2 is accepted i.e. Barter system is still prevailing in the marketing by rural artisans.

Table–7

Showing Area of Marketing for Rural Artisans

	Village Level	*District Level*	*Both*	*Total*
Kumhar	7	2	1	10
Jullaha	8	1	1	10
Khati	8	1	1	10
Mochi	8	1	1	10
Lohar	8	1	1	10
	39	6	5	50

It can be seen from the Table–7 that there are 39 artisans out of 50 i.e. 78 per cent whose marketing area does not extend to the village level and there are 6 artisans out of 50 i.e. 12 per cent whose marketing area is upto district level and there are also 56 artisans out of 50 per cent i.e. 10 per cent whose marketing activities covers the area both for village and district level.

Table-8
Showing Area Tools and Equipments used by Rural Artisans

	Traditional	*Modem*	*Total*
Kumhar	9	1	10
Jullaha	9	1	10
Khati	9	1	10
Mochi	10	-	10
Lohar	10	-	10
	47	3	50

Table-8 shows that there are 47 artisans out of 50 i.e. 94 per cent who are still using their traditional tools land equipments which are old and obsolete and adversely affecting the quality and quantity of their output. There are only 3 artisans out of 50 who are using modem tools and equipment which is just 6 per cent of the total. The rural artisans are still using old and obsolete tools.

Conclusion and Suggestions

This is a study of artisans in Kurukshetra district concerning the five villages. The evolution of planned development strategy for village industry is as old as the development planning in the country itself. However, adequate attention for the first time was paid only during the second five-year plan. It witnessed the evolution of the industrial policy resolution 1956, constitution of Khadi and Village Industries and introduction of 'pilot project' progrmme in certain selected areas. Efforts were made in the plan to crave out and independent status of the village and small industry sector.

Further, the rapid growth of media communication and transportation network transformed the rural culture into new life style among the rural masses. The new generations discontinued their family occupations and attracted towards the city in search of factory, office jobs. The media communication network exposed them to new glamorous entertainment means of life.

Technology, Technical Assistance and Training Technology

The rural artisan for instance is not a small industry but he has the potential to become one. As his technology is upgraded and his production goes beyond the subsistence level, he begin to think of expanding his operation and his own vision begins to widen. In fact, the whole object of rural development is to enable the rural artisan to grow and not to continue at low level of subsistence to which he has been used for centuries. This low technology has been growth of rural artisan.

Technical Assistance

The State Directorate of Industries, the SISIS and the one of the major constraints in the their associated facilities centers and small scale industries development. The technical advice available from State Khadi and Village Industries Board (SKVIB) is also available to the artisans through the specialized institutions, established by KVIC, while the Board itself appoints experts in various districts. Therefore, it may be stated that in the matter of technical assistance being provided to the rural artisans poorly served and are very much behind the modern small-scale sector. It is unfair to expect the rural artisans to accept new technology on their own, for this purpose continuous and co-ordinated efforts are very much required.

Financial Assistance

For the purpose of rural sector beside these schemes, there are a number of bankable schemes to meet the requirement of small rural artisans and self-employed persons. The Khadi and Village Industry Commission has also been helping the individuals and institutions from its budgetary allocations by providing loans through the Board and directly through its regional centers. These schemes are also designed to serve comprehensively the credit needs of small enterprises and artisans.

It is also evident from the fact that in the state of Haryana all the targets fixed by the government irrespective of amount of finance made available to the artisans. But the most of the bankable schemes are ill-prepared, ill organized and indeed ill-conceived. They failed to achieve the desired results and result in damaging the image of banks and the national economy. Also the low rate of interest and subsidy factor in the financial sector breed corruption in the system. As a result genuine borrowers may be rejected and fake borrowers may find it easy to get the loan. This is what happening in reality now-a-days particularly with those schemes which involve subsidy and low rate of interest.

On the basis of above discussion, it is clear that the availability, of finance assistance to the artisans is a tiring an complicated process. Therefore there is a great need to simplify this process and make it convenient for the rural artisans.

Supply of Raw Materials

The essential raw material, particularly the scarce once, are distributed through an allocation system. Small scale units and rural artisans can exercise lesser influence on government than their large counterparts. The position of the rural artisans and traditional sector is not good as its size is even small than modern small-scale sector and they have not any association of its own to influence the authorities or government policies in its favour.

But the availability of scarce raw material to the rural artisans is neither adequate nor regular in the state in spite of the establishment of raw material distribution centers by the Haryana Small Scale Industries and Export Corporation in different districts.

Marketing Assistance

To facilitate regular marketing arrangement, the government has been mainly undertaking the following measures:

- *(i)* Exclusive purchase of specific products of small scale units, cottage industry and rural artisans.
- *(ii)* Price percentage (of specified percentage) to small scale enterprises and artisans in public sector purchases.
- *(iii)* Provisions of quality control and testing facilities with a view to increase the competitiveness of the products of small scale units.
- *(iv)* Assisting in the sale of products of small enterprises, artisans (modern and traditional) by operating sale emporia under the state owned cooperatives and assisted cooperative societies.

This type of marketing assistance has been provided by the SISI located at Kamal, Haryana State Small Industries and Export Corporation through its various sub-centres located in different districts. Handloom 'Apex Society' at Panipat and many other outlets set up by the KVIC and HKVIB. These are state Emporia of HSSI and EC, Handloom and Handicraft Corporation and

Harijan Kalyan Nigam etc. in different cities and also even outside the state.

Last but not least education is the theme song of the picture entitled artisan and rural development at the grassroots level. Education and awareness are interlinked. We will have to revive our adult education centers to enable artisans to become more educated and aware. It should be mandatory for both male and female illiterate artisans.

- Training centers should be opened and these should be located in the villages themselves. The training centers should have a significance for rural orientations.
- The capacity building at the grassroots level is a pre-requisite for artisan capacity can be built through simple neighbourhood groups of Gram Sabha, Self-Help Group, Task Forces, Specialized Committee, NSS arid Voluntary organizations etc.

In democracy it is joint responsibility of the state and community at large to improve the lot of artisans the state will have to accept some responsibilities to facilitate to the artisans in rural area.

There is need to identify key communicators among rural artisans they can play crucial role in moderating them to accept new ideas.

The role of mass media in building awareness cannot be ignored. There should be concerted efforts to all mass media to evolve a greater role for artisans in the rural area.

17

Going Beyond Formal Processes to Empower the People: The Case of a Local Water Supply System

Dr. M. Rajivlochan

A doll with weighted feet is impossible to knock off. The same holds true for societies. Those that are weighted at the bottom tend to get upright despite the vagaries of circumstances trying to throw them off balance. The spirit behind the empowerment of Panchayats is much in line with trying to provide weight to the feet. Yet we need to make a distinction between the formal mechanisms envisaged for the empowerment of the people and the substantive efforts at doing so. It is not just the Government, following the constitutional directives that insists on elections to a number of village level bodies for running the government at village level. Even the directives from the World Bank today for various projects insist on having elected bodies to run different components of the projects funded by the Bank. "Or else you will not get the money", the Bank seems to be telling local communities. As a result we have seen the emergence of a plethora of elected bodies with adequate representation in them of women and SC/ST groups. How far these bodies are effective is anyone's guess. Yet, in practice, there could be many other ways, not necessarily through formal elections, of ensuring active participation of the people in decision making at the local level. In the is chapter we look at a case of how such non-elected systems of popular participation were created in a local community. That they have been effective and produced desired results for over two decades now would only suggest that when evaluating the quality of people's participation in decision making we need to give adequate importance to local contingencies, needs and abilities.

A Self-Reliant Community

The two small villages of Devka and Chikhalgaon in the tehsil of Dapoli in district Ratnagiri, lie next to the coast of Maharashtra about 400 km. from the city of Bombay. Yet despite the great distance, the city of Bombay reaches out and touches life in these communities in many ways. Nearly all the families here have at least one family member working in Bombay who still defines these villages as a home away from home. Bombay is merely the place where they work. All these men come back at least twice a year to celebrate the festivals of Ganpati and Holi at home. They regularly send money to support their families. Yet not many choose to sever the umbilical cord and shift their families to the city. Only when they retire do they move back to the village and send a new generation away to work. Those who come back at a younger age tend to experiment with new ideas, often with remarkable results.

One such man who came back was Ramchandra Laxman Gorivale, a man of the Tilori-Kunbi community, originally from the village of Devka. Gorivale worked as a typesetter in a printing press located in the Mazagaon Docks of Bombay for over fourteen years. He seems to have been something of a radical even in his Bombay days. He was the leader of the company union. He remembers distinctly leading a demonstration to the Government Secretariat at Nariman Point to demand a raise in Dearness Allowance.

Homeward Bound

Then in the year 1974, while still in his early 30s, Gorivale quit the city to help his brother set up a printing press in Dapoli. He participated in this venture till 1983 when the brothers parted ways. Meantime Gorivale had also entered public life in his native village of Devka. Devka was then and still continues to be, part of a Group Gram Panchayat of four villages which includes Chikhalgaon, Kinhad and Made. He was elected sarpanch of the combined Panchayat of these four villages for the first time in 1978 and again in 1982. These two tenures were put to excellent use as many people in these villages testify even today after the passage of twenty years.

Gorivale could see that one of the major problems facing the villages was the getting of drinking water. These are hilly villages and the source of water is invariably a stream at the bottom of the hill. This means that the village women had to walk down and up again with a head-load several times a day. One old lady recalled that they were used to doing as many as ten trips a day, each trip taking at least half an hour. So nearly half the working day used to be spent in the procuring of this essential item. The hills in these parts are rocky with little soil cover. Any slip could and often did result in injury. Moreover the villages were dispersed into many small wadis or independent settlements and often each wadi did not have an independent source of water, thereby increasing the distance the women had to walk.

Approaching the Government

Gorivale did what he could to remedy this state of affairs. He used the Panchayat funds to build wells closer to home for many of the wadis. But more needed to be done. He felt that the village could easily maintain its own piped water supply scheme without too much difficulty. How to find the funds for the initial capital investment was a major problem. He seems to have approached the local MLA and obtained sanction for a water supply scheme for Devka. Devka comprises the three wadis of Dattawadi, Ambikawadi or Varchiwadi (meaning the settlement at the top) and Baudhwadi (the backward caste settlement). Gorivale himself is a resident of Ambikawadi. The initial scheme covered only two wadis: the Dattawadi and Baudhwadi. This scheme was commissioned during his second tenure as sarpanch in 1982-83. But it never worked well. The pipes were galvanized iron pipes but evidently the material was not of particularly good quality. The pipes kept rusting. Besides they seemed to get continuously clogged up with mud. Gorivale says they eventually tired of cleaning the pipes every other day and finally abandoned the effort. Next time they would do better.

Meantime Gorivale suffered an upset in his public life. He was re-elected as member of the Group Gram Panchyat in 1986. But in the election for sarpanch, he was upstaged by a Ganpat Govind Bhuval of village Chikhalgaon who became sarpanch instead. We do not know the details of what happened but evidently it was enough to give Gorivale a permanent dislike of politics and everything associated with it. After completing his third tenure, he refused to stand for election again, despite repeated requests by many that he should do so. His own brother was elected to the Dapoli Panchayat Samiti in 1984-85. However, Gorivale continued to remain active in public life in many other ways. Till today, he is the Chairperson of the Adinath Varkari Sampradaya Mandal Dapoli.

We Can Manage

He spent this last tenure in making efforts towards establishing another water supply scheme, but this time he seemed to have made up his mind to have no further truck with the government. Clearly he felt that the village community, which already had a strong tradition of collective activity, could manage on its own. Outsiders have testified to the existence of such activity. Dinesh Dhondji Rane, Agriculture Assistant with the Agriculture University at Dapoli, who worked in this area between 1987 and 1997, recollects that in these villages, people had a tradition of gathering together on the night of amavasya every month. That night no agricultural operation was conducted and people simply gathered together to discuss their common problems. Attendance in these collective meetings seems to have been mandatory. At least that is the case today, so much so that those who do not come, have to pay a fine of Rs. 5 which is imposed and collected with some rigour. Perhaps the fine is of recent origin; the sabha clearly is not.

Meantime Gorivale used his own resources and those of his friends to conduct a survey for the water supply scheme and to prepare a plan estimate. He also seems to have decided that it would be better for the future of the scheme if it was implemented for and maintained by only one wadi rather than a combination of wadis. This scheme was to be for the Dattawadi in his native village of Devka.

Once the estimate was ready, it was time to start collecting funds. Gorivale succeeding in getting the electric pump for the scheme for free from his wife's nephew, Ramesh Daulat Bhaykar who lived in Mumbai. The names of all 59 donors to the scheme were duly inscribed on the pump-house next to the source well. Each household in the wadi was asked to contribute Rs. 1000 for the scheme.

The agricultural economy of this area however, being entirely dependent upon rainfed farming, is very fragile. Less than 1 per cent of the land cultivated in either Devka or Chikhalgaon is irrigated. The crops of rice and a local millet called nagli or nachni are grown in the monsoon months and that is the end of the farming season. This income is supplemented by earning from some mango, cashew and coconut trees but most households own just a few trees. In such circumstances, raising the money only on the basis of the village economy would have been far more time consuming. It was the Datta

Prasadik Vikas Mandal, the community of males from Dattawadi working in Bombay, who speeded up collection with the monthly remuneration which they sent home. This monthly amount today, ranges from Rs. 500 for those who work as domestics in Bombay to Rs. 2500-3000 for those in skilled jobs. The Mahila Mandal did its bit by donating some Rs. 1000 from the monthly saving of Rs. 2 per month of its members.

Some concessions were given to the few households in the village who were economically weak such as widows with little family support. However even these houses had to make some contribution in instalments. Gorivale says that everyone, however poor, was required to offer something. Eventually the Rs. 80000 required for building the scheme (including a well, a tank for holding the water and the pipeline) were gathered together and work began in earnest.

Much care was spent on locating a good site for the water tank. Large red stones called "jambha dagad" (dagad is Marathi for stone) characterize the landscape in this area. It is used extensively in construction in the Konkan. Gorivale says that they identified a site with an excellent foundation of this jambha dagad so that the tank would have a solid base and so that they would need to dig only very little. The site was located about 80 feet above the level of the water to get a sufficient head for distribution by gravity. The tank was built of bricks. Most of the pipes and other material required was bought at Mumbai. Gorivale himself supervised all activities but with the active support of the inhabitants of Dattawadi. Evidently they were tired of the daily struggle to get water and had confidence in his ability to deliver the goods. He justified their confidence.

All labour in constructing the scheme was contributed free of cost as "shramdaan" by the villagers. Once the pipeline was laid, Gorivale remembers that they left it uncovered in its pit (which was 1-1.5 ft deep) for one month so that they could check that the flow of water was clear. Only after this did they cover the pipes with soil. The scheme was completed successfully. Now it is over fifteen years old and the old tank and pipeline remains in good repair. The only trouble that they consistently had was with electricity. An unreliable and fluctuating electric supply meant that the switches often got burnt. The motor however functioned well for many years. Then it got burnt and it was replaced with a submersible pump of 5 HP rating. Otherwise, the scheme functioned well and continues to work till today. Except for some days during the monsoon when the electricity supply is invariably disrupted, the women no longer have to spend half their day getting water.

In like manner, a separate water supply scheme was constructed for Ambikawadi in Devka village in the year 2001. Baudhwadi did not participate in either of these schemes but now, in 2007, they are planning to set up one for themselves. Perhaps gathering so much money is a constraint. Gorivale says that Baudhwadi would ask for and get the government grant for backward caste settlements.

Replicating the Model

The success of the schemes inspired many people in the surrounding villages to attempt to replicate this model though they did try to obtain government help first.

In the mid 1990s, the villagers of Chikhalgaon seem to have approached the Zilla Parishad with a request for a water supply scheme. The Maharashtra Jeevan Pradhikaran (the State Water Resources Authority) then drew up a scheme which proposed to cover all eight wadis at a cost of Rs. 32 lakh. Pipes and material for the scheme were duly bought and supplied to the village. The engineers came and identified a spot for the new well for the scheme. This was to be near the dug well next to the nullah which was then the main source of drinking water for the village. However two years passed and there was no sign that the scheme would proceed any further. It is not clear whether the villagers were asked to make a 10 per cent capital contribution which they could not do or whether another reason was responsible for the delay. Whatever be the case, the people grew tired of waiting.

It was here that Agriculture Assistant Rane and the teachers at the local Zilla Parishad school stepped in to help. Two teachers in particular are remembered till today and of them, one continues to be actively associated with the scheme. One was the then Headmaster, a Shri Shigwan and the second was a Chandrakant Mahadev Ujad who was also a native of village Chikhalgaon and posted here at the time.

Rane had already been using the local tradition of monthly meetings on amavasya day to spread his message of extension. He had encouraged the people to start cultivating a kitchen garden by using waste water, as a means to supplement limited agricultural income. Mango, coconut, cashew trees were duly planted by most households but then they came across the problem of water scarcity. The only source of water in the village was the nullah flowing at the bottom of the hill on which it was located. And all the women had to carry the water in head-loads upto their houses.

Rane and the two teachers encouraged the Chikhalgaon people to plan their water supply scheme themselves. The two wadis of Ganeshwadi and Saiwadi located in the centre of the village, were the first to respond. The officials had impressed one thing upon them: that they would need to act collectively to be able to bring affordable water to their houses and they actively started looking for a technically feasible and affordable design for a water supply scheme.

The government agriculture university called the Konkan Krishi Vidyapeeth located at tehsil headquarters Dapoli, supplied the assistance required. No doubt the fact that Chikhalgaon is only about 18 kms away from Dapoli and is connected with a good metalled road, increased accessibility. Rane contacted Shri Sukhdev Kale, a faculty member of the agriculture university for help. Kale was an expert in Water Systems Management. The matter was of considerable interest to Kale who had worked on some such schemes earlier as well. He offered his services free of charge. Along with Rane, he conducted a site survey and designed a scheme for Ganeshwadi and Saiwadi which would cost about Rs. 1.87 lakh.

This included a water tank of 35,000 litres capacity, a 10 HP submersible pump and distribution of water by gravity. The tank would be enough to provide the seventy odd households of the two wadis with more than double the 40 litres per capita per day of water, which was the prevalent norm prescribed by the government. In addition, Kale says, he also factored in water to be used for the kitchen gardens. PVC pipes were to be used for the scheme. As Kale explains, the use of PVC brought down the cost considerably. PVC pipes can easily withstand heads of upto 60 metres (which was more than what this scheme required) and they have a life of 30-40 years. Equally importantly, this is a material with which farmers are used to working in their fields and repair is an easy task.

Before taking up the work of construction, the villagers visited three other schemes which had been set up before hand in the nearby villages in order to ascertain for themselves what were the strengths and weaknesses of each. In two out of three cases, the work on the water tank was not well done and the tank leaked. The Chikhalgaon people resolved that they would avoid these mistakes. The availability of local technical expertise had a significant impact on the quality of construction. The water tank of the Ganeshwadi-Saiwadi scheme does not leak while that of the Manewadi scheme does. We were told that the former had access to an expert mason who closely supervised construction and ensured that the cement work was properly done. Working with the jambha dagad apparently requires some skill.

The site for the well was located at some 10-15 feet distance from that identified by the engineers of the Maharashtra Jeevan Pradhikaran. The well and pump-house, so it is said, were on a private person's land. He, so the villagers report, donated the land for the well and pump-house and in return they promised him free water. A small sintex tank was installed next to the pump-house exclusively for the use of his family. However the revenue officials told us that being on the banks of the nullah, the well is legally public property. It was to get out of this problem that the villagers applied for an electric meter for the pump in the name of a private person.

Now the villagers began a fund collection drive in earnest. But the collection of so much money was no easy task. The two teachers from the Zilla Parishad seemed to have played a major role in mobilizing the community and helping gather the funds. Each household was asked to contribute Rs. 800. Those working in Mumbai sent money to their families and Rs. 50000 was gathered to begin with.

The various Mahila Mandals extant in the village were co-opted in the fund raising effort. Shri Chandrakant Ujad, the Zilla Parishad teacher, told us that the Mahila Mandals contributed Rs. 50000 for the scheme. The Utkarsh Mahila Mandal had existed in Chikhalgaon since the year 1984. This was followed by the Saiwadi Mahila Mandal in 1990 and then others. Parvati Pandurang Advilkar, a 65-year old lady from a Tilore-Kunbi family who is a founder member of the Utkarsh Mahila Mandal, recollects that they had formed the Mandal to address their collective problems and save Rs. 2 every month for an emergency. This monthly saving has now been raised to Rs. 5.

Given the meagre monthly savings of the Mandal, it seems a little difficult to believe that they could have contributed Rs. 50000. Sure enough, the talathi (revenue official) later told us that Ujad had attributed the Rs. 800 contributed by every household, to the Mahila Mandals. In these days of micro finance, he may well have thought that attributing so much effort to the Mahila Mandals was the politically correct thing to say. Whatever be the case, the Mandals undoubtedly contributed some cash for the cause. The ladies from the Mandal proudly remember how hard they worked to gather this money.

Eventually the villagers succeeded in collecting Rs. one lakh. This was not enough but they thought that they would begin by digging the well and then see how things went. So the scheme was implemented in stages. The money was used to purchase materials and the well was dug entirely through shramdaan. The villagers organized all the seventy participating families in a way that five were scheduled to work on Monday, five on Tuesday, five on Wednesday and so on throughout the week.

They succeeded in laying the pipeline and in bringing the water to the point of distribution. There was no money left to build the storage tank but water had been brought to one point in the wadis. The villagers thought that they would all come to this point and get their water. At this point, help arrived from an unexpected quarter.

One of the persons from the village worked for a seth in Bombay as a driver. This seth had earlier donated Rs. 1.5 lakh to help them build a Ganesh Mandir. He was to come to the village to inaugrate the mandir. Instead the people decided to ask him to inaugrate the water supply scheme. He enquired whether it was complete and how much money was needed for completion. And the man donated Rs. one lakh to the water supply scheme. This was enough to build the storage tank and eleven stand-posts.

In most of the stories from these villages, the city of Bombay figures again and again and it seems to be the connection with the city which makes all the difference. In Manewadi, also of village Chikhalgaon, the males of the wadi working in Mumbai organized an Udaya Natya Mandal which put up many cultural performances at Azad Maidan so they say, to gather funds for their water supply scheme. Manewadi too found a patron seth who financed the building of their water supply tank.

However, Gorivale's memories of the seths of Bombay are not so happy. He too at one time approached the Bombay seth who had helped out the people of Chikhalgaon. But the seth, so he reports, asked for the 80 C certificate needed to claim tax exemption. Gorivale could not give the certificate and so he did not get the money. He says that this seth was a Non resident Indian whose Chikhalgaon employee provided him significant managerial help for his Bombay business.

Whatever the seth's reasons for helping, his contribution undoubtedly played a major role in the Ganeshwadi-Saiwadi water supply scheme. It was commissioned in the year 1998 and functions successfully till today. Chandrakant Mahadev Ujad, the Zilla Parishad teacher who helped construct the scheme, is now the Secretary of the Ganeshwadi-Saiwadi Water Supply Scheme though he is no longer posted at Chikhalgaon.

Shigwan retired from government service and is no more but he lives on in the memory of all those whom he helped.

Sustaining the Effort

Even more interesting than the story of how these schemes were built is the story of how they were maintained. The villagers maintain that it is co-operative effort and trust in each other that was crucial to their success. No doubt this is true but the trust was nowhere blind. In fact these communities have set up a complex system of checks and balances which ensures that no one person can create difficulties for the collective.

And while there are minor technical differences in the schemes and some differences in the sources of funding, the management systems are remarkably similar in all cases.

Firstly, each water supply scheme uses an electric pump with a meter registered in the name of a private person. Nor was the person so chosen only because he or she lived closer to the facility. This was a collective decision and the villagers might choose anyone whom they feel they could trust. All these persons were made to sign a letter stating that they had no right to the pump which remained the property of the village water supply scheme.

Secondly, each water supply scheme is maintained by a Mandal which has two office-bearers: the President or Adhyaksha as he is called and the Secretary who is responsible for all record keeping.

But the scheme funds are kept in the bank account of a third person entirely. The Dattawadi scheme keeps its funds in an account in the Bank of Maharashtra branch in Burundi which is about 3 km away. The villagers do not reimburse the travel expenses of anyone for going to Burundi for the scheme, either to deposit money or to withdraw it from their bank account. Instead they ask the others as to whether they have work of their own in Burundi the next day and anyone who is going for his own work, is assigned the task of conducting the transaction.

Thirdly, the working of the scheme is reviewed and water taxes collected in the monthly meeting which is held on a fixed day of the month. In Ganeshwadi-Saiwadi for instance, the meeting is held on the Sunday following the first of every month. Women and men sit jointly for this meeting in all the wadis. Attendance is rigorously enforced. As mentioned earlier, anyone who fails to turn up has to pay a fine of Rs. 5. Proceedings of the meeting are written on the spot which is very different from what happens in the case of Gram Sabha meetings where proceedings are often written months later and which may not be accurate in their reportage.

In these meetings, each household has to pay the monthly water tax prescribed by the community. This rate varies from Rs. 25 to Rs. 50 in the wadis. Most of the wadis have revised the rate upwards in successive years.

Finances of the Schemes

The Table–1 gives an idea of the rate of increase in these self-imposed taxes over the years.

Clearly the rates have risen consistently over the years. Only in the case of Kamblewadi was the initial rate of Rs. 50 found to be unnecessarily high and it was later revised downwards to Rs. 30. In none of the wadis, has any distinction been made in the matter of tax assessment between households availing of water through a household connection and households availing of water through the stand-post. The residents of Ganeshwadi-Saiwadi explained that this was unnecessary as they had already charged a deposit of Rs. 2500 from all the 50 households which had taken house connections and some cash balance remained from these deposits. The wadis of Devka have not charged any such amount from private connections but the Ambikawadi residents say that they have decided to charge Rs. 5000 from anyone who applies for a fresh connection.

Table–1
Rate of Water Tax Per Household in Wadi—Specific Water Supply Schemes

Village / *Year*	*Devka Dattawadi*	*Devka Ambikawadi*	*Chikhalgaon Ganeshwadi-Saiwadi*	*Chikhalgaon Manewadi*	*Chikhalgaon Kamblewadi*
1992	10				
1993	10				
1994	10				
1995	15				
1996	15				
1997	15				
1998	15				
1999	15	20	20		
2000	20	20	20		
2001	20	20	25		
2002	20	30	25	25	
2003	20	30	25	25	
2004	20	30	25	50	50
2005	20	40	25	50	30
2006	20	40	30	50	30
2007	30	40	50	50	30

Some wadis make concessions to the weaker households in the matter of payment. For instance, Saiwadi has four widows with minor children and they are offered a concessional rate of Rs. 25 per month against the Rs. 30 payable by others. However, the difference of Rs. 20 has to be made up for by the wadi as a whole, i.e., the concession holds for the widows and not for the wadi. In the Ganeshwadi-Saiwadi scheme, Saiwadi has to contribute Rs. 810 per month and Ganeshwadi has to contribute Rs. 1000 per month. Any concessions they might make to some houses are internal to the wadi and have to be made up for by the rest. As a result, the communities are quite strict in evaluating anyone's ability to pay. Some of the women of Saiwadi said that there was a widow with a minor son who was as disadvantaged as the four other widows in their wadi but she was still asked to pay Rs. 30 per month. Others from the wadi said that she might be disadvantaged but she still had some support from her father and brothers and so she could pay the normal rate.

All wadis supply drinking water free of charge to the local Zilla Parishad school and to the mandir.

One matter about which all villagers uniformly complained was the ever rising electricity bill. In the case of the Ganeshwadi-Saiwadi scheme, the running cost of the 10 HP motor installed initially was found to be so high that the villagers gathered together some more money to purchase a fresh motor of 5 HP rating within three years of commissioning the scheme. Now they run the pump for about three hours daily which is sufficient to fill up the water tank and allows them to release water for about half an hour in the morning everyday.

The water tax collected seems to be sufficient to cover the routine expenses of the scheme. However occasional non-routine expenditure such as the purchase of a new pump might entail a round of fresh contributions.

There are three main components to the maintenance expenditure: Staff, Electricity and Repair. TCL is provided by the Village Panchayat free of cost. However the wadis have to hire someone both to add the TCL to their tanks and also to run the pumps. The Table–2 gives an idea of the current maintenance expenses of the various schemes:

Table–2
Monthly Maintenance Costs for Water Supply

Village Description Item	*Devka Dattawadi*	*Devka Ambikawadi*	*Chikhalgaon Ganeshwadi-Saiwadi*	*Chikhalgaon Manewadi*	*Chikhalgaon Kamblewadi*
Households covered	44	60	69	36	15
Population covered			260	113	42
Electricity Bill	1000	1200-1500	850	400-650	185-250
Staff Cost	400	350	400	250	100
Repair (all wadis gave this as an annual figure and we divided this by 12)	40	40	100	100	60
Average M & R bill for the month	1440	1740	1350	875	377
Average Maintenance cost per household per month	33	29	20	25	25

The costs of repair have been brought down in recent months in some of the wadis which succeeded in developing indigenous skills. Thus Ganeshwadi-Saiwadi now has a local boy named Rajesh Keshav Ghod who received two years of training in a private facility in Dapoli. So when they needed to replace the 10 HP pump with a 5 HP pump and they got an expenditure estimate of Rs. 45000 from a Dapoli shop, they got Ghod to obtain and install the pump at less than half this cost in Rs. 20000.

These communities have also established norms which ensure that their living space remains clean. Each house maintains a kitchen garden to use up the waste water. One tree has been planted near every stand-post for the same purpose. No doubt they are helped in this by the hilly topography which ensures that the water drains off very fast. In some wadis, we also found that many houses had compost pits to recycle waste. However there is no segregation of waste in general.

Social Homogeneity

It is also possible that all this collective effort is helped by the relatively uniform social structure of these villages. 95 to 100 per cent of the population belongs to the Tilore-Kunbi caste group, which is listed as a backward caste in Maharashtra. The caste structure of the wadis is given Table–3.

Table–3
Caste Structure of Villages

Village *Caste*	*Devka* *Dattawadi*	*Devka* *Ambikawadi*	*Chikhalgaon* *Ganeshwadi-Saiwadi*	*Chikhalgaon* *Manewadi*	*Chikhalgaon* *Kamblewadi*
Tilore-Kunbi	44	60	67	36	15
Baudh					
Maratha			2		
Teli	1		1		
Brahmin					
Total Households	45	60	70	36	15

Economically speaking, there are no great inequalities in these villages. The landholding structure of the wadis is as follows:

Village Size Class of Land	*Devka Datta-wadi*	*Devka Ambika-wadi*	*Chikhalgaon Ganeshwadi*	*Chikhalgaon Saiwadi*	*Chikhalgaon Manewadi*	*Chikhalgaon Kamblewadi*
0-1 hectares			7	11	24	5
1-2 hectares			5	2	15	8
2-3 hectares			13	4	4	2
3-4 hectares			7	2	6	1
4-5 hectares			4	4	2	1
Over 5 hectares			6	4	5	0
Total number of cultivators			42	27	56	17

A religio-moral undercurrent is clearly visible in these wadis. Nearly all wadis contributed some money to refurbish their village temples. The residents of Ganeshwadi-Saiwadi also said that they had built a tank next to the well for the animals and birds to drink from. When any lady goes to the well to wash clothes, she routinely puts in a bucket of water into the tank so that it remains topped up. They claimed that two years ago when the summer was quite severe and the water in all the wells had dried up, their well still had about six feet of water. Perhaps this happened, so they said, because they were kind to nature and nature returned their generosity.

Attempts at prohibition have been made in many of these wadis. In both Chikhalgaon and Devka, villagers claim that there are no liquor stalls any more. Couns elling people to give up alcohol is a constant activity. Gorivale said that he had made a lot of effort in this regard but it was too difficult to enforce. Chikhalgaon people said that the Village Panchayat peon had been a habitual drunkard at one time but then he went to Pandharpur with his wife and he had sworn off liquor since then. Not only that, he had also succeeded in persuading thirty other boys in the village to give up liquor.

Another self imposed restriction that we found in Chikhalgaon was that two days are fixed in the week for harvesting of cashew. In the previous year the village sold about ten tonnes of cashew in the market so it is a significant crop for them. They say that this restriction ensures that there is no thievery and peace is maintained in the village.

Further any disputes are sorted out in the Village Sabha. People never go to the police as a first resort.

Our Motto: Self-Reliance

One thing which the villagers repeatedly said was that handing over their scheme to the government was not an option for them. Certainly this would help reduce their electricity bill. Taking a private electric connection means that they have to pay Rs. 3.60 per unit of electricity instead of the subsidized rate the Gram Panchayats pay. But it was not worth it. Government procedures, they all said, were far too cumbersome and time-consuming. They could not afford to wait a month to float a tender if their scheme needed repair just to satisfy audit objections. To maintain their scheme satisfactorily they feel instant decision-making is a must and this is something which they do not think is possible in the government.

Nor has any wadi drawn support from any NGO in all these years. Rather some of the villagers of Chikhalgaon were hostile to a local NGO called the Lokmanya Sarvajanik Dharmadaya Nyasa which has run a high school in the village for many decades now. The ex-sarpanch Ganpat Govind Bhuvad said that the NGO tries to take unfair credit for work that others have done. The Zilla Parishad teacher Ujad felt that he was transferred out of the village at the instance of this NGO since he had contributed a great deal to the success of the village scheme and probably they did not like that.

These villages seem quite apolitical in atmosphere. We visited the villages about two days before elections for the Zilla Parishad and Panchayat Samiti were to be held and apart from the occasional poster or two and a campaign vehicle, there seemed to be little heat generated by the campaign. Some of the women could not tell who the current Chief Minister of the State was. Most people reported that they go to vote but that is the extent of interest they take in matters political. Perhaps the fact that most males in the village are part of the voter lists in Mumbai and not locally, has made a difference.

Conclusion

Empowerment of local societies that followed 73rd and 74th Constitutional Amendment brought about with it a variety of benefits to the people at the grass roots. Yet, local contingencies have resulted in such an exercise in empowerment being refracted through the lens of local concerns. In the present chapter we discussed the manner in which the people of a village went beyond the institutional mechanisms of elections to the PRIs in order to obtain essential services. By doing so they went contrary to many of the institutional restraints envisaged by the government and other donor agencies. Yet, in the specific context of the problems that the people of the village were addressing, going beyond institutional mechanisms was important. There are a number of notable features to be noticed here. These villagers began their exercise in local empowerment much before the Constitutional Amendment that set up the institutional mechanisms of the PRI came into existence. For this purpose they drew upon the many decades long experience of Panchayati Raj already prevalent in Maharashtra. The knowledge for working collectively and for the common good seems also to have been helped by the extensive experience that the men-folk had of working in Mumbai. Some help from their employers in Mumbai too was welcome in overcoming funds shortages. Also, while the existing PRIs provided some help, much of the self-help that these villagers resorted to was done in the context of the village and away from the hurly burly of Panchayat politics. Much before the World Bank and other donor agencies began to insist on the need for involving women in the local policy making processes and system maintenance, these villages had already begun to take active help of their local women's collectives, the Mahila Mandals. There was also a canny understanding that for the services to be effectively maintained it would be important to arrange adequate funds. If these could not come from the government then they had to be collected locally. Also user charges were increased from time to time keeping in line with the rising maintenance costs. Most important of all, these people had a fully transparent system of account keeping. Thus they were able to record in detail the contributions made by various persons and institutions as also the expenses undergone. All this was routinely placed before all the villagers and discussed at length in the monthly amavasya meetings. That this way of working has yielded considerable benefits to the people cannot be doubted. Neither is it possible to find fault with the absence of formal elections to the various bodies that were set up to put the water supply schemes in place and maintain them. Yet, despite the absence of elections these people were able to generate an adequate amount of consensus among themselves on how to create their water supply scheme and how to maintain it. In this way they were able to root their schemes firmly on to the ground. They may not have followed all the formal institutional steps that are envisaged in the Constitutional Amendments. Yet, they were able to implement the spirit of these amendments in the full. After all, is not the proof of the pudding in the eating?

Index